A World to Build

A WORLD TO BUILD

New Paths Toward Twenty-First Century Socialism

Marta Harnecker

Translated by
Fred Fuentes

AAKAR

A WORLD TO BUILD
Marta Harnecker

First Published in India 2015

ISBN 978-93-5002-346-4 (Pb)

Published in agreement with Monthly Review Press, New York for publication and sale only in the Indian Subcontinent (India, Pakistan, Bangladesh, Nepal, Maldives, Bhutan & Sri Lanka)

Published by
AAKAR BOOKS
28 E Pocket IV, Mayur Vihar Phase I, Delhi 110 091
Phone : 011 2279 5505 Telefax : 011 2279 5641
aakarbooks@gmail.com; www.aakarbooks.com

Printed at
Sapra Brothers, Delhi 110 092

Contents

Introduction 7

PART 1 LATIN AMERICA ADVANCES **12**

1. The Pioneer in Rejecting Neoliberalism 13
2. Correlation of Forces 30
3. Typology of Latin American Governments 46
4. "Left" Governments Facing More Objective Limitations 49

PART 2 WHERE ARE WE GOING? TWENTY-FIRST CENTURY SOCIALISM **56**

5. Why Talk about Socialism? 57
6. Recovering the Original Socialist Thinking 62
7. Some Current Reflections on Twenty-First Century Socialism 68
8. Transition and Its Varieties 98
9. Making Progress When the Government Is In Our Hands 113
10. A Guide to Judging How much Progress is Being Made 158

PART 3 A NEW POLITICAL INSTRUMENT FOR A NEW HEGEMONY **162**

11. Building a New Hegemony 163
12. A New Political Instrument 173

Bibliography 197

Notes 205

Index 217

To Comandante Chávez, whose words, orientations, and exemplary dedication to the cause of the poor will serve as a compass for his people and all the people of the world. It will be the best shield to defend ourselves from those who seek to destroy this marvelous work that he began to build.

Introduction

I completed this book one month after the physical disappearance of President Hugo Chávez, without whose intervention in Latin America this book could not have been written. Much of what you will read here is related in one way or another to the Bolivarian leader, to his ideas and actions, within Venezuela and at the regional and global level. Nobody can deny that there is a huge difference between the Latin America that Chávez inherited and the Latin America he left for us today.

By the time Chávez won the 1998 presidential elections, the neoliberal capitalist model was already foundering. The choice then was whether to reestablish the neoliberal capitalist model—undoubtedly with some changes, such as greater concern for social issues, but still motivated by the same logic of profit-seeking—or to go ahead and try to build another model. It was President Chávez who had the courage to call this alternative to capitalism "socialism," in spite of its negative connotations. He called it "21st century socialism," adding the adjective "21st century" to differentiate this new socialism from the errors and deviations that occurred in implementing twentieth-century socialism. This new socialism should not "fall into the errors of the past," and commit the same "Stalinist deviations" whereby the party became bureaucratized and ended up eliminating popular protagonism.

Like Peruvian socialist José Carlos Mariátegui, Chávez believed that 21st century socialism could not be a "carbon copy"; rather, it had to be a "heroic creation," which is why he spoke of a Bolivarian, Christian, Robinsonian, and Amerindian socialism. He conceived of socialism as a new collective way of life, where equality, freedom, and real and profound democracy reign; where the people play the role of protagonist; where the economic system is centered on human beings, not on profits; and where a pluralistic, anti-consumerist culture exists, in which being takes precedence over owning.

The need for people's participation was a recurring theme in the Venezuelan president's speeches and was an element that distinguished his proposals for democratic socialism from others. He was convinced that participation in all spheres is what allows human beings to grow and achieve self-confidence, that is, develop themselves as human beings.

But these would have remained mere words if Chávez had not promoted the creation of suitable spaces for participatory processes to flourish. That is why his initiative to create communal councils (self-managed community spaces), workers' councils, student councils, and peasant councils was central to the emergence of a truly collective structure; one that ultimately should express itself as a new form of decentralized state, with communes as its fundamental building blocks.

Chávez was not naïve, as some might think. He knew that the forces opposed to this project were tremendously powerful. However, being a realist does not mean one must accept the conservative vision of politics that sees it as simply the art of the possible. For Chávez, the art of politics was to make the impossible possible, not by sheer willpower, but by taking the existing reality as one's starting point and working to build favorable conditions and a correlation of social forces capable of changing that reality. He knew that to make possible in the future what today appears impossible required changing the correlation of forces at both the national and the international level. While in government, he worked masterfully to achieve this, understanding that to build political power, agreements among top leaders were not enough—the most important task was building up the correlation of social forces. The Venezuelan leader understood that an alternative society to capitalism simultaneously required an alternative globalization to neoliberal globalization. He never sought to build socialism in one country. Chávez was completely clear that this was not possible, which is why he put such an emphasis on shifting the correlation of forces at both the regional and international level.

He quickly perceived the particularities of the transition process under way in his country, one that served as a precursor for similar processes in other Latin American countries. Among them was the understanding that the transition process did not start from zero; its starting point was the inherited state apparatus, the inherited economic system and the inherited culture. In order to take the institutional road, the first step therefore had to be to change the rules of the institutional game. From there, the immense obstacles on that route, which he knew would arise, had to be overcome. He understood that a strong state is required in order to progress toward a society in which the state is no longer an institution dominating society but is instead an instrument serving society, and controlled by society. Starting with this strong state, it would become possible to create the international conditions to achieve national sovereignty and continental integration. This state drives forward the transition from the inherited institutions toward new ones that can create the conditions for building the new society—a new constitution, a new body of laws, greater development of local powers, etc. And the most important thing is that from this inherited state, now staffed by revolutionary cadres, encouragement can be given to promoting people's organizations and protagonism, essential elements for building a new state from below.

Many of these ideas will be further developed in this book, which updates, expands upon, and delves deeper into topics I addressed in "Latin America and Twenty-First Century Socialism: Inventing to Avoid Mistakes," published in the Summer 2010 issue of *Monthly Review*. I have incorporated into this new version paragraphs from my most recent articles.[1]

The book consists of three parts. The first part, *Latin America Advances*, is a brief recounting of what has occurred in Our America during these last decades: the modification of the political map, the social mobilizations that explain these changes, the indications that there has been a change in the correlation of forces between the United States and our region, and the attempts being made by the largest imperial power in the world to recolonize and dominate our subcontinent. Part One finishes with a typology of Latin American governments, because I think that rather than framing governments within a certain classification, it is more important to evaluate their performance, always keeping in mind the correlation of forces in which they operate. This requires us to focus less on the pace at which these governments are implementing change and more on the direction in which they are heading, as the pace will largely depend on how they deal with the obstacles they encounter.

Part Two, Where Are We Going: Tweny-First Century Socialism, tries to help the reader understand the value of talking about socialism even if the word has such a negative connotation; which parts of the original Marxist thought ought to be rescued; which new ideas have arisen out of the experiences of some of the Latin American governments; the characteristics of the transition we are living in; what these governments can do in spite of the big limitations facing them; and finally, what criteria to take into account in assessing their performance. I believe all these elements can help us find our way.

Part Three, A New Political Instrument for a New Hegemony, deals with the topic of how to achieve the necessary correlation of forces for overcoming obstacles in building the new society, and the relationship this has with the topic of the new hegemony. I argue that in many places of the world, the cultural hegemony of the bourgeoisie is breaking down, but this does not necessarily mean that a new popular hegemony has emerged in its place. This will not occur spontaneously. A political instrument is needed, a political organization that can help us construct this new hegemony. Aware of the existing, widespread rejection of politics and politicians, I explain that here I am not talking about the traditional parties of Old Left, but of a new political form that does not manipulate the social movements but rather puts itself at their service. I outline why the existence of a political instrument is necessary for the construction of 21st century socialism, what its main tasks are, and what kind of activist and political culture we need today. In doing so, I argue that it is fundamental to combat the bureaucratic style that leaders of political organizations and governments usually fall into and defend the need for public criticism to prevent this from happening.

It should be noted that the basic ideas in this book do not come from reading numerous texts—although it is evident that I have incorporated ideas and research from valuable intellectuals. Rather, this work is a result of having been able to study firsthand the diverse struggles and practical experiences of various countries of Our America.

Many anonymous collaborators have contributed to this book. I would like to give a special mention to my compañero Michael Lebowitz, many of whose ideas I have incorporated into this book, and Ximena la Barra who read over the final version of the book and provided me with some invaluable suggestions and contributions. I thank all those who, true to their revolutionary passion, whether in the area of research or activism, have made this book possible. My great hope is that this effort contributes a grain of sand in making possible a future—now not so distant—which a quarter of a century ago seemed impossible.

PART 1

Latin America Advances

1. The Pioneer in Rejecting Neoliberalism

Latin America was the first region in which neoliberal policies were introduced. Chile, my country, was used as a testing ground for neoliberal policies before prime minister Margaret Thatcher's government implemented them in the United Kingdom. But it was also the first region in the world that gradually came to reject those policies which only served to increase poverty, aggravate social inequalities, destroy the environment, and weaken working-class and popular movements in general.

It was in our subcontinent that left and progressive forces first began to rally after the collapse of socialism in Eastern Europe and the Soviet Union. After more than two decades of suffering, new hope was born. At first this took the form of struggles to resist neoliberal policies, but after a few years, people went on the offensive and began conquering spaces of power. Within Europe, itself in crisis and decline, sections of the impoverished masses have begun to see Latin America as a ray of hope.[1]

For the first time in Latin American history—and with the crisis of the neoliberal model as a backdrop—candidates from left and center-left groupings managed to win elections in most of the region's countries.

Let us remember that in 1998, when Chávez won elections in Venezuela, this country was a lonely island in a sea of neoliberalism that covered the continent, except, of course, for the honorable exception of Cuba. Shortly after, Ricardo Lagos was elected in Chile (2000), Luiz Ignácio Lula da Silva in Brazil (2002), Néstor Kirchner in Argentina (2003), Tabaré Vázquez in Uruguay (2005), Evo Morales in Bolivia (2005 and 2009), Michelle Bachelet in Chile (2006), Rafael Correa in Ecuador (2006, 2009, and 2013), Daniel Ortega in Nicaragua (2006 and 2010), Cristina Fernández in Argentina (2007 and 2012), Álvaro Colom in Guatemala (2007), Fernando Lugo in Paraguay (2008), Mauricio Funes in El Salvador (2009), José Mujica in Uruguay (2009), Dilma Rousseff in Brazil (2010), and Ollanta Humala in Peru (2011)—and Chávez was reelected for the fourth time in 2012.[2]

I agree with Cuban theoretician Roberto Regalado that these leaders are heterogeneous. "In some countries such as Bolivia, Ecuador and Venezuela, the collapse or extreme weakness of neoliberal institutions brought to power leaders who capitalized on the left's organizational and political capital to win the presidency. Then there were situations like in Honduras and Argentina where, because there were no presidential candidates from the popular sectors, progressive people from traditional parties won elections."[3]

Popular Movements: the Great Protagonists

We can say that in each and every country, albeit in different ways, popular movements and not political parties were at the forefront of the struggle against neoliberalism. Even in those countries where the role of left political parties was important, they were not in the vanguard of the fight against neoliberalism; the popular movements, however, were. These movements developed in the context of the neoliberal model's crisis of legitimacy and the crisis its political institutions were facing. In many cases, they grew out of the dynamics of resistance present in their communities or local organizations.

Overview of Key Mobilizations

Let us briefly look back at some of the most important social struggles that helped pave the way for what we see today in Latin America. Without a doubt, this new reality stands in stark contrast to the solitary struggle waged by Fidel Castro in 1985 for the non-repayment of foreign debt.[4]

El Caracazo, Venezuela. On February 27, 1989, a tremendous social explosion took place in Venezuela in opposition to a package of neoliberal economic measures demanded by the International Monetary Fund and imposed by the government of Carlos Andrés Pérez. According to renowned French intellectual Ignacio Ramonet, the Venezuelan people "were the first in the world to rise up against the tyranny of neoliberalism," and they did so at a time when the neoliberal model was on the rise globally.[5]

The package included, among other things, cuts to public spending, liberalization of prices and trade, promotion of foreign investment, and the privatization of state companies. But the most immediate cause for the popular rebellion was the increase in transport costs that resulted from the hike in petrol prices.

Residents from the poorest *barrios* (neighborhoods) came out onto the streets in huge numbers and began to burn buses, as well as loot and destroy supermarkets and shops. The military were called out to impose order. The *Caracazo*—as it was referred to because the rebellion had as its epicenter the capital of Venezuela, even though similar protests occurred in various other states—ended in a massacre of epic proportions and was a determining factor in the politicization of many young military officers.[6]

Ecuador's indigenous peoples spearhead the struggles of the 1990s. By 1986, the disintegration of Ecuador's workers' movement and the Frente Unitario de los Trabajadores (United Front of Workers, FUT) as a result of neoliberalism was evident. Water, sewerage, and rubbish collection services were all privatized, and thousands of municipal workers were fired. Yet while the workers' movement was on the decline, the level of conflict in the countryside was on the rise. The early 1990s saw the country become a powder keg, with a wave of land occupations occurring against latifundios and in favor of land reform.

The indigenous movement erupted onto the scene in 1990 with the occupation of the Santo Domingo Church. The occupation, which lasted ten days, gave national prominence to the demands of the indigenous people and forced the Rodrigo Borja government to open up a dialogue with the movement.

Shortly afterward, the indigenous movement began to raise demands of national concern such, as opposition to oil privatization, as well as other privatizations. Non-indigenous sectors, including neighborhood-based social movements and radical youth inspired by the ideas of liberation theology, began to accompany them in their protests. The broad Frente Patriótico (Patriotic Front) was initiated, within which CONAIE, the most important indigenous organization in the country, played a leading role.

In 1995, a broad coalition of social movements—indigenous, urban sectors, youth—formed the Coordinadora por el NO (NO Coalition) and successfully defeated a government-initiated referendum that sought to institutionalize neoliberalism. The proposal was rejected by 75 percent of voters.

Thanks to indigenous resistance against neoliberalism, the government was unable to privatize strategic companies in the areas of oil, electricity, and telecommunications. In 1997, the indigenous movement rose up and deposed President Abdalá Bucaram. The indigenous movement's proposal for a Constituent Assembly was accepted, but the right organized itself and successfully co-opted the process. Even though the June 1998 constitution recognized some rights for indigenous peoples, it also improved the institutional framework for deepening neoliberalism.

At the start of 2000, a peaceful indigenous uprising against privatization led to an occupation of the National Congress and forced the ouster of President Jamil Mahuad. The indigenous movement gradually transformed itself into one of the central axes of political action and an indispensable factor for any attempt to transform the country.[7]

Chile's Mapuche movement—in the front line of the struggle against neoliberalism. The Mapuche, an indigenous people that inhabit the Araucanía region of Chile, were greatly affected by neoliberal agricultural policies imposed by the military dictatorship and successive Concertación—coalition of center-left—governments. Mapuche communities were not only driven off lands granted to them under the land reform program initiated by the Christian Democratic government of Eduardo Frei (1964–70) and continued by the Socialist government of Salvador Allende (1970–73), but were also affected by the process of economic liberalization and foreign direct investment in forestry, tourism, and energy mega-projects carried out in their territories. The immediate result of all this was the forced migration of entire communities, an increase in logging to the detriment of agricultural activities, soil degradation, water contamination, and environmental destruction.

At the beginning of the 1990s, the Consejo de Todas las Tierras (Council of All the Lands), a Mapuche organization, carried out various symbolic occupations of ancestral Mapuche lands that were now in private hands. Up until 1997, the demands of this social sector were confined to individual communities; however, from that year onward, "other forms of demands for territories emerged, where issues of land, natural resources, participation and development were all integrated." This allowed the Mapuche movement to "develop a new discourse and construct supra-community alliances." As Chilean investigator Víctor Toledo Llancaqueo said, the situation went from one of "lands in conflict" to "territories in conflict."[8] "They were no longer simply demanding land, but rather a spatial continuum, a territory with its own water, species and cultivable soils, as well as their right to participate in decisions that affect their territory."[9]

In order to contain these struggles, Concertación governments and the recent government of Sebastián Piñera made efforts to co-opt the movement through paternalistic welfare policies. Unable to defeat the Mapuche people via this route, they turned to open and systematic repression against Mapuche communities and leaders, a number of whom ended up in prison.[10] From there emerged another form of struggle: hunger strikes. A hunger strike begun in March 2006 by three indigenous leaders and a theologian, Patricia Troncoso, who became a symbol of the Mapuche struggle against the state, had big repercussions across the world. Since then, these types of protests have represented a continuous form of pressuring the government to listen to their demands.

Referendum against privatization triumphs in Uruguay. In December 1992, one of the first successful struggles against neoliberalism took place: the little known triumph of the Uruguayan people in a referendum that repealed a law passed the previous year authorizing the privatization of large public companies.[11]

The Frente Amplio (Broad Front) waged a formidable propaganda campaign, including via numerous televised debates, to explain what privatization entailed and the reasons why it was dangerous. This meant that when people voted, they knew what project for the country they were voting for. That is why various commentators dubbed this Uruguay's first modern election.

The referendum united 70 percent of voters, from a truly diverse political background, behind a movement with tremendous political potential. This broad base of support was due to the fact that, following big debates within the leadership, the Frente Amplio decided not to challenge the entire law and its thirty articles, as the more radical currents were proposing, but rather to focus on the five key clauses that referred to strategic companies.

At the same time, this political organization understood that a media campaign was not enough, that it was necessary to meticulously campaign, going neighborhood to neighborhood, and, as much as possible, house to house. Retired workers, who represent a significantly large part of the Uruguayan population, played a big role in this task

Two years later, in 1994, the government attempted to modify the constitution in order to facilitate the deepening of neoliberalism. Retired workers, a social sector severely affected by the privatization of the social security system, were once again one of the forces to oppose this, carrying out a tremendous grassroots campaign, particularly in the interior of the country. A large number of experienced and excellent trade union leaders helped create the Organización Nacional de Jubilados (National Organization of Retired Workers), which prepared itself for battle and mobilized across the country. As all their members were retired, they had all day to actively campaign.[12] In the end, the government's initiative was rejected.

EZLN fights against NAFTA in Mexico. On January 1, 1994, in the indigenous southeastern Mexican town of Chiapas, the Ejército Zapatista de Liberación Nacional (Zapatista National Liberation Army, EZLN) erupted onto the scene, raising the banner of opposition to the North American Free Trade Agreement (NAFTA). Irrespective of how successful their struggle has been, I believe that this movement was critical to shedding light on the oppression and discrimination that Mexico's indigenous peoples have endured. Moreover, everyone recognizes the spectacular initiatives the ELZN has promoted on the international sphere, provoking great sympathy and support for their cause, especially among intellectuals and students. The EZLN has been capable not only of building social force in the areas they operate in, but also of influencing public opinion at the national and international level, something that, on many occasions, the left has not been able to do.[13]

Brazil's MST—the key national movement in the fight against neoliberalism. In Brazil, the Movimento dos Trabalhadores Rurais Sem Terra (Movement of Rural Landless Workers, MST) consolidated itself as the key national reference point in the struggle against neoliberalism, promoting the coming together of all those sectors excluded by the system: the landless, the homeless, the unemployed.[14] Attacked from the right for its radicalism, the MST is nevertheless respected by an increasingly broad cross-section of society that finds in this movement a political coherence and concern with ideological aspects largely lacking in leftist political parties.

Although its struggles date back to the mid-1980s, the movement started to gain national and international prominence following its third congress in 1995, at which it put forward the proposition that there would be no land reform in Brazil unless the neoliberal economic model was changed, and that it was only possible to advance in that direction if all of society began to see the struggle for land as a legitimate and necessary struggle.

The MST understood that to halt the advance of neoliberalism, it was necessary to establish a broad policy of alliances at both national and international levels. Going beyond mere words, the MST transformed itself into one of the most prominent promoters of important mobilizations. Referendums on foreign debt and against the Free Trade of the Americas Agreement (FTAA), and its struggle against genetically modified organisms (GMOs), have allowed the MST to establish alliances with campesino organizations the world over.[15]

Water War in Bolivia. In 2000, the so-called Water War exploded in Bolivia, the country that had most faithfully implemented the neoliberal structural adjustment model in our subcontinent, according to one of the model's key architects, Jeffrey Sachs.[16]

Following a series of privatizations of public companies, the city of Cochabamba, the third largest in the country, rose up against water privatization. The revolt ended only when the Bolivian government decided to backtrack and revoke the concession granted to Aguas de Tunari.

According to Mexican investigator Ana Esther Ceceña: "Within a short timeframe, the entire city had organized a revolt which brought together all social sectors. The multitude took over the city and impeded the entrance of security forces until the government backtracked on the concession and agreed to the city's water being jointly managed with representatives of the mobilized populace."[17]

This rebellion was the first in a wave of broad popular mobilizations: the uprising of the Aymara indigenous peoples in the Altiplano; protests in defense of coca by the *cocaleros* (coca growers) of the Chapare region, led by Evo Morales, who went on to gain national and international prominence; the police rebellion; the gas war; and other uprisings in El Alto and by indigenous campesinos in 2003. All of these mobilizations culminated in Evo Morales's victory in the 2005 presidential elections.

Referendum against foreign debt and the FTAA in Brazil. Within the framework of the Jubilee 2000 campaign, six million Brazilians participated in a national referendum against the foreign debt, with more than 90 percent voting for non-payment.[18] A number of the groups that organized the campaign—which included a considerable number of popular movements and some parties and religious entities, such as the Conferência Nacional dos Bisbos do Brasil (National Conference of Bishops of Brazil) and the Consejo Nacional de Iglesias Cristianas (National Council of Christian Churches)—went on to lead another initiative that soon took on a continental character: a national referendum against the FTAA. This informal referendum was held in September 2002 and signified both an important mobilization and unquestionable success: around 10 million people voted, of which 98 percent opposed the FTAA. This result can be explained by the huge educational campaign and mobilization prior to the popular referendum, carried out by more than 150,000 volunteer activists who facilitated pre-prepared educational courses and a grassroots campaign, many times going door-to-door to talk about the negative effects of the FTAA.[19]

Similar events, but on a smaller scale, were held in various Latin American countries, all asking the same question: Are you in favor of the government signing the Free Trade of the Americas Agreement?

Without a doubt, this campaign of popular consciousness-raising and broad-based mobilization weighed heavily on the minds of Latin American leaders when, in 2004, they voted to reject this nefarious economic initiative being promoted by the U.S. government.

Popular mobilizations in Argentina bring down four presidents. Between 2001 and 2002, Argentina's popular sectors awoke from their slumber and, led by the *piqueteros*, an unemployed workers' movement that had emerged as a result of the effects of neoliberal measures, rose up against "dubious financial maneuvers, political cynicism and gross levels of governmental corruption, and brought down four presidents, one after another, within the space of a month. The protests extended and became generalized to include opposition to the whole political system, leading to a shared sense of satiety and sentiment that 'all of them must go.'"[20]

Chilean student revolt against the neoliberal system and its education model. In April 2006, Chilean high school students, feeling the effects of a deficient public education system, overcame the fear that continued to prevail in Chilean society following the long years of dictatorship and rose up across the country to question the education system. The "Penguin Rebellion," as it was known due to the dark pants and white shirts worn by students, was a watershed moment for Chilean society.

Although the movement was ultimately co-opted by the Bachelet government, these struggles became engraved in the minds of their protagonists. A number of leaders of the 2006 movement reappeared on the political scene during the 2011 university rebellion, with high school students soon jumping aboard. This new student uprising was neither spontaneous nor a creation of then student leader and Communist Party of Chile member Camila Vallejo, as the international media tried to portray it; rather, it was the result of a "process of accumulation of social struggles," such as the struggles for democratization in the 1990s, the first student uprisings of 2001, and the aforementioned Penguin Rebellion.[21]

Around 100,000 people came out to the streets in solidarity with the student movement and its struggle for an education system that was not geared toward profit-making, a level of national support not seen in recent times. This issue garnered a great deal of sympathy with the population. "Indebtedness," said current Federación de Estudiantes de la Universidad de Chile (Federation of Students of the University of Chile, FECH) president Andrés Fielbaum, is not something that only affects students, but all of Chilean society, as this is "the manner in which people are paying for all their basic rights."[22]

"It is not only the students that are rebelling, but also their family and all the people are definitely behind them."[23] To use Chilean sociologist Tomás Moulián's phrase, "Credit Card Man" is beginning to liberate himself from neoliberalism's extremely well executed process of domestication.[24]

The 2011 mobilizations represented a qualitative leap forward. "Years ago we were only able to mobilize those that were already convinced, leftist activists or agitators, those that go to all the marches. This time around, many of the people that came on board had never in their life been on a march," said FECH ex-president Gabriel Boric.[25] They also revealed the separation that exists between traditional political leaders and popular sentiment.[26]

The Chilean student movement has rejected the traditional way of doing politics. It no longer tolerates being manipulated by political parties. Decision making is carried out in a very democratic manner. In what has been referred to as an assembly process, ideas are openly discussed and decisions are made collectively. Moreover, leaders must constantly report back to the grassroots on how they have gone about implementing decisions that have been made. The role of *veedor* (overseer) has been created, a kind of political commissar, but this time a commissar not linked to a political party, but to the popular movement. Their role is to exercise control over the leaders.

Another important achievement has been the movement's capacity to accept differences between various student groups and understand that it is necessary to unite in order to strike together and best advance the needs of the movement.

In the heat of the struggle, the student movement began to radicalize its demands: it not only questioned the nature of the education system and fought for free public education for all, but also began to question the global political system, placing on the political agenda the need for a constituent assembly to transform the rules of the political game (still intact from the dictatorship era). They also demanded the re-nationalization of copper, whose revenue could cover the costs of a free and quality education for all. That is, its basic aim was in the direction of "transforming the essence of the model."[27]

Mexican state of Oaxaca rebels and establishes its own self-government. In Mexico, the entire population of the state of Oaxaca rose up in June 2006 in opposition to the repression meted out against protesting teachers and demanded the resignation of the governor. The Asamblea Popular de los Pueblos de Oaxaca (Popular Assembly of the Peoples of Oaxaca, APPO) was formed, and for six months this Mexican territory "was converted into the Oaxaca Commune, with town meetings in the central plaza."[28]

Mobilization of "los forajidos" in Ecuador. In 2006 we also witnessed the mobilization of *los forajidos* (the outlaws) in Quito, Ecuador, protesting against Lucio Gutiérrez's betrayal of the anti-neoliberal program he campaigned for when he was first elected president with the support of popular and, in particular, indigenous movements.[29] There were a number of interesting elements in this popular rebellion. First, the main protagonists were not the social sectors that had supported Lucio and subsequently suffered a big blow as a result of this negative experience; instead it was a mobilization "without a particularly defined reference point, and with a strong youth presence." Second, it was characterized by "its network mode of organizing, above all between middle-class sectors, and including upper-class sectors motivated by a dose of racism." Third, radio stations, in particular Radio La Luna, played the key role of collective organizers.[30]

A number of these mobilizations raised the demand for a constituent assembly, conscious of the limitations inherent in the existing institutions.

The constituent processes in Venezuela, Bolivia, and Ecuador, and endorsed by popular referendums, were able to count on a combination of effective leadership by popular and charismatic individuals elected to office and strong pressure from the popular bases capable of uniting, organizing, and mobilizing around their own agenda of justice and sovereignty.[31]

The main lesson of these mobilizations. Although many lessons can be drawn from these popular struggles, in my opinion one of the most important is the proven validity of a strategy of a broad coalition of forces that seeks to unite all those who can be united. The concrete objectives for the struggle are to elicit understandings among all these diverse groups, all with their own very different traditions and political practices.

Social Movements, Old and New

What we saw in these resistance struggles was the emergence of new social movements alongside older ones, especially peasant and indigenous movements. These are pluralistic, in which elements of liberation theology, revolutionary nationalism, marxism, indigenism, and anarchism coexist. Having moved beyond focusing on specific, immediate issues that affected them as in the past, these movements took up national issues. This not only enriched their struggles and demands but also allowed them to unite with diverse sectors, all of which were feeling the effects of the same system.

Missing in much of the Latin American political scene, except on rare occasions, was the traditional workers' movement, hit hard by the implementation of neoliberal economic measures such as precarious labor conditions and subcontracting. And on those occasions when workers did participate, it was not on the front lines of the political scene.

These movements generally started out from a position of rejecting politics and politicians, but as the process of struggle progressed, they gradually shifted from an apolitical stance of simply resisting neoliberalism to an increasingly political one of questioning established power, and in some cases, such as those of Pachakutik and Movimiento Alianza PAIS in Ecuador and the Movimiento al Socialismo (Movement Toward Socialism, MAS) in Bolivia, went as far as to build their own political instruments.

Neoliberalism loses legitimacy in Latin America

Neoliberalism's heyday in our subcontinent has long gone. The "end of history" announced by Francis Fukuyama in 1989 never arrived.[32] The current global economic capitalist crisis is but one of the factors dealing a *coup de grâce* to that statement.

It is interesting to recall that though the fall of the Berlin wall, which occurred only months after Fukuyama made his statement, and the subsequent collapse of Soviet socialism seemed to prove him right, that same year the first social explosion against neoliberalism occurred in Venezuela, and was quickly followed by all the other social explosions mentioned above.

Although most governments in the region still hold to the general tenets of neoliberalism, very few defend this model. It lost legitimacy because it proved incapable of solving the most pressing problems facing our countries.

According to Emir Sader, there is a "hegemonic crisis" in Latin America, in which "the neoliberal model and the power bloc that led it are worn down, weakened, and only manage to survive by implementing the model in a toned-down form—for example in Brazil, Argentina, and Uruguay."[33]

Given this, there appears to be only two alternatives: either capitalism is given a makeover, or we move towards an alternative economic project focused on satisfying human needs and making possible the kind of economic development in our region that benefits the overwhelming majority of our people, not the elites.

Bourgeois Liberal Democracy Loses Prestige

The inability of the neoliberal economic model to obtain positive economic results for our peoples has also negatively affected the credibility of the political model of bourgeois democracy. People no longer have confidence in this form of government and are increasingly less willing to accept the enormous gap between those who get to elect and those who get elected.

As democratic regimes were losing credibility, traditional political parties began to face a crisis. People became cynical about politics and politicians. You can see this in the polls taken every year in Latin America by Latinobarómetro. In 1998, when Hugo Chávez was elected, only 37 percent of people in Latin America were satisfied with the democratic system; in Venezuela, the percentage was even lower (35 percent). Up until 2007, the average level of satisfaction in Latin America remained at 37 percent, whereas the level in Venezuela rose to 59 percent.

The 2008 Latinobarómetro poll shows satisfaction with democracy has risen to 82 percent in Venezuela.[34] It is somewhat paradoxical that in a country accused of being a dictatorship, such a large percentage of the population expresses its satisfaction with democracy. Moreover, it is interesting to see that the average level of satisfaction in other countries has gone from 37 percent to 57 percent. It doesn't seem out of place to conclude that, when the policies implemented by left-wing governments begin to show results, people begin to have a different opinion about the democratic system. The 2011 Latinobarómetro report noted that support for democracy diminished somewhat across most Latin American countries, and that one of the causes may have been the economic problems faced by the region. Nevertheless, it is worth noting that although it fell 7 points in Venezuela (84 to 77 percent), this nation continues to have the highest satisfaction rating for democracy in the region, followed by Uruguay (75 percent) and Argentina (70 percent).

Another interesting phenomenon that the report highlights is the contrast between internationally held perceptions of certain governments and how their own people perceive these same governments:

> In 2011, we saw how a citizen's demand emerged, leading to hundreds of thousands of Chileans coming onto the streets, firstly for [free] education, and afterward for many other motives including a demand for structural change, all of which has left a question mark hanging over the [government's] declared success and how it defines this. The Chilean case clearly demonstrates that there is no road to development that can ignore the collapse in confidence and unjust redistribution. Chile's good macroeconomic performance has done little to convince the population that things are going in the right direction. At the same time, we have the contrary case of Venezuela, where there is large popular support for the actions taken by the government of President Chávez, while the world views them in a negative light. There is little doubt that a high level of incongruence exists between what people think of their own development and how the world sees the evolution of a country.

In Chile there has been an undeniable growth in the size of the "cake," but each day opposition grows to the unequal way in which it is being shared around.[35]

Despite the media war, we have seen that, in reaction to the injustices caused by neoliberalism, people's consciousness has taken a qualitative leap forward. It has done this very rapidly and manifested itself at election time as support for governments that propose anti-neoliberal programs.

2. *Correlation of Forces*

Evidently, Latin America's political landscape has been radically altered since Chávez was elected in 1998. A new correlation of forces has been established that makes it more difficult for the United States to achieve its objectives in the region. At the same time, the U.S. empire has attempted to stop this advance by stepping up its attacks on our countries.

The U.S. government no longer has the same freedom it once had to maneuver in our continent. Now it has to deal with rebel governments whose agenda often clashes with the White House's agenda. Valter Pomar, a member of the national directorate of the Brazilian Partido de los Trabajadores (Workers' Party, PT) and executive secretary of the Foro de São Paulo (Sao Paulo Forum), argues that between 1998 and 2013, a new correlation of forces capable of limiting foreign intervention in the region was established.[36]

Let us look at some of the facts that indicate this to be the case.

Facts Indicating the Advance of Progressive Forces

The United States suffers its first important defeat: FTAA rejected, ALBA created. The U.S. government has been unable to impose its FTAA. As an alternative to the FTAA, the Bolivarian

Alternative for the Peoples of Our Americas, better know as ALBA, was created on December 14, 2004, first as an agreement between Cuba and Venezuela.[37] Since then several Latin American countries have joined: Bolivia (2006), Nicaragua (2007), Honduras (2008), Dominica (2008), Antigua and Barbuda (2009), Saint Vincent and the Grenadines (2009), and Ecuador (2009). Honduras withdrew following the coup against Zelaya in 2009, while Uruguay, although not a full member of ALBA, signed up in March 2013 to use the ALBA currency, the sucre.

According to Ximena de la Barra, the FTAA's defeat "was consolidated at the OAS (Organization of American States) Summit in Mar del Plata at the end of 2005, where the United States carried out its last attempt to rescue this trade project aimed at imperial domination. For the first time ever, this country was challenged by an institution of its own creation. For their part, the social movements won at the summit the right to be protagonists in the regional political processes." From then on, "integration stopped being simply an issue for governments that were more or less subservient to foreign capital and the designs of the imperial metropolis, and became an issue for the people."[38] Faced with this situation, the White House has sought to sign bilateral treaties with Latin American countries such as Chile, Uruguay, Peru, Colombia, and with a group of Central American countries via the Dominican Republic–Central America Free Trade Agreement (CAFTA). Moreover, it is promoting the Alianza del Pacífico (Pacific Alliance) among its unconditional supporters as a way of counteracting the counter-hegemonic processes of integration underway.

Ecuador closes the Manta U.S. military base. On November 1, 2008, Ecuadorian president Rafael Correa announced he would not renew the contract that allowed the U.S. Southern Command to have a military base in the Ecuadorian city of Manta. The treaty, signed in 1999, was due to expire in 2009. This was a big blow for the Pentagon, as this base was the biggest U.S. center of operations in Latin America.

There were plenty of reasons to make this decision, but there is no doubt that the event that triggered it was the flagrant violation of Ecuador's sovereignty that occurred on March 1, 2008, when a Colombian army squadron crossed the border and launched an attack against a Fuerzas Armadas Revolucionarias de Colombia (Revolutionary Armed Forces of Colombia, FARC) camp in the Sucumbíos region. Twenty-five people were killed in the attack, including the FARC commander Raúl Reyes and several Mexican and Ecuadorian civilians.

Shortly before announcing the non-renewal of the contract, Quito released an official report about CIA infiltration in the Ecuadorian armed forces that indicated the Colombian attack on Ecuadorian territory relied on support from a U.S. plane stationed at the Manta base.

Two other examples of the Ecuadorian government taking an independent and sovereign stance preceded the closure of the base: the February 7 expulsion of Armando Astorga, a customs attaché at the U.S. embassy, following a government decision to no longer allow the U.S. embassy to have the final say when selecting the top brass of the police intelligence unit, including the commanding officer; and the expulsion ten days later of Max Sullivan, the first secretary of the U.S. embassy, over unacceptable interference in internal affairs.[39]

In response to the closure of the Manta base, the Pentagon transferred its ships, weapons, and high-tech spying devices to Colombian bases.

Cuba joins the Rio Group. Cuba's official entry into the Rio Group was announced on December 16, 2008, during the Latin America and Caribbean Summit held in Salvador Bahía, Brazil, with thirty-three heads of state in attendance. Cuba's presence in the region was thus strengthened.

OAS reaches consensus on lifting sanctions against Cuba. On June 3, 2009, the foreign ministers at an OAS meeting in Honduras agreed to repeal the 1962 decision to expel Cuba from the organization. Ecuadorian foreign minister Fander Falconí said the decision "had been approved by all the representatives," and added that this agreement "reflects the change of epoch that Latin America is experiencing."[40] For its part, Cuba graciously declined the proposal to rejoin.

Brazil buys French, rather than U.S., military equipment. On September 7, 2009, Lula signed an agreement with Nicolas Sarkozy that enabled Brazil to obtain strategically important military equipment (five submarines and fifty military transport helicopters) totaling $12 million in value. This was on top of the thirty-six fighter planes Brazil had previously purchased.

Uruguayan journalist Aram Aharonian wrote that this agreement appeared "to complete the strategic shift brought about by the decline of U.S. hegemony and the rise of Brazil as a world power," adding that "an autonomous military-industrial complex had emerged in what was once the empire's backyard." The aim is to build a protective shield around the Amazon region and the oil and gas reserves (approximately 50 million barrels' worth) that were discovered just off the Brazilian coastline in 2008. This measure was passed by the Brazilian parliament with the support of the opposition in a record time of less than 48 hours. Aharonian said this was not a measure taken by a government, but rather the decision of a state. The sector with most at stake in this agreement is the military sector, which was very worried about its technological weaknesses if Western powers decided to intervene. Foreign powers have been trying to impose "shared sovereignty" in the Amazon region since 1990. There is also additional information that Brazil is able to manufacture atomic weapons.[41]

Paraguayan president refuses Southern Command's presence in his country. In another gesture of sovereignty, and in the context of growing rejection of U.S. military presence in the subcontinent, Paraguayan president Fernando Lugo decided, on September 17,

2009, to refuse U.S. troops entry to his country, even if they were accompanied by professionals engaged in humanitarian activities. The U.S. Southern Command's proposed program would have seen 500 U.S. civilian and military personnel stationed in Paraguay.

Growing number of meetings without U.S. participation. Latin American and Caribbean leaders have begun meeting without the United States. The first South American Summit took place in Brazil in 2000. Two years later there was another meeting in Ecuador, and in 2004 the summit was held in Peru. The following year, Brazil hosted the first summit of the South American Community of Nations. Then, in 2006, a second summit was held in Bolivia, during which the foundation stone was laid for what became the Union of South American Nations (UNASUR). It adopted this name at the energy summit held in Venezuela in 2007. The founding treaty for this organization was approved in Brazil the following year.

Second Africa–South America Summit. Latin American countries are not only coordinating more and more between themselves (and without the presence of U.S. representatives), they are also increasing coordination with Africa. The Second Africa–South America Summit was held on Margarita Island on September 26–27, 2009. Twenty-seven heads of states attended. The summit issued a call for a return to democracy and the restoration of the constitutional government in Honduras, and a proposal was made to draw up a 2010–2020 Strategic Plan as part of setting up a framework for collaboration between the two regions.

Bank of the South gets off the ground. On September 28, 2009, Chávez's 2006 proposal to set up the Banco del Sur (Bank of the South) linked to UNASUR came to fruition.

This historic event took place during the Second Africa–South America Summit. Seven South American leaders from Venezuela, Brazil, Ecuador, Paraguay, Bolivia, Argentina, and Uruguay signed the Banco del Sur's founding statutes and launched it with seven billion dollars in start-up capital.

The original plan was to create a multilateral financial entity in South America that could act as an alternative to the IMF and other credit-granting institutions controlled by industrialized countries. The bank was set up with some specific projects in mind, but the idea has evolved over the course of several meetings that have been held to get it up and running. Peruvian economist Oscar Ugarteche, a supporter of the proposal, believes that insofar as it can capture international reserves from central banks and use them intelligently to promote development in the poorest regions and above all for ecologically and socially sustainable projects, the bank could be a first step toward a new kind of South American integration.[42]

Despite statements of good intentions, the process of setting up the Bank of the South has encountered a number of hurdles, including reticence on the part of Brazil, which has preferred to promote the regional role played by its own Banco de Desarrollo Económico y Social (Economic and Social Development Bank, BNDES). By the start of 2013, the Bank of the South was still not operational.

On the other hand, the ALBA Bank, which was initiated at the Sixth ALBA Summit held in January 2008, has proven to be much more agile. With an initial start-up fund of $1 billion, it is based on the ALBA principles of complementarity, solidarity, cooperation, and respect for sovereignty. The idea is that member countries contribute according to their capacities and have equal representation in the democratic procedure for decision making within the bank, and that the bank contributes to accelerating the creation of decent jobs, decreasing excessive emigration, and reducing wealth concentration, inequality, poverty, and social exclusion, all the while promoting sustainable human development.[43]

The ALBA Bank also aims to develop internal financial markets, channel resources toward productive projects, revitalize fair trade, develop regional integration infrastructure, promote sovereign control over the economy and finances, reduce vulnerability to external financial crises, keep resources within the region, and activate a virtuous cycle of cultural, social, economic, and political transformation in the region. This focus on compensating asymmetries is something that the Bank of the South has put a lot less emphasis on, due to resistance from some of its member countries.

The sucre—an attempt to break the hold of the U.S. dollar. With the unanimous support of leaders and representatives of countries that make up ALBA, the Sistema Único de Compensación Regional de Pagos (Unified System for Regional Compensation, SUCRE) was created in April 2009. It was initially established as a virtual currency that could act as an accounting mechanism for trade, with the idea that at some later stage it would become a regional hard currency.

A substantial quantitative increase in trade using the sucre has occurred: from 10 million sucres in 2010 to approximately 216 million in 2011, and around 850 million in 2012. The majority of trade in 2011 and 2012 was between Ecuador and Venezuela. There has also been a good deal of trade between the latter and Bolivia.

There has been progress, albeit slow, toward involving small-scale productive structures (cooperatives, communal companies) in order to diversify the variety of agents trading in the sucre.

Creation of CELAC. In December 2011, the Comunidad de Estados Latinoamericanos y Caribeños (Community of Latin American and Caribbean States, CELAC) was created in Caracas. Present at the meeting were all the presidents of the region, including Cuba's. Of the thirty-five countries in the continent, only the United States and Canada were excluded, converting CELAC into a direct challenge to the OAS.

The creation of CELAC constituted an event of great historic proportions, and it was the direct result of all the advances mentioned above. President Ortega from Nicaragua believes it represented a death sentence for the Monroe Doctrine, the policy that said that America was for the Americans, that is, those from the United States. I would add that it signified the beginning of the end for the OAS and the Washington Consensus, which imposed neoliberalism in the region. The hope is that out of CELAC the Latin American and Caribbean Consensus will emerge; that is, our own agenda, one that is not subordinated to U.S. interests.[44]

It is also significant that the second term of the *pro tempore* presidency was designated to Cuba, a previously excluded nation whose re-integration has been consolidated through this new way of inserting a sovereign Latin America into the global chessboard.

Significant growth in economic relations with China. Given China's growing need for raw materials and the fact that Latin America has plenty of them, relations between the two regions have become closer. Today, China is one of the main trading partners for Peru, Chile, and Brazil. It has begun to form strategic alliances with several other countries in the region. According to Spanish expert in international relations Tito Drago, "Within a few years, [China] has become the third-largest trading partner with the region and the first when it comes to Brazil, Chile and Peru. These three countries have also led the way in terms of economic growth over the last few years, while big countries such as Mexico, that are still closely tied to the U.S., did not grow as much."[45]

Drago adds that the Economic Commission for Latin America and the Caribbean (ECLAC) foresees trade with China continuing to grow and that the country will become the second-largest destination for exports from the region by 2014 and the second most important source of imports by 2015, in both cases overtaking the European Union.

It is worth noting that trade agreements with China do not impose conditions like those enforced by the United States or the European Union.

Since the end of 2009, trade and economic relations between China and Venezuela have been tightening. Agreements have been signed in agriculture, energy, and industry, and a deal has been struck to increase the amount of capital in the China-Venezuela Development Fund, doubling it to $12 billion. This is the biggest loan given by China to any country since 1949.

Diego Sánchez Ancochea, an economics professor at Saint Anthony's College, Oxford, says that the fund has generated new resources and opportunities for Brazil, Argentina, Venezuela, and other Latin American countries. However, it also creates serious risks and threats, including a steep rise in the trade deficit with China, a reinforcement of "the traditional way Latin America, especially the Andean countries and those of the Southern Cone, participate in the world economy," and a heavy blow to labor intensive sectors such as textiles, with small and medium-size companies at risk of being edged out by competitors who benefit from China's high productivity and low real wages.[46]

After running through this long list of events, I believe we can say, without equivocation, that U.S. influence in the region has declined.

The U.S. Empire's Power and its Plan for Recolonization and "Disciplining"

Although there has been a marked change in the correlation of forces to the benefit of left and progressive governments in the region, we should not exaggerate this. The U.S. loss of ideological and political influence, plus a reduction in its regional economic power, has been partially compensated by its increased influence on the media and growing military power.

Today there are twenty-three U.S. military bases across our subcontinent, and multilateral joint-military exercises are still held every year for the purpose of training troops in the region. The Fourth Fleet has been reactivated and U.S. intelligence networks have been extended in an effort to keep a watch over and control the dynamics of popular movements in the region. The

U.S. empire is trying to prevent the emergence of national forces capable of confronting U.S. policies of domination and vassalage.

There has been a huge increase in U.S. military aid to Colombia, its faithful ally and beachhead in the region.

To weaken any government it does not control, the United States has supported separatist movements such as in Bolivia (the eastern states of Santa Cruz, Beni, Pando, and Tarija), Ecuador (the city and province of Guayaquil), and Venezuela (the oil-rich state of Zulia).[47]

The Pentagon Kicks Off a New Strategy in 2008

Faced with the unstoppable advance of left forces in Latin America, especially over the last two years, the Pentagon, according to Mexican researcher Ana Esther Ceceña, has begun implementing "a plan to recolonize and discipline the whole continent," with the aim of trying to stop and, as much as possible, reverse the process of building a free and sovereign Latin America set in motion by President Chávez.[48]

The empire cannot accept the fact that, despite the enormous economic, political, military, and media power it has deployed in the region, Latin American countries are designing their own independent agenda that run counter to those of the empire.

The U.S. attack on Ecuador. The March 2008 attack on the Sucumbíos province in Ecuador was, according to Ana Esther Ceceña, the start of a "new phase in U.S. strategy to control its living space: the American continent." It represented the first stages of a state policy that did not change with Obama taking office, although it has adapted itself to the new continental situation.

The military action—which had the support of the Pentagon but was denounced by the OAS as a violation of Ecuadorian sovereignty—triggered a breakdown in Bogotá-Quito diplomatic relations.

Attempted civilian-prefectural coup in Bolivia. In response to Morales's overwhelming victory in the July 2008 recall referendum, the oligarchic right entrenched in the eastern departments that make up the Media Luna (Half Moon) attempted to mount what the Bolivian government denounced as a civilian-prefectural coup. Using their control over the prefectures of Santa Cruz, Beni, Pando, and Tarija, and with support from the elite-dominated civic committees in the region, they violently took over state institutions. Paramilitaries soon appeared on the street as part of a plan to create a situation of ungovernability and force the government to resign or bring the military out onto the streets, thereby contributing to further deaths and chaos and potentially providing a pretext for foreign military intervention.

As there was plenty of evidence that the plot had been prepared with the direct support of the U.S. embassy in La Paz, the Bolivian government decided to expel the U.S. ambassador on September 9. Chávez also decided to expel the U.S. ambassador to Venezuela that same day. Bolivian social movements responded by setting off on a march to Santa Cruz to confront the coup plotters.

This was followed by the massacre in Pando, where dozens of peasants were murdered. This event was so strongly condemned throughout Bolivia that the government, together with the social movements, decided to declare a state of emergency in Pando and sent the armed forces to restore order. The plot was finally defeated thanks to Santa Cruz being encircled by the social movements and the unequivocal statements issued by UNASUR that member countries would only recognize the legitimate government of Morales. For the right, this represented a new political-military defeat to add to its political defeat in the June referendum.

Institutional coup against Zelaya in Honduras. Fifteen months after the attack on Ecuador and six months into the Obama presidency, the Honduran president, Manuel Zelaya, was kidnapped and thrown out of the country in the early hours of June 28, 2009. Zelaya was a liberal political leader who, during his time in office, had become radicalized, joined ALBA, and proposed a constituent assembly. The National Assembly ordered the military operation that ousted him.

This institutional coup was almost unanimously denounced. Brazilian researcher Theotonio dos Santos reported that this was the first time the United States condemned a coup d'état in Latin America.[49] But what did this condemnation entail? Did it signify a change in U.S. imperial policy toward our subcontinent? Unfortunately, the answer is no. Nothing has fundamentally changed.

In spite of Obama's formal condemnation, there is clear evidence of the Pentagon's hand in the preparations for this coup. This comes as no surprise, as throughout the 1980s Honduras was the U.S. regional operations center for its fight against Nicaragua's Sandinista government and the Salvadoran guerrillas. Moreover, the Soto Cano military base was of strategic importance for military and intelligence operations in the region.

According to Costa Rican analyst Álvaro Montero, the Honduran army was used by Reagan and Bush to support the Contra military bases in Honduras and in the north of Nicaragua. The army collaborated with the CIA to transport and sell drugs as part of financing the dirty war against the Sandinistas. It was said that if a sheet of paper rustled in the barracks of the Honduran army, U.S. intelligence officers would hear it.[50]

The big question is how committed President Obama was to this coup. Opinions are divided on this matter. There are those who wonder if this was also a coup against Obama.[51] Others believe that it was a move aimed at reinforcing the militarist position of Hilary Clinton within the overall context of government policy toward the region. Venezuelan journalist and former deputy president José Vicente Rangel observed that two levels of U.S. government policy operated in Honduras; one was the White House's and the other was that of the machinery left in place by the Bush administration, operating from the U.S. military base in Palmerola.[52]

Clearly, the U.S. empire placed vital importance on stopping the advances being made toward integration, in particular the ALBA project initiated by Chávez, which had been gaining more and more supporters. So the Pentagon decided to attack the integration process at the weakest link, Honduras, by promoting a military coup with a "legal" face that was more in tune with the new era.

Ana Esther Ceceña writes that this was "the first operation carried out as part of re-launching an escalation" of the process of recolonization, which was then followed by the decision to install new military bases in Colombia with the concomitant immunity given to U.S. troops on Colombian soil.[53]

Space does not allow for a deeper analysis of events in Honduras. However, I want to state that in the short term, the big winner out of all this has been the Pentagon. At the same time, the abrupt interruption of Honduras's popular democratic process has sown the seeds for a resistance movement that sooner or later will see the Honduran people reconquer democracy and take steps toward building a fairer and more solidarity-based society. Honduras today is not the same as it was yesterday. Never before in its history have the popular sectors been so united. The struggle to hold a constituent assembly, instead of tapering off, is stronger than ever. One day the Honduran people will give thanks for this momentary setback.

New military bases in Colombia. The U.S. response to the closure of its Manta base was to transfer ships, arms, and high-tech spying equipment to Colombian bases as per the agreements signed in early March 2009 between the Colombian Ministry of Defense, the head of the Pentagon, and the CIA. This expanded U.S. military presence sought to turn Colombia into a virtual land-based U.S. aircraft carrier located in the heart of the region.[54]

It is no coincidence that the bases that will receive most of this military equipment are located very close to Colombia's borders with Ecuador and Venezuela.

Colombia's decision to allow U.S. soldiers and civilian personnel to be stationed in five bases within its territory created a domestic uproar that extended to the country's neighbors, especially Venezuela and Ecuador, and unleashed widespread criticism at the international level.

Negotiations surrounding the agreement were secretly held in the United States. The agreement was signed on October 30, 2009, by Colombian foreign minister Jaime Bermudez and U.S. ambassador to Colombia William Brownfield. The agreement is known as the "Complementary Agreement for Defense and Security Cooperation and Technical Assistance." According to a State Department internal document dated August 18, 2009, the Defense Cooperation Agreement is designed to facilitate bilateral cooperation in matters concerning Colombian security.

Instead of creating new military bases, the agreement grants U.S. personnel access to seven Colombian military installations: two naval bases, two military installations, and three air force bases located in Palanquero, Apia, and Malambo.

Colombia, South America's black sheep, is an occupied country. Like Mexico, it suffers from a "comprehensive occupation," to use Pablo González Casanova's term, involving the "occupation of social, economic, administrative, cultural, media, territorial and strategic spheres." Pentagon strategists call this phenomenon "full spectrum dominance."

Attempted coup against Rafael Correa. On September 30, 2010, a National Police strike was called in Ecuador in opposition to the Public Service Law approved the day before that sought to introduce labor reforms in the public service deemed to be detrimental to police officers.

Elements within the ranks of the National Police began a protest inside their barracks, went on strike, blockaded roadways, and impeded entry into parliament. Elements within the Ecuadorian Air Force also joined in, using their bodies to blockade the runway at the Mariscal Sucre International Airport.

Correa has said the police rebellion was an "attempted coup" orchestrated by the opposition and certain groups embedded in the armed forces and police with links to Sociedad Patriótica (Patriotic Society, PSP). While the president was detained in the Police Hospital in Quito, most of the countries across the world came out to condemn the attempted coup.

There are no indications that the United States was behind this coup, but it is well known that Lucio Gutiérrez maintains a close relationship with the U.S. government.

Institutional coup brings down Lugo in Paraguay. With thirty-nine votes in favor and only four against, the Paraguayan Senate voted in June 2012 to impeach Fernando Lugo for poor performance of his duties. He was accused of being responsible for the massacre carried out by Paraguayan security forces when attempting to evict some 100 campesinos occupying lands belonging to a member of the Partido Colorado (Colorado Party) during the Stroessner dictatorship. Eleven campesinos and six police officers were killed, and dozens more injured and detained. Vice President Federico Franco was sworn in as Lugo's successor.

As was to be expected, the United States accepted Lugo's sacking, while UNASUR and MERCOSUR condemned it.

A U.S. embassy cable made public by WikiLeaks revealed that the U.S. State Department knew the opposition was planning a coup in Paraguay. A confidential diplomatic cable dated March 28, 2009, and sent from the U.S. embassy in Asuncion to the State Department, noted: "Rumors persist that discredited General and UNACE party leader Lino Oviedo and ex-president Nicanor Duarte Frutos are now working together to assume power via (mostly) legal means should President Lugo stumble in coming months."[55] The cable points out the plan included Federico Franco taking over as president. According to the cable, the Paraguayan opposition was waiting for any kind of mistake by the ex-bishop in order to carry out a political trial against him.

Obama Government: More of the Same

The coup in Honduras and subsequent developments in that country, the increased number of military bases in Colombia, the continuing economic blockade of Cuba, keeping the base in Guantanamo open, and the other aforementioned events have been a particular disappointment for those who, like me, hoped for greater consistency between Obama's discourse and his actions. There is no longer even the slightest doubt that the aims pursued by the imperial apparatus remain the same, with the added factor that the Pentagon has begun to pay more attention to Latin America. Previously, its gaze was fixed on wars in Iraq and Afghanistan.

3. *Typology of Latin American Governments*

Previously I discussed how during the past ten years, progressive and left sectors have been winning governments in more and more countries across the region. Various analysts have made an effort to classify governments by drawing up different typologies. We can initially distinguish two large blocs: right or conservative governments that seek to give neoliberalism a makeover and governments that define themselves as "on the left" or "center left" and are looking for alternatives to the existing state of affairs.

Governments That Want to Give Neoliberalism a Makeover

Some Latin American countries want to give neoliberalism a makeover by implementing a series of reforms that "make it possible to further deepen the transnationalization and denationalization of their economies, by increasing incentives for big capital and continuing to regressively redistribute income."[56] These governments implement what Roberto Regalado has called "neoliberal reforms."[57]

The governments of Colombia, Mexico, Chile, and most Central American countries fall into this first group.

Governments Looking for Solutions That Offer an Alternative to Neoliberalism

Left or center-left governments in the region include those who were elected on platforms offering an alternative to neoliberalism. These governments, even though very different from each other, have at least four identical planks in their platforms: the struggles for social equality, for political democratization, for national sovereignty, and for regional integration. They can be further classified into two subgroups:

Governments that, without breaking with neoliberal policies, emphasize social issues. These governments seek to balance liberalism with progressive social policies such as subsidies, rather than structural changes. This includes the governments of Brazil, Uruguay, and Argentina. Former Mexican Foreign Minister Jorge Castañeda refers to them as the "good left." Aram Aharonian characterizes them as governments "with post-neoliberal, developmentalist policies, which without breaking with neoliberal economic policies place a fresh emphasis both on the social sphere and on policies that promote productive domestic capitalism." Roberto Regalado says these governments implement reforms that "try to alleviate the economic, political and social contradictions of today's capitalism without breaking with the systems."[58]

Governments that want to break with neoliberal policies using the support of popular mobilization. Some analysts have classified these governments as anti-imperialist, because they have adopted social and economic protectionist measures against the United States. They include the governments of Bolivia, Ecuador, Nicaragua, and Venezuela, governments that Jorge Castañeda calls the "bad left" and which Aram Aharonian describes as "governments based on social and popular mobilization that have an expressed desire for change, are in favor of a break with neoliberal policies and have a new understanding of the economy, of regional integration and of integration of the peoples."[59] According to Roberto Regalado, these governments implement "reforms whose strategic direction and intent are anti-capitalist" and therefore are reforms that might lead to revolution.[60]

U.S. intellectual James Petras, renowned for his radical views, considers these governments to represent a pragmatic left, in contrast to those he labels "the radical left," which includes the FARC.[61]

4. *"Left" Governments Facing More Objective Limitations*

Henceforth I shall speak of "left" (in quotation marks) governments to refer to the group of governments that won elections by raising anti-neoliberal banners, and leave it to the reader to classify them according to the criteria listed below.

However, before continuing I shall specify what I mean by left. In the 1960s, there was a tendency to define the left not so much by the goal it was pursuing but by the means it used to reach that goal. The implicit goal was socialism, the means were either armed struggle or institutional struggle, and the left was branded revolutionary or reformist according to which method it pursued.

In the 1990s, the term "New Left" was sometimes used to refer to those on the left that abandoned the armed struggle and joined the institutional struggle. At other times, this term was applied to the "social left," composed of a large number of diverse actors, such as indigenous peoples, women, environmentalists, and human rights defenders.[62]

I would like to suggest a stricter definition that is derived from the goal pursued. Such a definition requires us to ask ourselves if the objective is to give capitalism a makeover, so that it is more humane, or if the goal is to build a society that can replace capitalism.

Therefore, I use the label "left" to refer to the set of forces that struggle to build an alternative to the exploitative and oppressive capitalist system and its logic of profit. That is, a society of workers organized around a humanist and solidarity-based logic, with the aim of satisfying human needs. A society free from the material and spiritual poverty that capitalism engenders. A society that does not issue decrees from above but rather builds from below, with the people as protagonists. In other words, a socialist society.

These forces are therefore not motivated solely by a struggle for equality that manifests itself as a war on poverty—although this may be one of their most distinctive features—but also by the rejection of an aberrant societal model based on exploitation and the logic of profit: the capitalist model.

I should add, nevertheless, that I fully agree with the Uruguayan researcher Beatriz Stolowicz, who maintains, "One is not left just because one says one is; rather one is left because of what one does to achieve these necessary transformations and constructions. That is how one comes to be left."[63]

But why is it so necessary to use the criterion of practice to decide who is on the left? Because—as I wrote in 1999 in *The Left on the Threshold of the Twenty-First Century: Making the Impossible Possible*—the right has unscrupulously appropriated the left's language, which is particularly obvious in the way it formulates its programs.[64] Words like "reforms," "structural changes," "concern over poverty," and "transition" are today part of an anti-people, oppressive language. As Franz Hinkelammert says: "The key words of the oppositional popular movements of the 1950s and 1960s have been transformed into the key words of those who ruthlessly destroyed them."[65] He goes on to say a little later: "The night, when all cats are gray, falls. Everyone is against privilege; all want reforms and a structural change. Everyone is in favor of a preferential option for the poor."[66]

Today—in the midst of the crisis of neoliberalism—this appropriation of the left's language has reached the point where even capitalists have adopted the left's criticism of neoliberalism. The role of the market has begun to be challenged; there is talk of the need for the regulatory power of the state.

We have to acknowledge, as Beatriz Stolowicz says, that "in the sphere of discourse, capitalist strategies are not dogmatic, they change their arguments, they criticize what they previously proposed when the negative effects can no longer be hidden and are generating political problems." To win people over, "they show solidarity with *the discontent over globalization* (Stiglitz dixit) and join in the anti-globalization zeal." Thus, for them, "neoliberalism" is simply speculation, and financial capital is to blame for the irresponsibility of "bad executives," thus protecting the credibility of capital. Some have raised the suggestion that neoliberalism must be overcome by counteracting financial speculation with more productive investment. Capitalism thus presents itself as neo-developmentalism and against both laissez-faire and populism.[67]

Electoral Victories, but Less Room to Move

Returning to the subject of our governments, it is important to briefly examine the situation that existed when the government was elected, that is to say, the reality it had to deal with, so we can evaluate their performance as objectively as possible. When analyzing the correlation of forces in the subcontinent, I mentioned the efforts made by the Pentagon to retain military control over the region and reverse the process of integration taking place. Three other elements are important for a better understanding of the context in which these governments have had to operate:

1. **Key decisions made outside of government and parliament.** It is obvious that the new heads of government have had less room to maneuver in recent decades than in earlier periods, because today the important decisions are not made by parliaments or executive branches.

   Although the eligible voter population has increased enormously in recent decades and electoral fraud has become more and more difficult, making it possible for left candidates to be elected, this has, paradoxically, not led to an expansion of the democratic system. This is because most important decisions are not made by parliaments, nor by elected presidents, but by bodies they cannot control: large international financial institutions,(IMF, World Bank), autonomous central banks, big transnational corporations, national security bodies, etc.[68]

2. **Opposition-controlled media.** Then there is the role played by the media, which is concentrated in the hands of large economic groups.[69]

Noam Chomsky said the media are instruments for "manufacturing consent" and make it possible to "shepherd the bewildered herd." According to Chomsky, propaganda is as necessary to bourgeois democracy as repression was to the totalitarian state.[70] As such, bourgeois political parties can accept a defeat at the polls as long as they continue to control most of the mass media. It is the media that, from the moment of defeat, and even before, carries out the role of winning back the hearts and minds of those who made the "mistake" of electing a leftist head of state.

This is the reason for the visceral reactions we have seen in a number of our countries to measures taken by left governments to punish media disinformation campaigns or campaigns to incite violence, or to create legal instruments that protect the people's right to receive accurate information. The powerful international media echo these reactions. They know that today's political battles are not won with atomic bombs but with "media bombs."

An example of these "media bombs" is the campaign carried out to make people think Venezuela is engaged in an arms race that threatens the region. The media supports its argument by alluding to Venezuela's weapons purchase from Russia. However, if CIA data are consulted, it is clear the situation is the complete opposite. Using this data, Belgian economist Eric Toussaint reports in October 2009 that "Venezuelan military spending is the sixth highest in the region behind that of Brazil, Argentina, Chile (a country with a much smaller population than Venezuela and considered to be a 'model country'), Colombia, and Mexico. It relative terms, comparing military spending to GDP, the Venezuelan military budget is the ninth largest in Latin America." Have people been able to read this in the most important international papers? Not at all. Instead, the media reported in August 2009 that Sweden was asking Venezuela to respond to Colombian allegations that it was supplying arms to the FARC guerrillas. Sweden had in effect told Colombia that the SAAB missiles found in a FARC camp had been supplied by Sweden to Venezuela. However, was anyone able to find an article reporting the detailed and concise reply given by Hugo Chávez stating that the missiles in question had been stolen from a Venezuelan port in 1995, four years before he took over the presidency?[71] Who had the chance to read his reply?

3. **Inherited baggage.** These governments have also inherited a lot of cultural baggage: an individualist culture based on the idea of survival of the fittest; a paternalist culture that prefers to wait for the state to solve our problems instead of organizing and fighting to resolve them ourselves; a consumerist culture based on the belief that the more we have, the better we are, rather than feeling bad for owning unnecessary stuff when there are people around us who lack enough for a dignified life.

In sum, it seems today that the election of left candidates is better tolerated by conservative forces, so long as they remain within the established institutional framework, because ultimately they have fewer real possibilities of changing the existing situation.

Being Aware of the Correlation of Forces

Given everything I have said up until now, we must be careful when the time comes to judge "left" governments in the region. If we are to judge them by what they do, we must be very clear about what they cannot do, not because of lack of will but rather because of objective limitations. We have to begin with a correct analysis of the inherited economic structure, of the cultural baggage they inherit and within which they must operate, and of the correlation of forces, national and international, they face. These are things that more radical left sectors, which demand that their governments take more drastic measures, often fail to take into account. They point to Venezuela as an example of a government that should take more drastic measures because of its great economic potential due to natural resources, particularly oil, something that probably no revolutionary process has had in its favor before.

I share Valter Pomar's opinion when he states that the existing situation may oblige a revolutionary government to adopt capitalist measures, but that these measures take on a different strategic meaning depending on whether a capitalist or socialist government adopts them.[72] I would add that these capitalist measures must also create conditions for advancing afterward toward socialist relations of production.

Therefore, by looking first at the existing situation in each country and analyzing the correlation of forces, we can better understand what these governments can and cannot do.

Correlation of Forces: Chávez and Lula

Let us consider for a moment Lula's government in Brazil. Although he won the presidential elections in 2002 with a bigger vote than Chávez obtained in 1998, we should not forget that this result came about because of a policy of broad alliances that were necessary for winning at the polls, and even more so for governing the country. We have to remember that the PT is not "the hegemonic force within Brazilian society," having only a minority in both houses of the legislature and, although it controlled, and still controls, a significant number of capital cities and important state governorships, it is in the minority at the provincial, municipal, and national level. To all this must be added the fact that Brazil depends to a much greater degree on international finance capital than Venezuela does, with its huge oil revenues. Moreover, Lula doesn't have the same level of support within the armed forces as did Chávez. The latter defined his revolutionary process as peaceful but armed. As Pomar said in a recent interview, we are dealing with "a country marked by the effects of neoliberalism, [and] hegemonized by big capital and center-right forces, but this does not mean we cannot or should not criticize [the Lula government], particularly in regard to the way it has sought to overcome the legacy of neoliberalism and the hegemony of the center-right and big capital."[73]

Taking as our starting point the objective conditions in Brazil, I agree with Pomar when he says that the correlation of forces, institutional mechanisms, or economic situations that could allow the Brazilian government to operate similarly to the Venezuelan government do not exist.[74] He does, however, acknowledge that Lula's government could have done more than it has done to date.

It's Not the Pace, It's the Direction That Matters

If we keep in mind all the factors mentioned above, rather than classifying Latin American governments according to some kind of typology as many analysts have done, we should try to evaluate their performance, always keeping in mind the correlation of forces within which they operate. We should pay less attention to the pace with which they are advancing, and more attention to the direction in which they are going, since the pace will, to large extent, depend on how these governments deal with obstacles in their path.[75]

PART 2

Where Are We Going? Twenty-First Century Socialism

5. *Why Talk about Socialism?*

You might be asking: why refer to *socialism* if this word has such negative connotations? Following socialism's collapse in the Soviet Union and Eastern Europe, leftist intellectuals the world over fell into a state of confusion. We seemed to know more about what we did not want socialism to be rather than what we wanted it to be. We rejected any lack of democracy, totalitarianism, state capitalist methods, and bureaucratic central planning. We opposed collectivism that sought to standardize without respect for differences, and productivism that emphasized the expansion of productive forces without taking into consideration the need to preserve nature. We also wanted nothing to do with dogmatism, intolerance toward legitimate opposition, attempts to impose atheism by persecuting believers, and the belief that a sole party was needed to lead the process of transition.

Today, the situation in Latin America has changed. We have a rough idea of what we want. Yet, why is the region clearer today on what kind of future society we want to construct? I believe this is largely due to:

1. The practical experience of what we have referred to as "local governments of popular participation." Profoundly democratic governments have opened up spaces for people's empowerment

and, thanks to their transparency, contribute to the fight against corruption.

2. The rediscovery of communitarian indigenous practices, from which we have much to learn.
3. The lessons we can learn from those Latin American governments that have proposed moving toward an anti-capitalist society, even if each government has given this society a different name.

These beacons that radiate throughout our continent were strengthened by the resounding failure of neoliberalism, increased resistance and struggle by social movements, and, more recently, by the global crisis of capitalism. An alternative to capitalism is more necessary than ever. What should we call it?

President Chávez was the first to have the courage to call this alternative society socialism. He called it "21st century socialism," reclaiming the values associated with the word *socialism*: "love, solidarity, equality between men and women and equity among all," but adding the adjective "21st century" to differentiate this new socialism from the errors and deviations of the socialist model that was implemented during the twentieth century in the Soviet Union and Eastern European countries.[1]

We should recall that the world's first experiment with a socialism that differed from the Soviet model began in Chile, with the triumph of President Salvador Allende and the leftist Unidad Popular (Popular Unity, UP) coalition in 1970. Allende and the UP proposed a peaceful transition via the institutional road but were defeated by a military coup three years later. If our generation learned anything from this defeat, it was that to travel peacefully toward our goal required rethinking the socialist project that had been implemented until then in the world, and that it was necessary to develop a new project suited to the Chilean reality and find a peaceful way to build it. That's what Allende seemed to sense when he coined his folkloric metaphor of "socialism with red wine and empanadas," alluding to the idea of building a democratic socialist society rooted in popular national traditions.[2]

Chávez Coins the Phrase "21st Century Socialism"

On December 5, 2004, at the closing ceremony of the World Meeting of Intellectuals and Artists in Defense of Humanity held in Caracas, Chávez surprised the audience by declaring for the first time, "It is necessary to review the history of socialism and rescue the concept of socialism."[3]

Why was this a surprise? Because when he began his term in office, he thought he could carry out social transformations while leaving capitalism untouched, via a "Third Way." But he soon realized this was not possible. The Venezuelan oligarchy was unwilling to give ground on anything. They only had to sense that the package of laws decreed at the end of 2001 might affect their interests a little bit to decide to organize a coup to overthrow Chávez. Once this plan failed, they tried to paralyze the country's economy by sabotaging the oil industry. This experience, and two other factors, convinced the president that he had to find another way. Two other factors—coming to an understanding that the heartrending problems of the Venezuelan people could not be solved quickly enough using the bourgeois state apparatus he had inherited, and an awareness that within the framework of the capitalist model it is impossible to solve the tragedy of poverty and inequality—convinced him he had to move toward a different kind of society, toward what he subsequently called "21st century socialism."[4]

A few weeks later, when he spoke at the World Social Forum on January 30, 2005, in Porto Alegre, Brazil, he reiterated the need to overcome capitalism and build socialism, but warned, "We have to reinvent socialism. It can't be the kind of socialism we saw in the Soviet Union." It is not a case of "resorting to state capitalism," because if we do that, we will fall "into the same distortion as the Soviet Union did."

Then, at the Fourth Social Debt Summit on February 25 that same year, he said there was no other alternative to capitalism besides socialism. However, he warned it would have to be different from previous socialisms, that we would have to "invent 21st century socialism." This was the first time the phrase "21st century socialism" was used in public.

We can say, without a doubt, that Chávez was the person who coined the phrase. I say he "coined" it in the sense that he was responsible for popularizing the name, because some authors had already used it; for example, the Chilean sociologist Tomás Moulian in his book *21st Century Socialism: The Fifth Way*, which was published in 2000.[5]

Conscious of the negative baggage that came with the term, the Bolivarian leader decided to explain to his people, via numerous public interventions, all the benefits that this new society would bring for them, contrasting this with the situation created by capitalism. His pedagogical efforts were so successful that, according to polls, more than half of the Venezuelan population currently prefers socialism to capitalism.

A Socialism That Is Neither an Imitation nor Copy, but Rooted in Our History

However, it's not a matter of copying foreign models or exporting our own; it is necessary to build a model of socialism tailored to each country. Naturally, all models will share some common features that give it a socialist character.

The three basic features Chávez pointed to were: economic transformation, participative and protagonistic democracy in the political sphere, and socialist ethics "based on love, solidarity and equality between women and men, everybody."[6]

These socialist ideas and values are very old. According to President Chávez, they can be found in biblical texts, in the Gospel, and in the practices of our indigenous peoples.[7]

Chávez believed, as Mariátegui did, that 21st century socialism could not be a carbon copy of other models; it had to be a "heroic creation." That is why he talked of a "Bolivarian, Christian, Robinsonian, Indoamerican socialism . . . a new collective existence, equality, liberty and real, complete democracy."[8]

Other leaders refer to communitarian socialism, a society based on the logic of *buen vivir*, a society of complete life. I agree with Bolivia's Vice President Álvaro García Linera, who says the name is not what matters, what matters is the content.

Chávez concurred with Mariátegui that one of the principle roots of our project can be found in the socialism of our indigenous peoples. He therefore suggested that those indigenous practices imbued with a socialist spirit must be rescued and empowered.

Moreover, when people in Bolivia speak of "communitarian socialism," they are proposing that we rescue what García Linera has called "communal civilization, with its technological procedures based on the power of the masses, on managing family and communal land and on the way economic and political activity meld, a civilization which has its own authorities and political institutions which give more importance to normative action than to electing, and in which individuality is a product of the collectivity and its past history."[9]

All this should lead us to renounce any Western paternalist culture that believes indigenous communities need our help. Chávez maintained we should instead "ask them for help . . . so that they cooperate with us in building the socialist project of the 21st century."[10]

6. *Recovering the Original Socialist Thinking*

This socialism of the 21st century, which seeks to guard its distance from the practices of twentieth-century socialism, has recovered some of Marx and Engels' original ideas. These ideas were not only distorted by the actions of the Soviet regime and the Marxist literature disseminated by that country, but were also downplayed or ignored by those who rejected socialism given what was done in its name.

Let us proceed to outlining some of these principle ideas.

Integral human development. According to Marx and Engels, future society will facilitate the integral development of all the potentialities of human beings, something that can only be achieved in a "cooperative society."[11] In place of the fragmented human beings that capitalism produces, there will be integrally developed human beings. This development will be achieved through revolutionary practice (in transforming circumstances, the person transforms themselves), which is why Marx also affirmed that it is through revolutionary struggle that workers begin to throw off the muck of ages and start a process of self-transformation.

Friedrich Engels wrote in his "Draft of a Communist Confession of Faith," an early draft of what would become *The Communist Manifesto*, that the goal was "to organize society in such a way that every member of it can develop and use all his capabilities and powers in complete freedom and without thereby infringing the basic conditions of this society." In Marx's final version of the *Manifesto*, this new society was presented as an "association in which the free development of each is the condition for the free development of all."

Canadian Marxist Michael Lebowitz has amply elaborated this idea in a number of his books dedicated to the issue of 21st century socialism.[12] He has been the most consistent in emphasizing integral human development as the goal, and the relationship between human development and revolutionary practice.

Human beings as social beings. Another of Marx's often-ignored ideas has to do with the social character of human nature. Yet this is something he first talked about in the *Third Economic and Philosophical Manuscripts of 1844*. According to Marx, the communist society will allow individuals, who are social beings, to fully realize their social character.[13] When he put forward the proposition that human beings were social beings, he was not proposing the negation of the individual, he was saying that individual human nature is eminently social. There is a complementary, dialectical relationship between the individual being and the social being that makes it impossible to establish a separation between the individual character and social surroundings of a human being.

As the French philosopher Henri Lefebvre noted, there is no such thing as an abstract citizen, who is above everything, who is neither rich nor poor, neither young nor old, neither male nor female, or all of those things at once. Yugoslav writer Miodrag Zecevic said, "What exist are concrete persons who live among and depend on other people, who associate with and organize in various ways with other people in communities and organizations in which and through which they make real their interests, rights and duties."[14]

This implies the rejection of "collectivism," which suppresses differences between each member of society in the name of a group.

Collectivism is a flagrant distortion of Marxism. Remember, Marx criticized bourgeois law for trying to make people artificially equal instead of acknowledging their differences. By pretending to be the same for everyone, bourgeois law ends up being an unequal right. He said that any truly fair distribution had to take into account people's differentiated needs. Hence his maxim: "From each according to his ability, to each according to his needs."[15]

From where did Marx get these "scarce" ideas regarding what the alternative society to capitalism (which he calls communism) should look like? I say *scarce* because there are not many references in Marx's works to socialism. The German thinker dedicated himself to scientifically studying the capitalist mode of production, and even here he was unable to fully develop his ideas on the various areas he proposed to study. Moreover, even if he had the time to dedicate himself to studying what an alternative society might look like, he would not have been able to advance much in this direction given that scientific knowledge cannot precede reality.

Marx's ideas about the nature of future society did not fall from the sky, nor are they the result of speculative thought; rather, they arose from an analysis of the internal contradictions of capitalism itself. Marx argues that capitalism creates the material conditions of this new society. One of these is the technical need for the existence of the collective worker; another is an increase in the productive capacity required to respond to people's most pressing needs.

But Marx not only indicated the conditions that favored the emergence of an alternative society. He also studied the contradictions and negative effects of capitalism on workers and the environment, to indicate what must be negated (reversed or transformed into their opposite) if we are to move forward with the task of building socialism.[16]

Thanks to these inversions, Marx could envision the new society that would replace capitalism.

Social property. It is necessary to end capitalist private ownership of the means of production, which has come into conflict with the increasingly social nature of production. This socialization of production reveals the need for property to become collective or common property in order to overcome the economic anarchy of capitalist production. Similarly, the economy should not be orientated toward self-interest but toward the interests of society as a whole.

Eliminate the division between manual and intellectual labor. It is necessary to end the growing division between manual and intellectual labor—the result of capitalist dispossession of workers' knowledge and skill—and transform labor into a comprehensiv, simultaneously manual, and intellectual activity. In order to achieve workers' maximum productive potential, it is necessary to end the alienated and mandatory character of labor that fragments and transforms workers into one more cog in a machine. These inversions establish the centrality of workers as protagonists in the production process.

Govern nature in a rational way. Marx also stated it was essential to end capitalist relationships of production and the antagonism between city and countryside, because they were responsible for an "irreparable rift" in the interdependent process of social metabolism between human beings and nature.[17] He noted that only in a communist society would "the associated producers, govern the human metabolism with nature in a rational way, bringing it under their collective control. . . ."[18]

I want to briefly expand on this topic, given the misrepresentations that have arisen based on a superficial reading of Marx's and Engels's texts, generally taken out of context, whereby these authors had a positive appreciation for capitalism's ability to develop productive forces and the perspective of promoting an even greater development of these forces within the socialist society. I say "taken out of context" because when they speak of the necessity of pursuing industrial development on a grand scale within the new society, they are not proposing unlimited development but a level of development sufficient to produce "enough goods to arrange distribution in such a way that the needs of all its members will be satisfied."[19]

We must remember that Marx lived in a time of crisis of land fertility provoked by capitalism's "blind desire for profits," a crisis that provoked a desperate search for natural fertilizers such as guano and then saltpeter, and that underpinned the second agricultural revolution associated with the notable advances made in the science of soil. Early on, Marx believed these innovations would contribute to solving the crisis, but he quickly reached the conclusion that the second agricultural revolution would only worsen the problems.[20]

In that context, more than 150 years ago, the author of *Capital* developed, according to Marxist ecologist John Bellamy Foster, "a critique of the environmental degradation that anticipated much of the present day ecological thought."[21]

In his masterpiece, Marx wrote: ". . . Moreover, all progress in capitalist agriculture is a progress in the art, not only of robbing the worker, but of robbing the soil; all progress in increasing the fertility of the soil for a given time is a progress toward ruining the more long-lasting sources of that fertility. The more country proceeds from large-scale industry as the background of its development, as in the case of the United States, the more rapid is this process of destruction. Capitalist production, therefore, only develops the techniques and the degree of combination of the social process of production by simultaneously undermining the original sources of all wealth—the soil and the worker."[22]

From all this, we can conclude that only an alternative society to capitalism will be able to reestablish the natural metabolism between humans and nature. This alternative is a socialist society in which people and not a privileged elite decide—through their delegates—what and how to produce to satisfy the population's true needs, and not artificial ones created by capitalism in its crazy pursuit of greater and greater profits.

Society, not the state, must take the reins of economic development. For Marx and Engels, socialism did not entail the simple handing over of the strategic means of production to the state, as this represents little more than a juridical change. The subordination of workers to an external force continues: there may be new socialist managers, but the alienated status of the workers in the production process remains unchanged. Though formally collective property, since the state represents society, real appropriation is still not collective.

Engels argued, "State-ownership of the productive forces is not the solution to the conflict" between the increasingly social character of production and private ownership over the means of production, although he added, "Concealed within it are the technical conditions that form the elements of that solution." What is the solution? Engels maintained "this solution can only consist in the practical recognition of the social nature of the modern forces of production, and therefore in the harmonizing of the mode of production, appropriation and exchange with the socialized character of the means of production. And this can only come about by society openly and directly taking possession of the productive forces, which have outgrown all controls, except that of society as a whole."[23]

Yet what does it mean for society to take possession of the means of production? Society is a highly abstract concept: it could mean all of humanity. This question will be answered later on in this book.

7. *Some Current Reflections on Twenty-First Century Socialism*

Obviously, we have to go beyond simply looking at the ideas of Marx and Engels. More than 150 years have passed, the world has changed, the new electronic-information revolution has brought with it new challenges and opportunities, and we face an alarming rate of environmental destruction. We are confronted with new questions that require new answers. We need to enrich these ideas with new reflections and proposals. Regarding this task, today we are in a better situation than we were a few years ago.

In what follows, I shall present some of the features that must be key characteristics of 21st century socialism.

Participatory and Protagonistic Democracy

Political Democracy and Social Democracy

As mentioned earlier, socialism came to be associated with a lack of democracy and freedom due to the actions of the Soviet regime. Factions of the left responded to this criticism by saying revolutionaries were only interested in real social democracy, not bourgeois pseudo-democracy. It was pointless to speak of democracy while people continued to die of hunger, while people were homeless, while people were unable to study, while people continued to die at a young age due to a lack of medical attention.

Today, the experience of these dictatorships has modified people's perceptions and forced many to start valuing political democracy. Some believed it was necessary to fill bourgeois political democracy with a social content.

Alfredo Maneiro, a Venezuelan intellectual and political leader, criticized this thesis, arguing it was not a question of adding a social thing to a political thing; rather, it was necessary to transform the very form of democracy by creating spaces that allowed for people's protagonism.[24]

Maneiro said it was not the same if a community managed to get a pedestrian bridge it had organized and fought for than if the bridge was given to them by the state as a gift. State paternalism is incompatible with popular protagonism.

I believe state paternalism tends to turn people into beggars. We must move from a culture in which citizens beg the state to solve their problems to a culture where citizens make decisions, and through struggle get results; where citizens implement, control, and manage things themselves, where citizens govern themselves. We have to go, as Aristóbulo Istúriz says, from a government for the people to people's self-government, that is to a situation where the people take power.

This participatory and protagonistic democracy is not a democracy solely for the elites, as bourgeois representative democracy is; it is a democracy for the great majority of the people. Within it, the common citizen can participate in a variety of matters, not only in formulating demands and supervision, but more fundamentally in making decisions and ensuring they are carried out.

As Uruguayan political leader Pablo Anzalone said, it is about constructing democratic processes in which the great popular majorities are incorporated into the political arena, both within institutions as well as in practice.[25] This requires a reformulation of the idea of politics, recuperating and emphasizing participatory mechanisms from the local to the national level.

Human Development through Popular Participation

Participation, protagonism in all spaces, is what will allow human beings to grow and increase their self-confidence, that is, facilitate human development.

I am almost certain that the Bolivarian constitution is the only one of its kind in terms of drawing a direct relationship between protagonism and integral human development, both individual and collective.

Although there are several articles in the constitution that refer to this subject, probably the most specific one is Article 62, which indicates how to bring about this development. It says, "People's participation in creating, implementing and controlling public policy is the necessary way to achieve the protagonism that ensures its full development, both individual and collective." It then goes on to say that it is "the state's obligation and society's duty to create the conditions most favorable to this participation." Article 70 points to other ways that allow people to develop "their capacities and abilities," such as "self-management, cooperatives of all kinds . . . and other forms of association that are guided by the values of mutual cooperation and solidarity."

As for participation at the local, territorial level, emphasis has been placed on participative diagnoses, participative budgets, and social auditing. Initially, local public planning councils were set up at the municipal level, composed of representatives from already existing institutions (mayors, councilors, members of the parish boards) and community representatives, who together carried out public planning.[26] It is important to note there was a greater percentage of community representatives, as opposed to institutional representatives, on these councils (51 to 49 percent), reflecting the clear political will that existed to encourage community protagonism.

Michael Lebowitz writes, "Only a revolutionary democracy can create the conditions in which we can invent ourselves daily" as fully developed human beings. He adds that the "concept . . .

of democracy in *practice*, democracy *as* practice, *democracy as protagonism*: protagonistic democracy in the workplace, protagonistic democracy in neighborhoods, communities, communes—is the democracy of people who are transforming themselves into revolutionary subjects."[27]

Protagonism and the Organization of Forces from Below

The need for popular protagonism is a recurring theme in the speeches of the late Venezuelan president Hugo Chávez and is an element that differentiates him from many other advocates of democratic socialism.

In the first program of "Theoretical Aló Presidente," broadcast on television and radio on June 11, 2009, he quoted at length from a letter that Peter Kropotkin wrote to Lenin on March 4, 1920. I think it is important to cite the most important ideas read out by Chávez, because they reveal his concerns.

> Without the participation of local forces, without an organization from below of the peasants and workers themselves, it is impossible to build a new life.
>
> It seemed that the Soviets were going to fulfill precisely this function of creating an organization from below. But Russia has already become a Soviet Republic in name only. The party's influence over people . . . has already destroyed the influence and constructive energy of this promising institution—the Soviets.[28]

President Chávez was convinced, and on innumerable occasions stated, that the problem of poverty cannot be solved without giving power to the people.

Creating Appropriate Spaces for Participation

Chávez's ideas would have never gone beyond mere talk if appropriate spaces had not been created where participatory processes could fully and freely take place. For this reason, his initiatives to create communal councils, followed some time later by his proposal for workers' councils, student councils, and peasant councils, were important steps toward forming real popular power. Today this power is also being expressed in the communes.

Only when a society based on worker self-management in workplaces and self-management by residents of their communities is created will the state cease to be an instrument that, standing over and above the people, serves the elites, and instead become a state whose cadres are composed of the best elements of the working people.

One of the most revolutionary ideas of the Bolivarian government was promoting the creation of communal councils, a form of autonomous community-based organization.[29] They are territorial organizations, unprecedented in Latin America because of the small number of participants: between 200 to 400 families in densely populated urban areas, 50 to 100 families in rural areas, and even smaller numbers of families in isolated, mostly indigenous, areas. The idea was to create small spaces that offered maximum encouragement to citizen involvement and facilitated the protagonism of those attending by making them feel comfortable and encouraging them to speak freely.

The idea for these territorially based organizations was arrived at after much debate and after looking closely at successful experiences of community organization like the Comites de Tierra Urbana (Urban Land Committees, CTU), which involved some 200 families organized around the issue of land ownership, and health committees, composed of some 150 families who formed committees to offer support to doctors in the most disadvantaged communities.

If we take a community to mean a group of families who live in a specific geographical space, who know and easily relate to one another, who can meet without needing to rely on transport, share a common history, use the same public services, and face similar problems, it is estimated that in Venezuela, which has about 26 million inhabitants, there are about 52,000 communities.

Each of these communities will elect a body that will act as a community government. This body is given the name of community council, and the people elected to carry out that task are called *voceria* (spokespersons), from the Spanish *vocero* or *vocera*, which in turn originate from *voz* (voice).

A Participatory Democracy Not Counterposed to Delegated Democracy

The Limits of Direct Democracy

We must also understand that direct democracy, that is, a democracy in which people debate and decide in assemblies, is not the only acceptable form of democracy. Direct democracy is one form of democracy, undoubtedly the richest and most protagonistic form, but it has its limits.

For everyone to be able to fully participate, the size of the group cannot be excessively large. It is difficult to imagine direct municipal democracy in a municipality with 200,000 people, much less direct democracy in large capital cities made up of millions of people.

Democratic participation cannot remain limited to experiences on a small scale; it has to transcend the community, the factory, and the classroom in order to go from local levels of power all the way to the national level. The same must occur in a factory: along with workers' councils in each workshop or sector, there must be workers' councils in each factory, and each branch of industry. The same must occur in centers of study, with councils in each classroom, faculty, university, and across all universities.

We have to create a system that allows citizens to participate in all decision-making processes concerning specific and general issues that affect their lives. This requires establishing some form of delegation of power that does not reproduce the limits and deformation inherent in classic bourgeois representative politics.

In this regard, revolutionary Venezuela has taken transcendental steps that mark a new high point in Latin American political history. They have abolished the classic idea of political representation in order to begin creating a political system that combines direct democracy with delegations, or *voceria*. Those that are elected to take part in the communal council are called *voceros* (spokespeople) because they are the voice of the community, and when they cease to be so, because the community no longer feels they are adequately transmitting the ideas and decisions of the community, these people can and should be recalled.

Combination of Direct and Delegated Democracy

In short, building a new political system of popular power or self-government combines direct democracy on a small scale with a whole system of assemblies of *voceros* or delegates at different levels, which then elect, orientate, and control the different organs of government.

A correct critique of bourgeois representative democracy should not lead us to reject all types of representation. What we reject is a democracy that is limited to five minutes of voting every few years, an elitist democracy that makes invisible important sectors of the population who today are beginning to appear on the political scene in different parts of the world, expressing open or implicit critiques of the current political system.

If we believe that big decisions have to be made by the people, we have to be coherent and point out how millions of people, living hundreds of kilometers away from one another, are going to make these decisions. I see no other alternative than delegating some people to represent the positions of their communities at higher levels. Moreover, we have to be clear that if they (in representation of their base) do not make these decisions, others will do it for them.

Denying the possibility of delegation is denying the possibility to participate in decision making on issues that transcend our local reality, that is, the community, workplace, classroom.

Those who today are made invisible will not become visible unless they themselves make their presence felt. This was the error committed by the Zapatistas, who despite having made themselves visible in 1994 through their armed insurrection have subsequently marginalized themselves from national politics and have to a certain extent become invisible once again.

Given this, it is possible to conclude that we need to create a political system of representation, or delegation, though one that is very different from the bourgeois democratic system. The latter views representatives as professional politicians and therefore expects they should be remunerated for their role. Their mandate is seen exclusively as a personal one, and not one that reflects their voters, who are only reached out to at election time.[30] The alternate system of delegation or *voceria* is the antithesis of this conception and practice: elected representatives, delegates, or *voceros* must remain tied to their base, which in turn must supervise and guide the work of that delegate and prevent his or her bureaucratization.

Delegates are not given a blank check for a certain period of time like bourgeois representatives are; rather, they must be guided by the decisions and orientations of their electors, who evaluate their performance in accordance with the tasks they have been assigned. This is what the Zapatistas mean by their idea of "governing by obeying."

Here we have to clarify that this is not the same as saying the delegate's mandate is binding. They are not robots that receive messages and simply transmit them; they are responsible and creative people who, faced with the realities of other communities, must be able to modify the mandate they have received once they have seen, for example, that a neighboring community is in a worse situation than their own and therefore should be supported, rather than simply defending one's own community. As they must account for their mandate in their community, the delegates will have to return home and explain their decision. They will have to win over their community to an understanding of why, based on reasons of solidarity that justified the decision made, the delegates chose not to comply with the mandate they were given. If the community is not convinced, it has the right to recall delegates because the delegates no longer represent its wishes. In this case, it could be said that the community has yet to mature and take onboard the value of solidarity, and therefore does not deserve a delegate who reflects those values. Let's recall that old saying, "The people get the government they deserve." The same could be said of this community.

García Linera explains this same thing using other words, and in his case referring to those governing at the national level:

> To govern by obeying is to affirm every day that the sovereign is not the state, that the sovereign is the people who do not express themselves only every five years through the vote, but rather they express themselves, they speak, they put forward each day their needs, expectations and collective requirements. What is required of the leader is to synthesize and to unite, because the voices of the people can be discordant. The people are not something homogeneous. No sir! There are social classes, there are identities, there are regions. The people are very diverse. The role of those in government is not to substitute for the people but to harmonize the voices of the people, only to synthesize in a sense their concerns. But that does not mean that they are substitutes for the people. To govern by obeying is that the sovereign is the people and the leader is simply a unifier of ideas, someone who articulates their needs, and nothing else.[31]

In order to comply with their roles as *voceria*, these people should be elected from their workplace or community and, as said above, be recallable if they lose the confidence of their electorate.

Moreover, they should not receive a salary, but instead continue working at their normal job. If it is necessary at certain times to dedicate themselves full-time to community work, it should be the community—via its own resources—that pays them a certain sum of money that allows them to cover their basic living costs. In this way, it is even clearer why the delegate should report back to the community. This also avoids transforming community work into bureaucratic tasks that are carried out simply to obtain a salary.

Finally, some communities have taken a healthy approach toward rotating cadres, to avoid a situation whereby certain people eternalize themselves in certain roles, impeding the ability of others in the community to learn how to carry those tasks.

And, of course, it is very important that delegates are correctly selected. Once again, the Venezuelan experience has provided us with some important insights. There, we have seen just how important it is that the election of delegates is carried out properly, with the people knowing the candidates, having seen them in action and thus not solely reliant on what the candidates say.

How do people know who the candidates are? The general practice within a communal council is that, before voting, candidates who nominate themselves for election collaborate in carrying out a socioeconomic and demographic census of the community. This has been very positive, because through the process they are obliged to contact each family in the community.

The elaboration of a brief history of the community, together with the people, has also been very useful, as it has allowed candidates to become more acquainted with the reality they have to deal with.

Another constructive activity has been the organization of a participatory diagnostic that allows them to get to know the real needs and dreams of the people who live in the community.

It is therefore not enough to be able to deliver beautiful speeches to be elected; the people in the community have seen just how dedicated each candidate is to their community. This helps avoid electing *voceros* who are simply looking for a launching pad for their own political career.

I believe that all this should lead us to conclude that the democratic system we want to build has to combine direct democracy and indirect or delegated democracy.

Decentralization Allows for Real Popular Protagonism

I have said that popular protagonism is central to socialism, but promoting participation can become little more than sloganeering if people do not have the opportunity to offer their opinions and make decisions in the areas where they spend most of their time (communities, workplaces, educational institutions, interest groups, etc). If the central state decides everything, there is no room for local initiatives, and the state becomes an obstacle or, as Marx said, ends up hindering the "free movement" of society.[32]

It is interesting to note that István Mészáros believes the Soviet state's excessive centralization led to "both the Soviets and the factory councils [being] deprived of all effective power."[33] We should not be surprised, then, when he argues that one of the aims to be pursued in the transition phase is "accomplishing a genuine autonomy and decentralization of the powers of decision making, in opposition to their existing concentration and centralization which cannot possibly function without 'bureaucracy.'"

Centralization Produces Bureaucratism

I agree with Mészáros that decentralization is the best way to combat the bureaucratic deformations of the state. This was not the way Lenin saw it: he always related the phenomenon of bureaucracy to the state inherited from capitalism.

Before his death, Lenin was concerned about the "bureaucratic ulcer" affecting the state apparatus.[34] In one of his last writings, he said, "Our state apparatus is to a considerable extent a survival of the past and has undergone hardly any serious change."[35] A few days earlier, he described it as a "bourgeois and tsarist hodgepodge."[36]

In his last article on the role of the unions, written in January 1922, he went as far as to say that "in no way could the strike struggle be renounced" provided that it was directed against the bureaucratic deviations of the proletarian state. He explained that this struggle was very different from the one waged under the capitalist regime, when the struggle was to destroy the bourgeois state; now the struggle was to fortify the proletarian state by combating "the bureaucratic deformations" of the state, its huge weaknesses, and "all kinds of vestiges of the old capitalist regime in its institutions, etc."[37]

As we can see, Lenin thought the bureaucratic deformations that characterized the Soviet state were a legacy of the past. I believe he was wrong, and this fact prevented him from prescribing the right medicine for this disease. As I understand it, the underlying causes of bureaucratism lay in the excessive centralization of the Soviet state. We know full well what happens when not only strategic decisions but nearly all decisions are made centrally: red tape, endless running around, slowness in enacting, lack of control, lack of response to local problems, brakes put on local initiatives, etc.

Only Social Control Can Prevent Corruption

One of the most important lessons learned by the Cuban government when it failed to meet its ambitious 1970 sugar harvest target was that it was impossible for the socialist state to administer everything centrally, especially so in an underdeveloped country like Cuba. Spaces were required where people could exercise control over the way the state functioned and ensure it operated more effectively.[38] Fidel Castro admitted this in his July 26 anniversary speech in 1970.

"The revolutionary process itself has shown," he said two months later, "the problems caused by bureaucratic and administrative methods."[39]

After pointing out the mistakes made as a result of identifying the party with the state administration and allowing mass organizations to become weak, he stressed the role the people should play in making decisions and solving problems:

> Imagine a baker's shop on a street which provides bread to all who live there and an administrative apparatus that controls it from above. How does it control it? How could the people not care how that bakery operates? How could they not care whether an administrator is good or bad? How could they not care if people there had privileges or not, if there was negligence or not, insensitivity or not? How could they not care about how it delivered its services? How could they not care about the hygiene problems there? And how could they not care about the production problems, absenteeism, the quantity and quality of the goods? They couldn't!
>
> Can anyone think up a more effective means for controlling that bakery than the masses themselves? Could there be any other method of inspection? No! The person who runs that micro-unit of production could become corrupt; the person who inspects it could become corrupt, everyone could become corrupt. The only ones who are not going to become corrupt are those affected [by all this], those affected!

These ideas were incorporated into Cuba's new constitution in 1976.

The new political model proposed decentralizing to the municipal level as many of the state's functions as possible. Although these institutions had to be subordinated to those above them, they could act autonomously within the established legal and regulatory framework and "should not be submitted to constant and restricting supervision by the institutions above them."

According to Raúl Castro, this mechanism, "in addition to making the higher level bodies work faster and better and more in tune with the demands made by the where and when of the decisions that have to be taken, frees them, and especially national institutions, of the heavy, voluminous burden of everyday administrative tasks which in practice they cannot properly carry out . . . and which, moreover, prevents them from attending to the important tasks they are truly competent to undertake in areas related to setting standards, control and inspection of the activities they deal with."[40]

As time went by, experience demonstrated it was necessary to decentralize government administration even further, leading to the creation of the People's Council in Havana in 1990. This was a government body that functioned in an area smaller than the municipality and whose objective was improving control and supervision over all administrative bodies and finding ways to involve all members of a community in solving their own problems. Jesús García said the idea was to have "a strong government body at the 'barrio' level that could organize community forces for solving problems that people had at that level."[41]

Unfortunately, the great economic difficulties that have beset Cuba over the past two decades placed huge limitations on the resources available for attending to people's aspirations. Similarly, the People's Power cadres began to burn out and grow weary, and people lost faith in the experiment, with participation diminishing and often becoming a mere formality. These, and other issues that we cannot go into here, meant that after a bright and creative start, the People's Power experiment gradually lost its shine.

All That Can Be Decentralized Must Be Decentralized

I am more and more convinced by historical experience that decentralization is the best weapon for combating bureaucratism; it brings government closer to the people and allows them to exercise social control over the state apparatus. I therefore share Marx's opinion that it is necessary to decentralize all that can be decentralized, keeping as functions of the central state only those tasks that cannot be carried out at the local level.

It is worth rereading Marx's thoughts on the Paris Commune contained in his book *The Civil War in France*. We know about his ideas on the need to destroy the bourgeois state apparatus, to destroy the army, the need to create a communal police, that all public officials be paid a worker's wage, that all officials be recallable, all these things.

But we have often failed to pay attention to the fact that when Marx talked about the need to destroy "state power" he was referring to "centralized state power." The word *centralized* is key, as this is the fundamental characteristic of the inherited state.

His statement is that "the old centralized governments in the provinces would also have to give way to the self-government of the producers."

And he adds something very important:

> The few but important functions which still would remain for a central government were not to be suppressed, as has been intentionally mis-stated. . . . The unity of the nation was not to be broken, but, on the contrary, to be organized by the Communal constitution and to become a reality by the destruction of State power which claimed to be the embodiment of that unity independent of, and superior to, the nation itself, from which it was but a parasitic excrescence.[42]

A Non-Anarchic Decentralization Impregnated with a Spirit of Solidarity

Of course, we are not talking about an anarchic decentralization. There must be a national strategic plan that coordinates local plans. Each of the decentralized spaces should be part of the national whole and be willing to contribute its own resources to strengthen the development of those spaces with the greatest shortages. This kind of decentralization must be imbued with a spirit of solidarity. One of the most important roles the central state can play is just that—implementing a process of redistributing national resources to protect the weak and help them develop.

A Socialist Conception of Decentralization

After everything I have said, it should be clear that I am not talking about the kind of decentralization that neoliberalism promoted as a global strategy to weaken national unity and the nation-state. What I am advocating here is a different way of looking at decentralization, a socialist conception of decentralization, enshrined in numerous articles in the Bolivarian constitution.[43] I am envisaging a decentralization that, by strengthening communities and communes as the foundation of the nation-state, helps to deepen democracy and strengthen the central state, the fundamental instrument for defending our sovereignty and leading the country toward the new society we want to build.[44]

A New Economic Model Directed toward Satisfying Human Needs

Twenty-first century socialism proposes to replace the neoliberal capitalist model with a new socialist model whose main characteristics are:

1. Human development as the center and focus. Socialism is to be governed by the logic of humanism and solidarity and have as its aim the satisfaction of human needs, not profits.
2. Respect for nature, and opposition to consumerism. Our goal should not be to live "better" but to live "well."
3. As Michael Lebowitz notes, socialism requires a new dialectic of production/distribution/consumption based on: a) social ownership of the means of production, b) social production organized by workers, and c) the satisfaction of communal needs.[45]

4. A new concept of efficiency that both respects nature and seeks human development.
5. Rational use of available natural and human resources through a decentralized participatory planning process that has nothing to do with the hyper-centralized bureaucratic planning of the Soviet state.[46]

Social Ownership of the Means of Production

As Marxists, we know full well that the distribution of the social product depends on how the means of production are distributed in society. For social wealth to satisfy the needs of everyone in a country, it is essential that the fundamental means of production are not monopolized by a few and used for their own benefit, but are instead put under collective, social ownership.

But state property does not equate to social ownership, even if twentieth-century socialism tended to identify them as one and the same thing. Even Lenin insisted on distinguishing between state property and socialization. In this regard, it is important to make the distinction between formal (legal) and real ownership. The state formally represents the collective, but for the people to actually appropriate the means of production (factories, mines, land, services), it requires much more than just a legal act of expropriation of the capitalists and the placement of these means of production under state control.[47]

What happened in the Soviet Union and the countries that followed its example was not real ownership of the production process by the workers, but merely the nationalization of the means of production. They ceased to be owned by a few to become property of the state, which supposedly represented the workers. However, the production process itself underwent very few changes: a big socialist factory differed little from its capitalist counterpart, with workers continuing to be mere cogs in the machine. They had little or no participation in decision making within the workplace. This mislabeled "state capitalism" retained the hierarchical organization of production, with the manager having "dictatorial" power and orders being delivered from above. I share Pat Devine's view that we should not use the term "state capitalism" for such situations where most of the surplus produced goes to the state, not private hands (leaders, managers), and is used largely to boost economic development and to satisfy pressing social needs.[48] I will develop the concept of social ownership more fully later on.

Production Organized by Workers

It is not enough for the state to become the legal owner of the means of production. In order to speak of social property, workers need to take the production process into their own hands (appropriate) and be involved in organizing it. Instead of feeling like just one more cog in the machine, they should be able to contribute with their ideas and knowledge acquired through practice, combining thinking and doing, and thereby fully develop as social human beings.

It is interesting to note that in Allende's Chile it was said that one objective of workers' participation in the management of state enterprises was "the integral development of the human personality," and that, since workers have the same rights as any citizen, "it would be paradoxical if they did not have equal rights within the workplace."[49]

Twenty-first century socialism cannot afford to leave intact work processes that alienate workers. It cannot continue to maintain the division between manual and intellectual work. Workers must be informed about the production process as a whole; they must be able to control it, to review and decide on production plans, the annual budget, and the distribution of the surplus, including its contribution to the national budget.

But can we say that workers are prepared to participate actively in the management of enterprises? Except in rare circumstances, this is generally not the case, precisely because capitalism has never been interested in providing workers with the necessary technical knowledge to manage enterprises. Here I am referring not only to production, but also to matters related to marketing and finance. Concentrating knowledge in the hands of management is one of the mechanisms that enables capital to exploit workers.

So one of the first steps for promoting self-management or co-management of enterprises is allowing workers to appropriate this knowledge. To do this, they must begin to engage in practical management, while at the same time acquiring training in business and management techniques.

Satisfying Communal Needs

Finally, if the means of production are to be socially owned, and this means owned by all, what is produced should satisfy the needs of the people. Moreover, the surpluses obtained cannot be monopolized by one specific group of workers, but must be shared with the local, national, and (why not?) the international community.

But who determines these needs? In twentieth-century socialism, the central state decided what social needs existed and what to produce to satisfy them. In 21st century socialism, it must be the people themselves who define and prioritize what is produced through a participatory planning process.

New Concept of Efficiency

Twenty-first century socialism requires a new concept of efficiency, a concept of "socialist efficiency."[50] This concept cannot replicate the capitalist vision, in which people are productive only insofar as they produce surplus value, and in which productivity is measured by the quantity of goods produced in a given period, regardless of whether or not these goods satisfy people's needs or are harmful to nature. The efficiency of Japanese multinationals in southern Chile is measured by the amount of timber obtained from the felling of trees in a given time. This measure does not consider the depletion of Chilean forests and the negative effects this has on the environment.

As Michael Lebowitz writes, efficiency under socialism must take into account two things.[51] First, an enterprise is efficient only if the production process does not destroy the future of humanity, if it does not destroy nature. The second, which is usually not taken into account, stems from the dual nature of what an enterprise produces. Though it might appear that when you transform raw materials into products you only produce commodities, there is another element that is transformed in the process of production, and that element is the workers themselves. When men and women work, that is, transform materials into products, they are also developing or deforming (crippling) themselves. In this sense, an enterprise will be efficient under socialism only if, in addition to being materially productive, it allows workers to develop themselves as rich human beings by combining their thinking and doing through participation in management. But for this participation to be real and not a mere formality, workers need to understand the production process.

Historical experience has taught us that without this education, it is not workers who tend to end up managing the companies that have become social property but rather technicians, who have more knowledge about the productive process.[52]

Investment in Human Development

Training and education should not be thought of as something separate from the workday. On the contrary, every workday should involve a determined amount of time, considered an integral part of work, that is dedicated to worker training and education. Under socialism, investment in the development of workers should be considered productive investment.

Efficiency in a socialist-oriented steel enterprise cannot be measured in the same way as efficiency in a capitalist steel enterprise. The first must dedicate time to preparing workers by providing technical and management training, and the second will dedicate the entire workday to producing products. If efficiency is measured purely in terms of production levels, the capitalist enterprise may come out ahead—although this cannot be taken as certain, because it ignores the benefits obtained when workers are aware of the meaning and purpose of their labor activity, something that can lead to greater motivation to work and have a positive impact on productivity. If, however, efficiency is measured not only in terms of labor productivity but also in terms of respect for nature and for workers self-development, there is no doubt that a self-managed or co-managed socialist enterprise will outperform a capitalist one.

Incentives and the Level of Consciousness in the Construction of Socialism

Getting workers to produce quality products efficiently is one of the challenges facing 21st century socialism. The Soviet system failed in this regard. Fidel Castro was also aware of this when, in a speech to the National Assembly of People's Power in Cuba made before the collapse of the Soviet Union, he argued that socialism had not yet managed to figure out how to replace the role of capitalist whip in encouraging production.

The solution that some have found for achieving this goal has been to use the dull instruments of capitalism, preferring to rely on individual incentives and private property. But are personal incentives or private property the only levers available for stimulating workers?

A sense of ownership over the means of production seems to be an important element in determining the attitude that workers may have toward their work. Why, then, did the classic Soviet slogans "Factories to the workers!" and "Land to the peasants!" fail to work in the Soviet model?

Cuban researcher Darío Machado provides us with an explanation. According to him, "Workers never felt that they were the owners of the means of production and services" in the Eastern European socialist countries. Though in legal terms they were owners, this did not come hand in hand with participation. While they worked, others above decided "what to produce and how to produce."[53]

There is a big difference between the state taking ownership of factories and land in the name of workers, and these factories and lands being subject to self-organization and self-management on the part of their workers.

Protagonism in the Workplace, an Important Incentive

Yugoslav President Tito understood protagonism. He rejected the Stalinist bureaucratic state model and tried to promote an economic model of broad worker participation, handing over the means of production for the workers to run under self-management.

Yugoslav workers in self-managed industries achieved positive economic results because they were able to participate in management, they had their views taken into account, and they knew that the results of their labor would be translated into benefits for themselves. Labor productivity greatly increased.[54]

That sense of belonging and commitment also occurred in Venezuela, among workers in the electricity sector.[55] Conscious that the opposition was targeting the electricity company Cadafe, the electrical workers organized to prevent any attempt to sabotage it. As a result of their long struggle against the privatization and virtual dismantlement of the company promoted by previous administrations, these workers began to raise the issue of co-management (*cogestión*) in their struggle to regain control over the company. This experience produced ideas that corrected some of the deviations that had occurred in Yugoslavia.

Since this company was strategically important for the country as a whole, it was necessary to avoid worker management becoming a vehicle for defending the narrow interests of particular individuals and groups. To avoid this, it was seen as vital that, together with workers and company managers, spokespersons from organized communities also participate in the process of co-management. The electricity company, after all, does not belong to the electrical workers alone, it belongs to all Venezuelans, and their voices also needed to be heard inside the company. They should have an opportunity to point out shortcomings, suggest solutions, and collaborate in their implementation.

In the Venezuelan state of Merida, this type of co-management was introduced in the regional electricity company and obtained excellent results. Service improved significantly. Electrical workers, who had previously been denounced by the community due to the poor service the company provided, are today greeted with affection. Revenue collection has increased dramatically, and illegal access to electric power by households has decreased. These results can be explained by a combination of factors: a district manager proposed by the workers; a general manager who supported this decision; a union leader who had good relations with both the workers and the manager; and regular meetings between workers and communities to discuss how to improve the service. Of crucial importance is the sense of joint responsibility that exists among all parties. However, for this to be viable, workers must have confidence in those running the company. That is why it is so important that the voice of workers be heard when it comes to designating managerial cadres.

"When workers feel that their views are being taken into account, they are willing to work three to four times harder, because they now work with joy," one union leader told me. "Before they worked for a wage; now it comes from the heart."

Being able to participate in decision making is the main way to stimulate workers to give their best. In this context, work ceases to be alienating, and the worker is spiritually transformed as he or she starts to feel useful and part of a much larger family that extends beyond his or her own enterprise. In this way, greater self-development can be achieved.

But this goal cannot be realized overnight. Individualism and consumerism have been inculcated into workers and, in general, their motivation to work is tied to economic stimulus. A process of cultural transformation is clearly required. To the extent that people are building the new society and participating in the management of their workplaces, their work becomes an expression of their potential instead of being a burden. To the extent that they are engaging in solidarity actions that create satisfaction, they begin to understand that it is more important to be than to have. As such, moral incentives can increasingly become a force that moves people into action. But this is a gradual process.

In reflecting on incentives and the motivation to work under socialism, it seems important to consider the experiences of the Chinese and Vietnamese agricultural communes. One can see in these experiences the need for a step-by-step process. Mistakes were made when, in the distribution of surplus, excessive emphasis was initially placed on forms of compensation intended for collective use (to meet the needs of the community, especially the children, the elderly, etc.) rather than remuneration according to the contribution of each peasant. As a consequence, peasants who had contributed more preferred to leave the cooperative while the remaining peasants found it necessary to reduce the share of collective compensation in order to lure them back.

How to Stimulate Some Workers and Not Be Unjust to Others

Equally important in regard to incentives and motivation is the experience of the MST in Brazil. Its initial policy was one of equal distribution to all households, regardless of what each contributed. This discouraged people who were making more effort and led to vagrancy, when what was needed most was increased production. So the MST shifted to a process of distribution based on days worked, and finally, according to hours worked. This formula proved to be better than previous ones in stimulating greater effort. It is, however, considered to be unfair, because the productivity of each cooperative member is not the same: a young man, with more strength, can harvest more corn in one hour than an older cooperative partner can. The MST leadership faces the challenge of finding the most effective way to measure the contribution of each working member.

Socialism and the Dull Instruments of Capitalism

It is important to take into consideration what Engels said in 1890 to Schmidt, in reference to a discussion on how distribution should be organized in the future society, and in particular, whether it should conform to the amount of work performed or otherwise. Engels expressed surprise that this discussion had not addressed the relationship that must exist between modes of distribution, on the one hand, and the quantity of products available for distribution, on the other: "The method of distribution essentially depends on *how much* there is to distribute, and that this must surely change with the progress of production and social organization, so that the method of distribution may also change."[56]

The great challenge before us, then, is how, considering the legacy of the past, we can build the future. Of course, in the beginning it is essential to find ways to encourage work and reward the greatest effort, because it is not fair if those who make a smaller effort earn the same as those who work with determination and enthusiasm. We must also encourage creativity and innovation. But I think there must be a gradual development of measures combining material and moral incentives that begins to change the culture and values of people, until they feel that the best pay, the best incentive for them, is to see that their work is helping to satisfy the needs of others, making them happy, to realize their work is helping to build a better society for all. We cannot build socialism with the dull instruments of capitalism, but we also cannot eliminate these dull instruments overnight. Instead, their role should be gradually decreased, to the extent that we are capable of creating conditions for cultural transformation that strengthen the role of motivations other than mere individual self-interest. From a society in which people receive according to what they give, we will move gradually to a society in which people contribute according to their capabilities, and receive according to their needs.

The Centrality of Participatory Planning in Socialism

Without participatory planning, there can be no socialism. If I place a lot of emphasis on this it is not only because we must put an end to capitalist anarchy of production, but also because it is only through such a process that society can truly appropriate the fruits of its labor. I will now try to demonstrate this assertion.

Means of Production: a Social Heritage

I argued previously that one of the essential elements of socialism is social ownership of the means of production and said this issue deserved to be developed further. It is time to do so. To understand this concept it is necessary to consider what gives rise to wealth. Marx argued there were two sources of wealth: nature and human labor, which produces use-values using raw materials derived from nature. We must remember, however, that along with living human labor, there is also what the author of *Capital* called "dead labor," that is, labor embodied in means of production. This past labor is an important factor of wealth production.[57]

The tools, machines, improvements made to land, and, of course, intellectual and scientific discoveries that substantially increased social productivity are a legacy passed down from generation to generation; they are a social heritage—a wealth of the people.

But who owns this wealth, these social assets? Capitalism, through a process of mystification, has convinced us that the rightful owners of this wealth are the capitalists. This is the basis for their accepting expropriation only if they are compensated for their loss. This also explains why bourgeois legislation does not hesitate to consider such compensation to be fair and natural. Socialism, by contrast, begins by recognizing that wealth is a social heritage that must be used in the interests of society as a whole rather than serving private interests. These assets, incorporating the labor of generations, do not belong to specific people or specific countries, but to humanity.

The question is: how do we ensure that this happens? The only way is to de-privatize these resources, transforming them into social property. But since the humanity of the early twenty-first century is still not a humanity without borders, these action must begin on a country-by-country basis, and the first step is therefore the handing over of ownership of the strategic means of production to a national state that expresses the interests of society.

Clarifying the Concept of Ownership

Before proceeding, we need to understand the concept of ownership of the means of production. This concept can be related to several issues, including the ability to use, to enjoy, and to dispose of the means of production, and therefore the products obtained in the production process. But it is also important to distinguish between juridical property and the actual power or possibility to use, enjoy, and dispose of property.

We will use "effective possession" to refer to the ability of holders of the means of production to put them into action, that is, to have control of or manage the labor process. We will use "real ownership" to refer to the situation in which the effective possession of the means of production is in the hands of those who also have the power to dispose of them and their products.

Marx tells us that in the manufacturing stage, even if the capitalist is the juridical owner of the means of production, he does not yet have complete control over them: the means of production still need to be adapted to humans, and the expertise of workers still counts. But with expanded industrial capitalism, the contrary occurs. The machinery makes the organization of production independent of the characteristics of the labor force. The workers lose all control of the work process, they are completely separate from the means of production, and the capitalist becomes not only the juridical owner but also the real owner, finally controlling the entire process of production.

On the other hand, it may happen that real ownership and juridical property are not in the same hands. Agricultural land, for example, can be nationalized—that is, transformed into state property (juridical property)—and the right to operate the process of production and to dispose of that land and its fruits can be delegated to communes or regional centers. The state would then have the juridical property, and real ownership would belong to the commune.[58]

However, there may be other combinations, such as when the right to dispose of the means of production and products are in the hands of people other than the producers. This is the case of servile production, in which the landlord has legal ownership of land and thus gets a share of the product, while the serf working with his own means of production creates the product and is therefore left with another part of that product. Here the direct producer, to whom the lord has granted a piece of land, has effective possession.

State Property: A Juridical Change

Under the initial phase of socialism, the placement of the principal means of production in state hands represents nothing more than a juridical change of property. The subordination of workers to an external force continues; there are new socialist managers, but the alienated status of the workers in the production process remains unchanged. This is formally collective property, because the state represents society, but real appropriation (ownership) is still not collective. That is why Engels argues:

> State ownership of the productive forces is not the solution of the conflict, but concealed within it are the technical conditions that form the elements of that solution. This solution can only consist in the practical recognition of the social nature of the modern forces of production, and therefore in the harmonizing of the mode of production, appropriation and exchange with the socialized character of the means of production. And this can only come about by society openly and directly taking possession of the productive forces, which have outgrown all controls, except that of society as a whole.[59]

Participatory Planning: How Society Can Take the Means of Production into Its Own Hands

But what does it mean for society to take possession of the means of production? Society is a highly abstract concept: it may be all of humanity. In my understanding, what we need to determine is who should have effective possession of those means of production, that is, who should be entitled to use, enjoy, and dispose of those assets. It is here that Pat Devine's contribution of distinguishing among different levels of social ownership seems important to me. Each level is associated with who is "affected by decisions over the use of the assets involved, in proportion to the extent to which they are affected."[60]

According to this logic, a bakery that produces bread and sweets for a given geographic area (for example, a commune), whose workers live in that area and whose raw material also comes from nearby farmers within the local area, should be owned by that commune. It makes no sense for that bakery to be owned by the nation as a whole.

In contrast, in the case of a strategic sector such as oil, it would be absurd for the oil workforce to claim ownership of a resource that belongs to all inhabitants of the country (or even to humanity as a whole). This doesn't mean, however, that those workers should not play a decisive role in the management of the enterprise, especially in the production process. Its surplus should be devoted to new investment in the enterprise, to improving the living conditions of its workers and the surrounding community, and should also provide a substantial contribution to the national budget. The legal ownership of this enterprise should be in the hands of the state; the effective possession or control of the production process should be in the hands of the enterprise's employees; but the destination of the product, once investments and labor remuneration have been deducted, should be defined by society as a whole.

How, then, does the commune (in the first case) and society (in the second) define what is to be done with the fruits of productive activity? Here is where the participatory planning process must play an essential role. This is very different from bureaucratic planning.

I share with Pat Devine the idea that the actors in participatory planning will vary according to different levels of social ownership. In the case of the community bakery, decisions on how much to produce, with what raw materials, what quality, what variety, when the product should be ready, how to distribute it, how much to invest in maintaining or expanding the enterprise, etc., should be made not only by those who work in the bakery but also by the people who produce the raw material used and by the consumers of bread and sweets. In the case of the oil enterprise, while its workers must participate in management, decisions concerning reinvestment, new investment, marketing, the destination of the rest of the surplus, etc., must involve the entire society. In both cases, the local society or the national society should be present through its various representatives or spokespersons.

Social ownership is one of the central features of socialism. To ensure that social ownership is not merely formal juridical property, society must "openly and bluntly take possession" of these means of production through the exercise of participatory planning. The manner in which this is done will depend on the level of social property in question.

8. *Transition and Its Varieties*

Up till now we have spoken about some of the characteristics of this new society that we want to build, but you may be asking, how long will it take us to reach this goal? History has shown that "heaven" cannot be taken by storm, that a long historical period is needed to make the transition from capitalism to a socialist society. Some talk in terms of decades, others of hundreds of years, and yet others think that socialism is the goal we must pursue but that perhaps we shall never completely reach.

We call this historical period "the transition to socialism." We should distinguish between three kinds of transition to socialism: transition in advanced countries, transition in backward countries where state power has been conquered, and finally, transition in countries where only the government is in our hands.

Transition in Advanced Countries

The most common interpretation of Marxism up until the Russian Revolution maintained that socialism would start with the more advanced countries, where capitalism itself had created the material and cultural conditions for it. Revolutionary access to state power was thought to be the *sine qua non* that would make it possible to expropriate the expropriators, create producer associations, and convert the state into an expression of society instead of a body above it. A high level of development of productive forces was also considered to be an indispensable condition.

This idea of transition—which never actually took place—has been used as an argument against Marx, but this only reflects that those who raise this issue have not read his later writings, in which he modified his initial vision and began to focus much more on the political, rather than economic, conditions for revolution.

In his September 27, 1877 letter to Friedrich Adolph Sorge, Marx maintained: "This time the revolution will begin in the East." Why did he say this? Due to the political situation he could see brewing in Russia at the time, everything seemed to indicate that a war between Russia and Turkey would break out, and that the Russian government would be defeated, with grave economic and political consequences flowing out of this defeat. All of this was to occur in a situation of complete economic, moral, and intellectual disintegration in which Russian society found itself.[61] But Marx not only foresaw the possibility of political revolution in a backward country; he also saw the possibilities arising out of the tradition of collective property in the countryside, which could provide the basis for a transition from the commune to socialism that bypassed a period of capitalist agriculture.[62]

Transition in Backward Countries Where State Power Has Been Won

History demonstrated that Marx was right. The construction of socialism did not begin in advanced capitalist countries that had a large and experienced industrial working class but in countries where capitalist development was only just beginning, whose population was predominantly peasant, and whose working class was a minority of the population.

Why did it happen like that? Because political conditions outstripped economic conditions.

The outcome of the February 1917 Russian Revolution was that the bourgeoisie gained power, but power was shared between it and the workers and soldiers soviets. This revolution was considered by Lenin to be an unfinished revolution, "the first stage of the first of the proletarian revolutions which are the inevitable result of war."[63] According to Lenin, it was the horrors of the imperialist war that had led to these proletarian insurrections, and these evils could only be cured if the proletariat took power in Russia and adopted measures that, even if not yet socialist, were steps toward socialism.

Lenin was fully aware that the backwardness of his country would prevent the immediate installation of socialism, but he also saw with total clarity that the only way they were going to be able to get the country out of the critical situation the war had led them into was by taking steps toward that goal.[64] He wrote:

> From April 1917 onwards, long before the October Revolution, that is, long before we took power, we declared publicly and explained to the people: the revolution cannot stop at this stage (the bourgeois revolution) since the country had moved forward, capitalism has advanced, misery has reached levels never before seen, which (whether you like it or not) will demand that steps are taken in the direction of socialism since there is no other way of moving forward, of saving the war-weary country, and of alleviating the suffering of the workers and the exploited.[65]

A few weeks before the October Revolution, Lenin gave an exhaustive explanation of the analysis he had often repeated in the preceding months:

> It is impossible to stand still in history in general, and in wartime in particular. We must either advance or retreat. It

> is *impossible* in twentieth-century Russia, which has won a republic and democracy in a revolutionary way, to go forward without *advancing* toward socialism, without taking steps toward it (steps conditioned and determined by the level of technology and culture: large-scale mechanized production cannot be "introduced" in peasant agriculture nor abolished in the sugar industry). But to fear to advance *means* retreating.[66]

The Russian Revolution thus shattered European Social Democracy's traditional preconceptions. The proletarian revolution was victorious when the objective premises for socialism did not yet exist in Russia, when the development of the productive forces had not yet reached the level of development that makes socialism possible. The leaders of the Second International drew the conclusion, therefore, that it was a mistake for the proletariat to have taken power and to have embarked on the construction of socialism, that it should have gone down the road of capitalist development and Western European bourgeois democracy.

Lenin, in one of the last things he wrote, in January 1923, railed against those who supported this thesis. He maintained that these people had not reflected on the reasons why the revolution first broke out in Russia and not in the advanced European countries. They did not realize that the war had created a hopeless situation in Russia and, concomitantly, the political conditions for a combination of a peasant war with the workers' movement, creating a balance of forces such that it made it possible to overthrow tsarism and big imperialist capital. What should they do next? Should they have rejected the road of the socialist revolution because they did not yet have all the material and cultural prerequisites for building socialism?[67]

"You say," Lenin said, referring to the Social Democrats' ideas, "that civilization is necessary if we are to build socialism. Very well. But why could we not first create such prerequisites of civilization in our country by the expulsion of the landowners and the Russian capitalists, and then start moving toward socialism?"[68]

Yet even if Lenin thought that Russia had to go down the socialist road because it was the only way to solve the serious problems caused by the war, he was not unaware that it was an extremely difficult task and knew that "the final victory of socialism in a single country is of course impossible."[69]

It was also the political conditions caused by the Second World War that allowed revolutionaries to take state power in Eastern Europe and then in Africa and Asia and use that power to begin the transformations designed to bring about socialism.

Transition in Countries Where Only the Government Has Been Conquered

Our situation in the 1980s and 1990s was in some way comparable to that experienced by pre-revolutionary Russia in the beginning of the twentieth century. What the imperialist war and its horrors were for Russia, neoliberalism and its horrors were for Latin America, in the extent of hunger and misery, increasingly unequal distribution of wealth, destruction of nature, and increasing loss of our sovereignty. In these circumstances, our peoples said "Enough!" and embarked on a new path, resisting at first, and then going on the offensive, making possible the victory of left-wing presidential candidates with anti-neoliberal programs.

These Latin American political leaders faced the same dilemma that confronted the Bolsheviks in Russia: either use capitalist measures to try to take our countries forward, which would mean more suffering for our people, or begin to build an alternative to capitalism, heading toward another model that makes our people the main builders of the new society.

In other words, faced with the evident failure of neoliberalism as it was being applied—and which had demonstrated itself as being incapable of resolving the problems of the people—there emerged the following dilemma: either the neoliberal capitalist model is rebuilt, evidently with changes, such as a greater focus on social issues, but still motivated by the same capitalist logic, or advances are made in constructing an alternative project. However, even if there are similarities between what happened in the USSR and what is happening in Latin America, the situation facing our "left" governments is even more complex than that which faced the Soviet government.

In advancing toward this alternative project, there are great differences between the diverse "left" governments in Latin America. Some have limited themselves to adopting important social policies but have not broken with the neoliberal economic model, even if they have made efforts toward developing a productive national capitalism.

Others have decided to embark on a truly alternative path—a path toward socialism—knowing that the objective economic conditions in which they find themselves oblige them to coexist with capitalist forms of production for a while to come.

How to Advance Having only Conquered Governmental Power

For this group, the dilemma exists as to how to move toward socialism when only governmental power has been won. This makes the situation much more complex. These countries not only have to confront backward economic conditions but also the fact that they still do not have complete state power.

It is not only that the economic, material, and cultural conditions in our countries are not favorable to building socialism, but also that the most important condition is lacking, one that until now has been considered indispensable: we do not have complete state power; we only have a tiny part of it. Let us remember that the power of the state is not limited to the executive branch but also includes the legislative and judicial branches, the armed forces, local government bodies (municipal and state governments), and other institutions.

The Difference between Becoming the Government and Conquering Power

Governmental power is not the same thing as conquering state power. This was one of the errors that some sectors of the left made in Chile. People said, ignoring the existing balance of forces, that we had conquered power and thus all we had to do was implement our program.

It cannot be denied that having won the government, we gained a modicum of political power, but equally, it must not be forgotten that, although we had very large left parties and a fairly strong labor movement on our side, we did not have the armed forces, and we had a minority in Parliament. We never won an absolute majority in any election. The Christian Democrats still had a large following, not only in the middle and upper classes but also among workers and peasants. This partly explains why the Popular Unity, the political coalition that supported Allende, never proposed holding a constituent assembly. What it did was to use the existing legislation and look for legal loopholes. Some laws passed in the 1930s by a socialist government that had existed for 100 days were still in effect. Using those laws, we were able to go ahead and nationalize the most strategic sectors of the economy, which was referred to by Popular Unity as the "areas of social property."[70]

I agree with those that believe achieving state power is a complex process, one of whose most important aspects is to achieve control over the armed forces, or what has been called "the monopoly of violence." This is why Hugo Chávez insisted that there was a fundamental difference between the process led by Allende in Chile and the Bolivarian revolutionary process: the first was an unarmed peaceful transition, whereas Venezuela's is an armed peaceful transition, not because the people are armed, but because the great bulk of the armed forces supports the process.

Using the Inherited State to Promote the Creation of a New State Built from Below

We should recognize that our governments inherit a state apparatus whose characteristics work well in a capitalist system but are not suitable for a journey toward a humanist and solidarity-infused society, a society that not only places human beings at the center of their own development, but also makes them the leading actors in the process of change.

Nevertheless, practice has demonstrated that, contrary to the theoretical dogmatism of some sectors of the radical left, you can use this inherited state and transform it into an instrument that collaborates with building the new society.

The fact that state institutions are run by revolutionary cadres who are aware that they should aim to work with the organized sectors of the people to control what the institutions do and press for transformation of the state apparatus can make it possible, within certain limits, for these institutions to work for the revolutionary project.

But we must be clear that this does not mean we can simply limit ourselves to using the inherited state. It is necessary that the foundations of the new political system are built up by the revolutionary government using the power it is able to employ, creating adequate spaces for popular participation, preparing the people to exercise power at all levels, from the most simple to the most complex. By doing that, they promote the creation of the new state from below, or a non-state that will replace the old state, "the government of persons replaced by the administration of things," as Engels wrote.[71]

There are people—like Valter Pomar—who think that as long as this condition does not exist, as long as the working class has not taken state power, it is only possible to speak of "the struggle for socialism but not of the transition to socialism."[72] I do not share this opinion because I think that what baptizes a process with the name *transition* is the aim that it pursues and the measures used to achieve it. Of course, these measures must be consistent with the aim pursued, as we shall see below.

I agree with Pomar that "conquering state power is a complex process," but I think this process can be initiated precisely by left forces taking government power.[73]

To Each Country, Its Own Transition

I have previously noted that some of our governments have begun a process of transition toward socialism, but undoubtedly each process is very different from the next.

As Michael Lebowitz says, "Socialism does not fall from the sky." Every society has its own unique characteristics that differentiate it from other countries, and therefore although there may be a shared goal, the measures that are taken in the transition process must be adapted to the specific conditions of each country. It must necessarily be rooted in a particular society.

History and Traditions

Every country has a unique history, its unique traditions (including religious and indigenous ones), its mythologies, its heroes who have struggled for a better world, and the individual capacities that people have developed in the process of struggle.[74]

Starting Points

The starting points of each transition process are different, too. The measures that are adopted will depend on the conditions that exist when the process begins: the specificities of the inherited economic structure, the level of development of the forces of production, the way in which daily life expresses itself, the population's educational level, etc.[75]

Correlation of Forces

What's more, each transition will be shaped by the correlation of forces that exists between those who want to move forward with the construction of a new society and those who want to prevent change, and by the level of class struggle at both the domestic and international levels.

Historical Actors

Finally, depending on the class structure of each country and the history of its struggles, the historical actors who work for the transition will be different. In some cases they might be working-class parties, in others, indigenous and peasant movements, in others, a sector of the military, and in others, charismatic leaders.

Implicit in all this is the idea that there cannot be a general theory of transition; rather, each country must design its own particular strategy for the transition. This will depend, among other things, "not only on the economic character of that country but also on the way the class struggle is waged there," and this strategy should guide the way the process advances.[76]

Nevertheless, even with all these variants, in the current situation in Latin America and the Caribbean, all of our transition processes, as we have seen, have one common feature: we are "transitioning" peacefully. This means starting out from what is inherited from the previous regime and, little by little, transforming it, first of all by taking over the government.

Duration of the Transition

For some, this process will last decades. For others, such as Samir Amin, it will take centuries, just as capitalism took centuries to consolidate itself. And there are those, such as myself, who see it as a utopian goal that lights the path, that orients the struggle, but one that we will never fully achieve. This is not being pessimistic, as some might think. On the contrary, a utopian goal that is well defined helps us chart our course and strengthens our resolve to struggle—and each step that brings us closer to the horizon, as small as it may be, is considered positive.

A Process Full of Challenges

This process of transformation, of advancing toward the new society we want to build from the government, is not only a long process but also a process full of challenges and difficulties, as can be seen from what was said above. Nothing ensures that it will be a linear process; there is always the possibility of retreats and failures.

Defeating the Conservative Offensive

We should always remember that the right only respects the rules of the game as long as it suits their purposes. To date, there has never been a single example anywhere in the world of a ruling group that willingly gave up its privileges. The fact that they agree to withdraw from the political arena when they think a retreat may be in their best interest should not deceive us. They may tolerate and even help bring a left government to power if that government implements the right's policies and limits itself to managing the crisis. What they will always try to prevent, by legal or illegal means—and we should have no illusions about this—is a program of democratic and popular deep transformations that puts into question their economic interests.

It may be deduced from this that the left must be prepared to confront fierce resistance. These sectors will oppose and maneuver to recover their lost power. The left must be capable of defending victories achieved democratically.

Electoral Agenda Collides with Popular Power

Another smaller, but no less important challenge has to do with the electoral cycle that left governments have to submit themselves to in order to re-legitimize themselves in the face of constant opposition attacks, while giving continuity to the process of change under way.

On many occasions, this agenda can clash with the agenda of building participatory democracy. The process of construction of popular power tends to be postponed or weakened to make way for electoral campaigning. Campaigns tend to be carried out in a populist manner in which priority is given to solving problems for the people rather than encouraging people to organize and solve their problems themselves.

In this sense, one of the first things that we must do is to avoid using the same techniques used to promote candidates in the bourgeois electoral system when seeking votes, and instead focus on educational, pedagogic campaigns that help raise people's consciousness and organizational capacity.

We also have to factor in that candidates do not always compete on an equal footing: those who have access to the media or use the state apparatus for their campaigns have an important advantage in relation to everyone else.

Contradiction between Political Conjunctures and Democratic Processes

At the same time, it is not easy to resolve the dilemma posed by the contradiction between political conjunctures that might best be dealt with immediately and democratic processes. On many occasions some have wanted to extend the time to debate laws or new constitutions, which could have helped enrich the democratic discussion but could also have put at risk the future of the democratic process.

This is what occurred with the constituent process in Venezuela and Ecuador. Both processes sought to achieve the greatest possible level of citizen participation in discussions about the new constitution. The popular response was so great that the timeframe set for the process turned out to be too short. As such, the issue of extending the deadline to allow for greater participation came up. However, this brought with it potentially negative political consequences, and in both cases it was decided to sacrifice the democratic process due to the political conjuncture.

In Ecuador the first deadline turned out to be too short, so it was decided to extend it, which was allowed under the regulations governing the Constituent Assembly. However, even this deadline turned out to not be enough, and Alberto Acosta, then president of the Constituent Assembly, tried to convince the political leadership of the socialist party Alianza PAIS to support a further extension. The political bureaucrats decided against this course of action, and Acosta resigned from his post. The argument used to defend this position was that if the discussion and dialogue process continued to drag on, the final product could potentially be at risk, as the opposition was using the deadline extension to wage a campaign against the government, arguing that its real motive was to assume full power and do away with Congress. It must be recalled that when the Constituent Assembly was elected, it was decided that Congress would go into recess until the new constitution was approved or rejected by the people in a referendum. Parliamentarians were sent home. This would ensure that Congress could not interfere with the Constituent Assembly, while stopping short of dissolving it.[77]

I believe that those who most deeply sense the dilemma of political conjunctures and democratic processes are the intellectuals, and that is why I want to recall what Carlos Matus wrote regarding the relationship between politicians and intellectuals: "While the dilemma for some intellectuals is to occupy their time with theorizing without giving up action . . . for some politicians it is about carrying out actions while continuing to theorize. This dilemma leads each of them to attack the other, and means they are unable to recognize the capacities and contributions that each group makes."[78]

These are all realities that we will need to face up to in the future. The great challenge we face is how to build alternative institutions. How do we maximize the positive aspects and minimize the negative ones in order to accumulate the forces we need to continue advancing down the path of change and avoid returning to the past?

Moreover, advances come at a slow pace and, confronted with this, many leftists tend to become demoralized. Many of them see the capture of governmental power as a magic bullet that can quickly solve the most pressing needs of the people. When solutions are not rapidly forthcoming, disillusionment sets in.

The Need for a Pedagogy of Limitations

I believe that, just as our revolutionary leaders need to use the state to change the inherited balance of forces, they must also carry out a pedagogical task when they are confronted with limits or brakes along the path—what I call a "pedagogy of limitations." Many times we believe that talking about difficulties will only demoralize and dishearten the people, when, on the contrary, if our popular sectors are kept informed, and it is explained to them why it is not possible to immediately achieve the desired goals, this can help them better understand the process in which they find themselves and moderate their sometimes politically unrealistic demands. Intellectuals as well should be widely informed so they are able to defend the process and also criticize it if necessary.

But this pedagogy of limitations must be simultaneously accompanied by the fomentation of popular mobilizations and creativity, thereby avoiding the possibility that radical initiatives from the people become domesticated and generate circumstances in which we come to accept unwarranted criticisms of possible faults within the government. Not only should popular pressure be tolerated, it should be understood that it is necessary to helping those in government combat errors and deviations that can emerge along the way.

9. *Making Progress When the Government Is in Our Hands*

Thus far, I have given a broad overview of the characteristics we see as essential to 21st century socialism. Now we will go into some of the concrete measures that can be taken in order to move toward that goal, using the state bequeathed to us. This requires a fundamental condition: that revolutionary cadres, instilled with the political will to do so, run the inherited state.

Move Toward a New Regional Integration

A lot of ground can be covered in the international sphere once in government. Imbued with the ideas of Simón Bolívar regarding the need to unite our countries, certain Latin American governments have begun creating institutions that have allowed them to reassert their sovereignty, depend less on global power blocs, and liberate themselves from the dictates of the Washington Consensus. The creation of ALBA, Petrocaribe, Telesur, Radio del Sur, Banco del Sur, UNASUR and its Defense Council, the sucre (ALBA's trading currency unit), CELAC, and many other initiatives means that we have moved quite a distance in this direction.

Changing the Rules of the Institutional Game

One of the first tasks of the more advanced governments of the region has been to change the rules of the institutional game by means of a constituent process that has allowed them to develop new constitutions.

On coming to power, the presidents of Venezuela, Bolivia, and Ecuador promoted constituent processes resulting in new constitutions being approved by referendum with majority support. Venezuela's Bolivarian constitution was passed in December 1999; Ecuador's new constitution was approved in September 2008; and the Bolivian constitution in February 2009. Honduran president Manuel Zelaya also wanted to push forward with a constituent process, a move that ultimately ended with his overthrow via a military coup.

One of the most notable elements of the Bolivian and Ecuadorian constitutions was the creation of plurinational states that for the first time recognized the historically excluded indigenous nations.

However, though it is not possible to build socialism via the peaceful road without carrying out a constituent process, this issue cannot be dealt with in a voluntarist manner. It only makes sense to promote a process of this type once revolutionary forces believe they can obtain the required electoral support required to ensure the approval of the necessary changes. It makes no sense to promote a constituent process if the end result is the approval of a new institutional framework that will act as an obstacle to change.

This was precisely why the UP in Chile decided against convoking a constituent assembly: they were unsure they could win. But I have always wondered, what would have happened if we had pushed our forces to the limit and gone door to door promoting this issue? It is important to remember that when the opposition in Venezuela proposed a recall referendum as a means to remove Chávez from power, the polls indicated they had a majority, and there was a real risk that the vote against Chávez would win.

Nevertheless, Chávez decided to accept the challenge and campaigned hard to build a correlation of forces capable of ensuring his victory.

That is why I have asked myself what the possibilities are for converting the generalized discontent that exists among Chileans toward the current institutional framework—something the youth of my country have so brilliantly exposed with their struggles—into a demand for a constituent assembly that no politician could oppose, if we tapped into this discontent by carrying out a consciousness-raising campaign on this issue, going door to door, classroom to classroom, workplace to workplace?

Conquering Spaces That Used to Be Capital's Domain

It is also possible, using the inherited state, to start a process of recovering spaces that were lost as a result of the privatizations undertaken during the neoliberal period and begin creating new spaces under the control of the people's government.

Advances in Venezuela

The clearest example of this in Venezuela was the recovery of the oil company PDVSA. Although formally in the hands of the state (it had been nationalized in August 1975 under Carlos Andrés Pérez), it was not run by the government but by neoliberal managers with their own agenda that coincided with the interests of the dominant economic groups. The sabotage of the oil industry in December 2002–February 2003 allowed the Venezuelan government to remove the coup-supporting, anti-national managers and replace them with new managers who supported the Bolivarian process. This meant the government could recover control of the company and use the surplus for social use.

The Venezuelan government has also been able to nationalize or re-nationalize important strategic companies such as the steel factory SIDOR as well as cement, plastic, and telecommunications companies and food processing installations, such as Conservas Alimenticias La Gaviota (a sardine tinning plant), Lácteos los Andes (Andes dairy products), sugar mills, silos, coffee-roasting plants, and refrigeration storage companies.

The state also took over one of the biggest private banks, the Banco de Venezuela, which belonged to the Spanish-owned Grupo Santander, and more recently took control of the Exito chain of supermarkets.

In 2010, further expropriations aimed at establishing food sovereignty were carried out. Among the companies nationalized were Sociedad Mercantil Molinos Nacionales (Monaca), a food company majority-owned by the Mexican group Gruma; Envases Internacional and Aventuy, which produce aluminum cans and food packaging, respectively; the Spanish-owned Agroislena, which, with its eighty-two outlets and eight silos, is the largest distributor of agricultural products and equipment in the country; and the Venezuelan unit of Owens-Illinois, a world leader in the production of glass packaging for foods, drinks, medicines, and cosmetics.

Advances in Bolivia

Bolivia has also made important advances in terms of nationalizations.[79] These have been a crucial component of the new economic model implemented by the Morales government and have included the return of the hydrocarbon sector to state hands. On May 1, 2006, the government decreed the nationalization of hydrocarbons, including gas, the main source of wealth for the country. The decree completely changed the way in which different players participate and benefit from the process of extraction. Under the new contracts, transnational corporations no longer appropriate 82 percent of the wealth, but instead receive between 10 and 18 percent. In a single year (2011), the Bolivian state received more income from the hydrocarbon sector than it had during the ten years prior to Morales's election. The state company YPFB was strengthened in order to take on the leading role in the nationalization process, and the Empresa Boliviana de Industrializaión de los Hidrocarburos (Bolivian Company for the Industrialization of Hydrocarbons, EBIH) was created.

The government has also taken steps toward industrializing gas, among them the construction of two gas processing plants, the first of which came online in 2013, while the other will begin functioning in 2014.

In terms of the other strategic sector, mining, the Posokini deposit in Huanuni was nationalized in 2006. But there have been a number of difficulties in this sector, largely as a result of neoliberal policies that saw large mines carved up and handed out to small operators, many of them cooperatives. At the same time, mineworkers in the private sector have opposed nationalization. This explains the conflicts that have arisen between private sector mineworkers and cooperative miners.

In May 2010, the Morales government nationalized four electricity companies: Corani, Guaracachi, Valle Hermoso, and the cooperative distributor Empresa de Luz y Fuerza Eléctrica in Cochabamba. Two years later, it expropriated the shares that Red Eléctrica de España (REE) owned in the company Transportadora de Elcctricidad (TDE) and expropriated shares in the La Paz and Oruro electricity companies. In doing so, the Bolivian state transformed itself into the key player in this sector.

The same occurred in the telecommunications sector. On May 1, 2007, the government decreed the nationalization of the telephone company Entel, an affiliate of the Italian-owned Euro Telecom International. Within four years (2008–2012), the telecommunications sector has grown by 326 percent.

Advances Made in Ecuador

Thanks to the resistance against privatization by various social and political fronts, the privatization trend in Ecuador did not affect strategic sectors as much as it did in Bolivia and other countries. Ecuador inherited state or municipal companies in the area of oil and electricity, but they functioned according to a private and privatizing logic. During Correa's government, a total of eleven public companies have had to be restructured, and ten new companies have been created. Ecuador and Venezuela have also joined forces to create the Gran Nacional Minera Mariscal Sucre (Grand National Mining Company Mariscal Sucre).

According to Ecuadorian economist Magdalena León, Ecuador has utilized its state control over strategic sectors to promote the government's vision of economic sovereignty, energy independence, and wealth redistribution.[80] That is why it was necessary to carry out deep changes to the legal framework inherited from neoliberalism that protected the control transnationals and private interests had over strategic resources.

In the oil sector, reforms have led to new contracts with private companies that until then were reaping extraordinary benefits from windfall profits due to high international oil prices. As of April 2013, 100 percent of windfall profits were being captured by the state, with state oil revenue jumping from $838 million to $1,639 million. The state is also promoting the construction of a new refinery (Refinería del Pacífico) and has improved the Refinería Estatal de Esmeraldas, thereby beginning to reverse the paradoxical and disadvantageous situation Ecuador finds itself in, exporting crude oil and importing processed derivatives.

The government has also attempted to bring together different institutions, norms, and public policies to deal with strategic sectors in an integral manner, not only in terms of recuperating state control but also promoting a change in the productive and energy model toward a post-extractivist economy. Within this framework, public investment in strategic sectors has already surpassed $10 billion. This includes funding to conclude the delayed construction of two large hydroelectric projects, which will mean hydropower's contribution to energy generation will rise from 48 percent to 94 percent by 2020.

Telecommunications services have also expanded and been democratized. Between 2007 and 2012, access to the Internet quadrupled, and the number of schools with access to this service went from four to 1,400.

A significant part of the resources obtained through state control over strategic companies has been redirected toward meeting the immediate needs of the peoples of these countries.

Changing the Relations of Production

These Latin American governments are capable of going about implementing a coherent strategy toward changing the relations of production. However, these changes won't happen overnight. It is a complex process that needs time. As Michael Lebowitz says: "It is not simply a matter of changing property ownership. This is the easiest part of building the new world. Far more difficult is changing productive relations, social relations in general, and attitudes and ideas."[81] It is therefore necessary to design a coherent strategy aimed at transforming the existing relations of production into the new relations that are the hallmark of 21st century socialism. The steps to be taken and the speed with which these can be implemented will depend on the starting point and on the existing balance of forces.

To explain this more clearly, I list below some of the steps that will have to be taken first, when dealing with state-owned companies, second, when dealing with cooperatives, and third, when dealing with capitalist companies.

1. State Companies

It goes without saying that the easiest transition is the one that can take place in state companies, because these are formally owned by society in general and are explicitly directed toward serving the interests of that society.

In such companies, it would be possible to move from formal ownership to real appropriation by:

- creating workers councils that allow workers to play a part in running the company;
- organizing production to satisfy communal needs;
- opening the books and ensuring complete transparency, thereby allowing workers to exercise a social accounting function and combat waste, corruption, and bureaucratic interest;
- electing managers who share this vision and who have the trust of the workers;
- applying a new type of efficiency in these companies that, as productivity improves, makes it possible for the workers to achieve more and more human development (introducing a workday that includes time for worker education so involvement in management is truly effective and not merely formal), and also respects the environment.

According to Michael Lebowitz, it is possible that specific companies that follow this type of social policy may not initially be profitable, but because these policies can be thought of as social investment, all of society should cover their costs.

2. Cooperatives

Cooperatives must be encouraged to overcome their narrow focus on the interests of the group that makes up the cooperative. How can this be achieved? One way to do it is to develop organic links with the rest of society.

In order to do this, it is important to encourage:

- forging links between cooperatives so they relate to each other in a cooperative and not a competitive way. In some cases it might be possible to integrate their activities directly without them being separated by commercial operations, and;

- forging relations between cooperatives and the communities. This is the best way to begin to move away from the private interests of each cooperative and focus on the interests and needs of people in general.

3. Capitalist Companies

It might be possible to gradually transform capitalist companies by finding various ways to subordinate their economic activity to the interests of the national economic plan. Michael Lebowitz has called this "socialist conditionality."

These measures could include:

- demanding transparency and open books, so that communities and workers can inspect them;
- using a system of prices and taxes that obliges companies to transfer a portion of their surpluses to other sectors of the economy, thus making it possible to set up new companies or to improve social services for the population;
- using competition with state companies or subsidized cooperatives to oblige the capitalist companies to lower their prices and reduce their profits;
- using government regulations that require companies to transform the workday so that a given number of hours is set aside for educating workers, and require them to implement specific ways for workers to participate in making decisions about how the company will be run.

But why would capitalist companies accept such impositions if they can move to other parts of the world where these costs do not exist? They might be willing to do so if the owners have a strong patriotic consciousness and if the revolutionary government rewards their collaboration with the national development plan by giving them easy access to loans from state banks and by guaranteeing that state companies or the state itself will purchase their products at prices acceptable to them. That is, the state can use its power to change the rules of the game under which capitalist companies can survive.

However, if the revolutionary government's aim is to begin to move toward a society without exploiters and exploited, why design a strategy to incorporate capitalist companies into the national plan, if they continue to exploit workers?

The reason is very simple: the state is not capable of running all of these companies overnight. It has neither the economic resources nor the managerial experience needed. Nevertheless, we must never lose sight of the fact that capitalist companies placed in this situation are continually going to try to reduce the burden of the aforementioned "socialist conditionality." At the same time, the revolutionary government, with the cooperation of workers and communities, will try to introduce more and more socialist features into these companies. There will be, therefore, a process of class struggle in which some will try to recover lost ground by returning to the capitalist past and others will try to continue to replace capitalist logic with a humanist, solidarity-based logic that makes it possible for all human beings to develop fully.

In general, we must strive to ensure that ownership of the means of production becomes increasingly social, while also ensuring that small-scale private property is allowed to exist.

Create New State Institutions

We have spoken about the need to work from within the inherited state apparatus, but this does not mean that we should not look for new ways to overcome it.

This was what the Bolivarian revolutionary government in Venezuela did to provide assistance to the most neglected sectors—it decided to create institutions to run programs outside of the old state apparatus. This was the objective of the different social missions created by the government: Misión Barrio Adentro, to provide health care in poor neighborhoods; Misión Milagro, to attend to those with vision impairments; Misión Mercal, to supply food and essential products at lower prices; educational missions at various levels (literacy, primary, secondary, and higher education); Misión Cultura, to expand culture to the whole country; Misión Guiacaipuro to attend to indigenous communities; and Misión Negra Hipólita, to provide services to the homeless and those living in extreme poverty. In the past few years, a number of new missions have been created, such as Gran Misión AgroVenezuela, which provides small and medium agricultural producers with the necessary inputs to produce; Gran Misión Vivienda Venezuela, created in April 2011 in response to the housing crisis; Gran Misión En Amor Mayor, to attend to elderly people in situations of poverty; and Gran Misión Hijos e Hijas de Venezuela, to help families in extreme poverty; Gran Misión Saber y Trabajo, which has the goal of generating three million jobs between 2011 and 2018.

Why did they have to create these missions outside of the inherited state apparatus? The example of Misión Barrio Adentro can help us understand why.

The Ministry of Health's bureaucratic apparatus was not able to respond to the health care demands of the very poor who lived in far away places or areas that are hard to get to, such as the *cerros* (poor neighborhoods located on hillsides in Caracas). The doctors working in the inherited health system didn't want to go to these places—they weren't really interested in providing health care; their aim was to make money. Additionally, they were not prepared to provide the type of health care that was needed, since they were basically educated as specialists and not as general practitioners. While a new generation of Venezuelan doctors was being educated to meet this demand, the government decided to create Misión Barrio Adentro, building medical clinics in the cerros and barrios to provide basic health care to the poorest people. The government sought the collaboration of Cuban doctors to help them in this endeavor. Whereas the poor joyfully welcomed these doctors, the opposition criticized the measure, saying they had come to take jobs away from Venezuelan doctors and nurses. They also said the Cuban doctors were not trained professionals and made other ridiculous accusations. However, the Misión has had such positive results and an excellent reception from the Venezuelan people that the opposition is now saying in their electoral campaigns that it will keep the missions but will make them much more efficient.

In the case of Ecuador, Misión Manuela Espejo was created to attend to people with disabilities and was placed under the supervision of Vice President Lenín Moreno. The tremendous work of this mission has been recognized at the international level, and various governments have asked Ecuador to provide advice on how to carry out similar projects in their respective countries. The Ecuadorian government recently decided to create a secretariat dedicated to providing attention to people with disabilities.

Transforming the Central Government's Management

Itinerant Cabinets: Bringing the Government Closer to the People

On beginning his first term as president, Correa decided to break out of the traditional bureaucratic mold whereby all decisions are made within the confines of four walls, and created the so-called *gabinetes itinerantes* (itinerant cabinets).[82] Every three weeks, meetings are held in different municipalities and parishes, far removed from traditional centers of power, involving the entire cabinet, representatives from national and local government institutions, and local parliamentarians who belong to Alianza PAIS. Small towns are prioritized over large cities. This was part of a proposal for bringing the government to the people.

The cabinet meeting begins on Friday morning, with the starting time dependant on how far away the place is. Regional and national problems are analyzed. In general, there is no break for lunch or to eat, although sometimes a break is allowed so that government functionaries can lunch at a local restaurant and have direct contact with people from the community. Ministers, secretaries, and directors of state institutions work throughout the day. Speeches given by each one of them are projected on a large screen and on smaller screens in front of the table they all sit around.

On Friday night, around 8:30, and once the cabinet meeting has finished, a cultural activity is held in the local stadium, where the people get a chance to interact directly with the president and his government team. There is generally a big turnout from the local population. The president says a few words and presents his cabinet, an event that allows him to get a sense of how the people feel about some of his closest collaborators. Afterward, some of the ministers play musical instruments and on many occasions end up dancing with the locals. More than a formal event, it is a "moment for communicating with the people."[83] The event tends to finish up in the early morning.

On Saturday at 8:30 a.m. on the dot, Correa and his government team meet up with local mayors. Each mayor is given three minutes to put forward his or her demands. The name of the mayor, the municipal council he or she is from, and the demands or issues they want to talk about are broadcast on a screen. A digital clock on the screen indicates how much time they have left to speak. Following their speech, there is time for discussion with the president and his ministers. Opposition mayors receive the same treatment as supporters of the government. All agreements are registered in a computerized system. Correa is always careful not to make any promise that cannot be kept.

That same Saturday, after listening to the mayors' speeches, and while Correa hosts his weekly radio and television program *Enlace Semanal*, ministers and heads of state institutions hold meetings with local citizens in a public school. Working groups are set up and presided over by the coordinating minister for each of the seven areas that ministries and secretariats are grouped into. All citizens can choose to participate in one of the working groups, putting forward their problems or suggestions. The ministers are open to receiving criticisms on how to improve their work.

Agreements reached with the different ministers are registered on a computerized system that the president has access to, with the aim of making sure promises are followed through. If there is anything that Correa strongly rejects, it is broken promises that undermine the credibility of the government.

Foreign minister Ricardo Patiño says these types of activities are enormously important, because if ministers simply stay inside their offices and make decisions from there, they will never be able to carry out what the people really want.[84]

Creating Spaces Where Officials Can Be Held to Account

President Correa insists a lot on the issue of public accountability of government officials. This is something that distinguishes his government from previous ones. It is also why he started up a weekly radio-television program, broadcast every Saturday. *Enlace Semanal* lasts for two or three hours, starting at 10 a.m. He always hosts it at different locations.

The program has three parts. In the first, Correa informs his audience of what he did each day of the week, hour by hour, in a pedagogical manner, explaining different topics. At the same time, he criticizes government institutions for errors or deficiencies that have occurred. According to Foreign Minister Ricardo Patiño, this is why "people respect him so much, because they know he does not pretend, hide or cover things up."[85] He makes public calls and brings matters of public concern to the attention of his ministers.

Following this, the show moves on to the second part, dealing with important issues that have arisen during the week. Correa usually takes up three or four issues of political interest and comments on international affairs.

The third part is dedicated to critically analyzing the messages sent out by the opposition media. This section, which lasts fifteen to twenty minutes, is called "Freedom of Expression Belongs to Everyone." Correa will pick out a news item from one of the opposition newspapers and outline, one by one, the lies contained in the article. He does the same with television news items.

On some occasions, the president will ask one or a few ministers or functionaries present to give details regarding some policy that has been recently implemented by their respective institution. On average, some 200 to 1,000 people, depending on the location and size of the venue, will attend the broadcast of the program, which is open to the public.

Carrying Out Pedagogical Work from Government

Another task that our governments must take on is utilizing the media outlets at their disposal to educate the people and raise their consciousness.

I referred above to Correa's radio program and its educational content. However, it was Hugo Chávez who first had the idea of making direct contact with the people via the media.

Chávez always concerned himself with providing ideological education for the people. On May 23, 1999, just three months after being sworn in as president, he inaugurated his Sunday radio program *Aló Presidente* as a means for direct communication with the people, who were able to call in and ask questions or give their opinions. Shortly after, the program began being broadcast on various television channels across the country.

The program was a vehicle to reach the people every Sunday for several hours. With a simple style and attuned to popular idiosyncrasies, he would patiently explain to the people the negative effects of capitalism and the benefits of socialism, using concrete examples that related to people's everyday life. On numerous occasions he used diagrams or maps to explain things. The increase in people's political consciousness was due, in no small part, to the pedagogical capacities of the president, which he used not only during his Sunday program but also in his long and frequent speeches.

Chávez also used the program to listen to the people, and through this he learned of many things that government authorities had kept from him. He always asked people from the area where the program was being broadcast from to speak.

Changing Course When the People Demand It

Another thing our governments can and should do if they are serious about building 21st century socialism is make themselves capable of changing course when the people demand it.

This is what occurred in Bolivia at the end of 2010, when Morales backtracked on his government's decision to remove subsidies on gas, a move that had the effect of sending prices skyrocketing (on average by 83 percent).

Although the measure had a rational justification (while the government was spending $380 million on fuel subsidies, around $150 million of this money was leaving the country via contraband to neighboring countries such as Brazil, Peru, Argentina, Chile, and Paraguay), it was taken without consultation. The following day, violent protests took place, and threats of further marches and strikes began to be heard. This popular reaction forced the president to rethink the move, and he decided in the end to repeal the decree in line with his attitude of "governing by obeying."

"The people did not come out in opposition to Evo, rather they mobilized to say no to any attempt to govern without consultation, to demand rectification and recognition," argues Isabel Rauber. In an act of humility, revealing both his great wisdom and his roots, Evo Morales changed course by withdrawing the decree and reiterating his decision to "govern by obeying," which, in strict terms, is not a question of either governing or obeying, but rather governing together, working jointly on key measures, and sharing responsibility for decisions made and their implementation.[86]

According to the Argentine investigation, this popular reaction, known as the "gasolinazo," converted itself into a kind of "political earthquake . . . which was capable of reversing the growing tendency within the government to make decisions from on high without taking those below into consideration, adopting the old political culture of power that believes governing to be the task of those who supposedly 'know and are right,' that it is something for those that know better, or that are 'tough' enough to put up with it."[87]

Transforming Parliament and Creating Forums for National Debate

The government is not only capable of creating new institutions more suited to the new tasks; it is also capable, up to a point, of transforming parts of the inherited state apparatus, such as parliament.

A New Form of Legislating: Social Parliamentarianism of the Streets

In Venezuela, they have experimented with a new conception of participation with regard to drafting laws. They have called this initiative "social parliamentarianism of the streets."

To carry out this initiative, it was necessary to redefine the role of parliamentarians, ensuring that they did not see their job as merely confined to the National Assembly and instead went out to make direct contact with the people, calling on voters to debate proposed laws. Pedro Sassone, an advisor to the National Assembly, recognized that this was not easy, as it would require a rupture with the prevailing culture.[88] Rather than discuss laws from a narrow corporatist vision by, for example, speaking to the private sector about economic laws, or discussing a housing law with experts in the field, attempts were made to create spaces where people could come together to discuss proposed laws and have their opinions and suggestions taken into consideration.

Sassone believes this should not be limited to discussing laws that have already been drafted, but should also focus on creating spaces for popular participation where people's suggestions on certain issues can be taken as the basis for drafting new laws from scratch. In this regard, he told us about one of the best experiences he witnessed, which occurred in Plaza Altamira, a place that has always been a gathering point in Caracas for the opposition. The meeting was called to discuss the issue of crime, one of the most deeply felt problems for many people. "We met with sections of the opposition, and reached an agreement with the [opposition-controlled] Chacao mayoral office to hold various social parliamentarianism of the streets meetings on this issue. They placed as a prerequisite that they also have the opportunity to participate in the debate, something which we agreed to. The mayor of Chacao came to our center and we went to Altamira to debate a national proposal for fighting crime."[89]

There is no doubt that if this legislative initiative is applied well, it could signify a real revolution in terms of drafting laws.

There is also a need to push forward with a proposal that Jesús Rojas, a Venezuelan sociologist and one of the main promoters of communal councils, was extremely passionate about: the establishment of local parliaments composed of popular spokespeople. The idea is that in the future, municipal councils will be made up of popular spokespeople elected by communal councils and other expressions of popular power, such as workers' councils, councils of shopkeepers, artisans' councils, communes, etc.

In El Salvador, there have not been big advances in this direction, but it should be noted that the parliamentarians from the Frente Farabundo Martí para la Liberación Nacional (Farabundo Marti National Liberation Front, FMLN) have implemented an interesting practice: they meet periodically with their constituents in a public place to report back on their activities and receive suggestions from the people.

Networks of Direct National Democracy

Bolivian political analyst Luis Tapia has an interesting proposal that in various ways coincides with Sassone's ideas, and can further enhance people's political participation and deepening democracy.

According to Tapia, "Participation in political life has as a first strong connotation, being present in public political spaces to debate issues of general interest, with the aim of discussing the direction that the government should take from the viewpoint of the collective we belong to, be it at the local, regional and national level.... In this sense, our first task is to consider what kind of spaces for participation we need before we start thinking about types of representation."[90]

Historically, in Bolivia, there have existed two main spaces and forms of political participation: "One of these is the communitarian space, that is, communities where certain types of self-government exist, which on many occasions come into conflict with the Bolivian state. The other space is civil society, which is composed of different organizations within society that generally reflect corporative interests."[91]

Luis Tapia has proposed an interesting idea: a "network of local assemblies of national direct democracy."[92] This would entail "creating political spaces for direct participation, not only in regard to local and municipal issues, but also national and plurinational issues." He believes that people who were born or choose to live in places distant from the capital should not be limited to discussing local issues; they should participate in discussions on national issues.

This would require organizing local spaces for direct democracy with the aim of discussing national issues. The national government would create these spaces in every part of the country, allowing people to discuss both local and national issues.

Luis Tapia believes that another complementary idea, one very similar to social parliamentarianism of the streets, could be to "consider making the agenda of parliamentary debates . . . public, so that once it is drawn up, it too can be the object of discussion in each of these assemblies, something which in turn would nourish the discussions both in parliament and those taking place in other assemblies at the national level with suggestions."[93]

"These 'national democracy local assemblies,'" as Tapia calls them, "would be the space in which citizens could exercise, in a permanent manner, their right to participate in governing the country."

To make this idea a reality, the government would have to formulate a plan for discussing the key issues on the country's political agenda and establish a timeline within which local assemblies could participate in the discussion before any policies are implemented.

According to Tapia, this collection of democratic spaces for direct democracy should have direct representation in the multicultural national parliament and the executive branch of the state:

> In this regards, a key feature of the proposal is that this network of assemblies for national and multicultural democracy be the principal form of political decentralization, within which citizens participate in local discussions about national issues on a regular basis and via a range of institutions that allow for communication and interchange between both levels. In this sense, the main form political decentralization would take is the organization of political spaces within which national politics can be carried out at the local level.
>
> The size of the assemblies might correspond with that of neighborhoods in the case of cities, or alternatively, to tasks covered by municipal councils, even if it is not a municipal issue. In any case, the possibility would have to be left open for the people themselves to designate the boundaries of these political spaces.
>
> The idea is to avoid this level becoming bureaucratized. It is essential to ensure that the infrastructure and a core group exists to make sure these assemblies function every month, and that the assembly itself elects, on a rotational basis, representatives to take all the decisions made in the assemblies to the national level, that is, directly to the Bolivian parliament.

> This implies avoiding the "professionalization" of politics at this local level. While delegates may receive some funds, this would not be in the form of a salary, and would be paid purely to cover costs incurred, for instance when traveling to and from meetings and even the national parliament.[94]

The use of public spaces for debate is becoming common in the global movement against neoliberalism. We have the example of the 15M movement in Madrid and the Chilean student movement, which have used public spaces for debates and have transformed themselves into a mass process of popular self-education.

Finally, alongside the system of collective construction of opinions and policies, where those most committed tend to participate, we should not rule out the use of mechanisms for carrying out popular, nationwide consultations, as have already occurred in some Latin American countries. However, we must be clear that these mechanisms for consultation are based on individual acts and lack the richness of collective discussions, which is why they should be seen as complementary instruments, and not as substitutes for collective discussions.

Pushing for the Construction of a New State from Below

Previously, we discussed that 21st century socialism required the construction of a new state from below, pointing to the emphasis that Chávez initially placed on the communal councils as the smallest organ of societal self-government. Later, it was decided that the ideal size in which to develop self-government was a geographical space smaller than a municipality but larger than the area of a communal council, a space that to some degree is economically self-sustaining, and to whose government certain functions and services, previously carried out by municipalities, could be transferred. The functions and services to be transferred included, among other things, the upkeep of electricity service, street and road upkeep, tax collection, rubbish disposal, and upkeep of educational and health installations. Chávez called this space the commune.

Inspired by his numerous public interventions and looking back at historical experiences of communes, I have come to formulate some ideas on this issue that are contained in the book, *De los consejos comunales a las comunas*. Below, I summarize some of these.

A Territory That Brings Together Several Communities

The commune is a populated territory within which exists a number of communities that share common historical-cultural traditions, problems, aspirations, and economic vocations and use the same services; they have the conditions to be self-sustaining and self-governing; and are willing to come together behind a common project that has been elaborated in a participatory manner and is constantly being evaluated and adjusted for new circumstances as they emerge.

These criteria should be contemplated when defining the territorial boundaries of a commune, as this is not something that can be done simply by reference to numbers of residents, which is often the case when it comes to the electoral districts or municipal subdivisions that exist in some countries. Nor can they be determined by whether an affinity exists between certain community leaders or whether good relations exist between certain communities as opposed to others. Much less can they be defined in an arbitrary manner, decreed from above without any consultation.

Economic Sustainability with a Socialist Orientation

The commune should be able to provide the necessary material and spiritual conditions for its productive development and the satisfaction of material, social, and cultural needs, as well as any other collective needs of its inhabitants. To this end, it must work toward combining efforts behind a communal development plan that has been elaborated in a participatory manner.

The commune should ultimately become self-sustaining, that is, it should strive to generate its own funds, allowing it to depend less and less on external resources. It should carry out productive activities or provide services within its own territory that provide it with the means for obtaining a significant part of the resources it requires to meet its needs and costs.

Each commune should strive to build up a system of production, distribution, and consumption with the participation of its communities, via communitarian organizations, cooperatives, social property companies with a socialist orientation, bartering systems, and many other innovative ideas that point in the direction of this new productive model based on popular power and control over production.

Logically, a key structural axis of the commune will be those units of production or service provision that are communal or communal-state property.

In terms of a rural commune, we could combine agrarian cooperatives involved in the cultivation of certain fruit and vegetables with the purchasing of these products and industrial processing by a communal social property company. Distribution would be in socialist-oriented stores within and outside the commune.

Attempts should be made to establish communal property companies in each commune, which could employ local residents and produce goods and services that are of communal use: bakeries, transport, companies that regulate water distribution and service payment, LPG cylinder refilling plants, gas stations, etc. The commune should financially support initiatives that generate local jobs during their initial phase, until they are financially self-sufficient.

A Communal Government

At the same time, we need to take steps toward communal self-government. The municipal council should gradually transfer an important part of its governmental functions and management of public affairs to the commune. It should only conserve in its power those functions that are justifiable on the basis that they are of a more general or complex character.

- A communal parliament emerges from the assembly of popular power of the commune.

  Within each commune, a communal parliament or communal legislative power should be created. This would be the decision-making body for those people—whom we could call *communeros*—living in the commune. This parliament would be made up of spokespeople from communal councils, workers' councils, issues-based councils, or interest groups that exist within the commune's boundary and that are willing to participate in the construction of the commune. It would be the commune's assembly of popular power.

  To facilitate the work of these spokespeople, I propose the creation of a legal advisory team for this parliament that could be brought together in three collegial bodies: a council of community popular power, a council of workers' popular power, and a council of issues-based or interest group popular power.

  Each one of these councils of popular power will work separately on their specific issues and come together in a grand assembly of popular power to discuss common issues and collaborate on those points that require doing so.

  The commune's assembly of popular power will be the highest decision-making body within its territory.

- Assemblies of popular power create their respective government organs.

  The commune should be capable of taking on a series of activities that until now have been carried out by the municipal council: local taxes, street cleaning, electricity, water, local roads, and maintenance of communal places. Doing so will require an apparatus that allows it to exercise these responsibilities.

In the future, the commune's assembly of popular power should become the communal government, creating for itself the necessary apparatuses and institutions that can allow it to take on the tasks that arise as a result of being transferred greater responsibilities.

This assembly would also be responsible for electing people to occupy posts in the remaining four branches of the state recognized in the Bolivarian constitution: the executive, judicial, moral, and electoral branches. These public servants should report back on their activities and be recallable in case they are considered not to be complying with the mandate they were given.

- Communal planning council.

  The commune should have a communal planning council that at the start of each governing term facilitates a participatory planning process for the elaboration of the commune's multi-annual strategic development plan and its annual plans. These plans should fit within the broader strategic national development plan and other local plans, while at the same time nourishing those plans with its own proposals and projects.

Communal Bank

The commune should also have its own financial entity or communal bank in which to deposit the funds it administers. There could also be other financing initiatives, such as rural banks, savings and loan cooperatives, and savings banks.

The national state should establish a fund to help kick-start the creation of communes, based on the principle of equity and solidarity. Those communes with the most needs and historically least attended to by the state should receive more funds that the rest.

While the communal bank is being established, communal councils that belong to a single commune can pool their funds into a single project, with each council taking on its financial share of the project. Alternatively, one of the already constituted communal council banks could be chosen to receive funds from a state institution willing to support one of the commune's projects. The disposition of communal councils to share their resources with other communal councils in the commune is a good indication as to whether the subjective conditions are being created to move in the direction of communal self-government.

Social Control over the Government

Efficient social control should exist over the functioning of the government, with different means and mechanisms available for citizens to speak out about the quality of services and the power to remove those functionaries whose performance has been questioned by a sufficient number of local residents.

Communes Cannot Be Decreed from Above

It is not up to the local governor or mayor to decide, without any prior research, when and where a commune should be created. It is not a question of seeing who has more communes in their region. Communes should not be created in an artificial manner simply to satisfy the desires of those higher up or in order to obtain resources from the state. The process of creating the necessary subjective conditions in these territories cannot be forced. Governorships and mayoralties should be facilitators of this process and not take over responsibility for things the people have to do themselves. They should provide technical assistance to aid the communes in their creation, with their handling and distribution of money, and in other areas in which they may need help.

Experimenting with a Different Way of Managing the State Apparatus

The experience of the communes should provide an opportunity to experiment with a different way of managing the state apparatus, putting it at the service of the people. Within the commune, state institutions should work in a harmonious manner, with the aim of meeting the needs of the respective commune. This requires, on the one hand, working together among themselves, and on the other, meeting with community spokespeople to ensure they are operating within the framework of the communal plan.

The actions of state institutions should be subject to some kind of communal social control, and if a state functionary is found not to be up to the task in terms of his or her respective responsibilities, there should be a commitment on the part of each local or national institution that such a functionary be removed from their post.

The process of building communes implies laying down the foundation of a new state, one that will no longer stand above the people, but rather be a state composed of the organized people who have taken their destiny into their own hands.

Coexistence of Two Types of State in the Period of Transition

It is necessary to understand—as Michael Lebowitz writes—that two states will coexist for a long time in the transition process: the inherited old state whose administrative functions have been taken over by revolutionary cadres that will try to use it to push through the process of changes and a state that begins to emerge from below through the exercise of popular power in various institutions, including the communal councils.[95]

Relationship of Complementarity

The uniqueness of the transition process is that the inherited state fosters the emergence of the state that will replace it, and thus a complementary relationship should be developed rather than one where one of the states negates the other. Of course, the assumption is that the organized movement must control and exert pressure on the inherited state to ensure that it moves forward. This is because it suffers from tremendous inertia and because the cadres that occupy leadership positions are not always imbued with a truly revolutionary spirit and so tend to slip into the same behavior patterns as officials of the past.

The Inherited Culture

It cannot be ignored that the seeds of popular power that spring up from below might be contaminated by the inherited culture and that they might deviate into bureaucratism or other things. As Gramsci says, and President Chávez never tired of repeating, a struggle exists between the old that cannot finish dying and the new that is being born.

Local Vision, Global Vision

One of the characteristics of the state that emerges from below is its tendency to have a "local view" of reality, seeing the trees but not the forest: a kind of local *esprit de corps* exists which, as with trade unions, that tends to focus on making economic demands on the company and loses its vision of the working class as a whole.

The inherited state, however, because of its national character, necessarily tends to have a "global view" of things. It should have a plan for the overall development of the country, designed with as much participation by the people as possible; a plan that allows it to push forward its project for economic, political, educational, and cultural transformation toward the society we want to build, a society that makes possible the full development of all humans, which is in solidarity with the poorest areas and which will lead to balanced national development.

Transforming the Armed Forces to Identify with Their People

One of the most important tasks facing our governments is that of transforming the military. However, is it possible for a body that has been part of the repressive, disciplinary apparatus of the bourgeois state, which has been impregnated with bourgeois ideology and whose high commands have been trained by the U.S. School of the Americas and indoctrinated in its national security doctrine, to transform itself into an institution at the service of the people and increasingly identified with the people?

Historical experience in the past few decades in Latin America allows us to think that this can happen. In the years following Hugo Chávez's election, the armed forces played an important role in defending the decisions democratically made by the Venezuelan people. It was the armed forces who were mainly responsible for Chávez's return to power when a group of top officers, most of whom commanded no troops, sadly played the role of pawns of big business interests in a frustrated April 2002 coup attempt.[96]

Transforming the military is no easy task, given that in most of our countries this has been a repressive institution at the service of the established order. What order are we talking about? Well, the order that has allowed capital to reproduce itself and is enshrined in the inherited constitution. Every time the popular movement, through various forms of struggle, has threatened the reproduction of the capitalist system, every time that its interests have been even slightly affected or an attempt has been made to reduce the privileges of the groups that have ruled up to that point, the armed forces have been called upon to impose order, that is to say, to keep bourgeois order, to defend the inherited system of institutions. It is symptomatic that in Bolivia "the armed forces had—and still do to some extent—concentrated their soldiers around the mines in the rebellious Altiplano and the Chapare, that is to say in the rebellious zones of the city and the country. Their logic was social containment."[97]

Today, however, an increasingly large number of left governments in our continent have understood the importance of changing this order, of creating new rules for the institutional game that can serve as a framework for making it easier to build the new society. For this reason, they have organized or are organizing constituent assemblies to draft new constitutions that will install a new way of organizing society and establish a social order that will serve the majority of the population and not the elites. These constitutions will ensure that the natural wealth of these countries, which was ceded to transnational companies, returns to state hands and will ensure the construction of independent and sovereign states. The military, by defending this new order, will thus be defending the homeland and the interests of the overwhelming majority of the population, not the interests of the elites.

That is what happened in Venezuela. The first gesture made by the newly elected government was to organize a constituent process to change the rule of the inherited game and to re-found the state by creating a new set of institutions better suited to the changes people wanted to make. The Constituent Assembly led to a new constitution. The new constitution became an important ally of the process, because defending the constitution means nothing if not defending the changes undertaken by the Chávez government. It was this constitution that allowed the majority of high-ranking officers—under pressure from the people—to rebel against the coup-supporting officers and decide to disobey the orders of their superiors. Many young officers and soldiers used this same constitution to organize the resistance from below by putting pressure on their officers to reject the coup.

How can our governments begin the process of transforming the armed forces into an institution willing to defend and implement the new institutional order in a consistent way?

Our governments have been implementing various measures. Let us examine some of them.

Give the Military Responsibility for Social Projects to Help the Most Destitute

One important means is assigning social projects to the armed forces so that they use their labor power, their technical knowledge, and their organizational abilities to help the most destitute social sectors. The most obvious example of this was the Plan Bolívar 2000, which President Chávez instigated in Venezuela when he began his mandate. It was a program designed to improve the living conditions of the popular sectors. The military cleaned the streets and schools, cleaned the neighborhoods to fight against endemic diseases, and helped restore social infrastructure in urban and rural zones. Venezuelan soldiers accepted this work with a great deal of enthusiasm, and direct contact with the social problems that the poorest sectors of the population were experiencing helped to raise the consciousness and social commitment of the young officers who worked in the program. These young solders are today among the most radicalized sectors of the process.

In Bolivia, the military has been given the job of providing the most destitute sectors with economic aid such as the Juancito Pinto bonus, provided to help with the schooling of children from the lowest-income families, and the Juana Azurduy bonus for single pregnant mothers.

Provide Educational Schools and Courses in the Spirit of the Constitution

It is important that top military officers and those under their command have a vision of the world that is consistent with the new society we want to build.

It is interesting to note that in Hugo Chávez's generation, most officers were not educated in the School of the Americas but in the Venezuelan Military Academy, which had undergone far-reaching changes in 1971. What was known as the Andrés Bello Plan raised the level to university equivalent. Army cadets began to study political science to learn about democracy theorists and analysts of Venezuelan conditions. For military strategy, they studied Clausewitz, Asian strategists, and Mao Zedong. Many of these soldiers ended up specializing in certain subjects in universities and began to interact with other university students. If any did go off to study in the U.S. academy, they went with their rucksacks filled with progressive ideas.

Give the Armed Forces Responsibility for Big Infrastructure Projects

Our armies and our peoples, even though they desperately wish to live in peace, must be prepared to defend our national sovereignty as long as imperial forces want to dominate the world and impose their vision.

It is worthwhile remembering that in the beginning, the Cuban Revolution wanted to turn barracks into schools but needed to change its plans and spend huge sums of money on strengthening its military might to prevent U.S. intervention. Faced with an unreasonable enemy, there is no option but to prepare for war as the best way to avoid it.

However, in countries like ours, which have so many development needs, it makes no sense for our armies to train only for war and then just sit around and wait for an invasion. Some of the soldiers can be used for strategic economic tasks.

It is important for the armed forces to feel they are not simply defenders of order and national security, but that they also consider themselves to be builders of the new society. Much of the knowledge they acquire to defend the homeland can be used to repair infrastructure that has fallen into disrepair for lack of maintenance (hospitals and public schools) or to collaborate in managing new strategic companies or undertake work that, for example, improves communication throughout the country.

By employing members of the military in economic tasks, Cuba has achieved excellent results. Companies run by the army have, on the whole, achieved better results than other state companies.

Democratize Access to the Top Ranks and Change Selection Criteria

It is also important that all discrimination impeding access to the highest ranks in the military is eliminated. In Venezuela, this was much easier because, unlike in most other countries, no military caste existed. Most high-ranking officers came from low-income families, both rural and urban, and knew firsthand the difficulties Venezuelan people had to deal with in their daily lives.

In Bolivia, as in most of our countries, an officer who trained in the United States used to have more chance of being promoted, but things now operate in the opposite direction: whoever shows the greatest nationalist sentiment, the greatest commitment to institutions, the greatest support for social and productive tasks has the best chance of being promoted in the armed forces.

Include the People in National Defense Work

Our nations must be prepared to defend themselves from any foreign interference. It is obvious that because of numerical and technological imbalances, our armies would not be able to resist an imperial invasion, unless our people join on a mass scale with military personnel in the task of defending our sovereignty. As Álvaro García Linera, vice president of Bolivia, says, the only option for surviving or resisting if faced with a possible invasion is if there are "strong links between the military and social structures. In Bolivia they are rediscovering a tradition of struggle from the past: something that was called *las republiquetas* [the little republics]. These arose to fight against Spain during the struggle for independence. In these *republiquetas* the military was merged into the local community structure. That was how they stood firm and developed during the fifteen years of the battle for independence and were able to build the Bolivian state. This is the logic being used by members of the military themselves to create Bolivian military doctrine."[98]

To defend the sovereignty of Cuba, a country that is only ninety miles from the United States, it was of fundamental importance to have, side-by-side with the standing army, people's militias trained to defend the homeland in the event of an external threat. In Venezuela, progress is being made in this area.

History has shown that, confronted by the elevated combative morale of our peoples rising up in arms, there is no empire that can be victorious.

Moreover, the decision to form the Defense Council of UNASUR has been another important step forward in the defense of our sovereignty as a subcontinent.

Recover Patriotic Symbols and Traditions

Another of the efforts that our governments have made is to restore traditions and values by modifying national symbols to better fit with the characteristics of each national reality. The most recent example of this is the decision by the armed forces of the plurinational Bolivian state to use the indigenous symbol of the Whipala as one of its flags.

Build Territorial Sovereignty in Regions Previously Neglected

There are countries in our continent that have not yet gained complete sovereignty over their territory. This is the case in Bolivia. Until a very short while ago, the state did not control about 30 percent of its national territory. In the eastern strip, from Beni to Santa Cruz, power was in the hands of landowners, drug traffickers, wood smugglers, and illegal raw material and mineral dealers. There was no state there; the strongest ruled—the drug trafficker's thug or the landowner's thug. "Now we are getting this territory back as never before in our history. The state's presence in this area has multiplied by 2,000," says the Bolivian vice president. "Previously a visit to Pando was a once-a-year visit for the president, now not a week goes by without a minister visiting. We have managed to assert the state's presence in all of these territories in the country. Now there is a permanent state presence with its armed forces, bringing resources, bringing health care, bringing education."[99]

A Model of Development That Respects Nature

Another important task our governments face is implementing an economic development model that is not based on the indiscriminate exploitation of natural resources, but instead seeks to gradually reestablish the necessary harmonic metabolism between humans and nature.

There exists a consensus among Latin American progressive governments that the growth rates experienced by advanced countries in the second half of the twentieth century cannot be maintained or imitated by other countries. This would "have irreversible and catastrophic consequences for the natural environment of this planet, including to the human species."[100] No one doubts that putting an end to this situation has become more and more urgent if we want humanity to have a future. Nevertheless, we all know that the solution won't come from advanced, developed countries, which are at the same time the most polluting nations. The 2012 Rio+20 Summit is further proof of that.

This is why the more advanced governments in our region should lead by example, not simply because this is a question of principles—that there will be no socialism if we do not respect nature—but because the survival of humanity demands it.

Venezuela, Bolivia, and Ecuador should implement their respective constitution's mandate and respect the environment. The new constitutions passed in these three countries place emphasis on this issue. In fact, the Ecuadorian constitution is the first constitution in the world to recognize the rights of nature.[101]

This is a far from easy task. The big dilemma these countries have in front of them is how to raise their people out of poverty and attend to their basic needs, while respecting nature. To aim for some kind of "zero growth," as some propose, to avoid the consumption of polluting energy and its degrading consequences for the environment, would mean enshrining existing inequalities between rich and poor countries, that is, between developed societies that have reached a high standard of living and the majority of humanity that are a long way from reaching those conditions. It is much easier to ask others to stop growing if one's own needs are already satisfied.

Transform Natural Resources from a Curse into a Blessing

We have to confront the challenge of finding a strategy that allows us to build the good life (*buen vivir*), taking advantage of nonrenewable natural resources and transforming them into "a blessing," as Nobel Prize winner Joseph Stiglitz has recommended, but without depending exaggeratedly on them. Only in this way will we be able to leave the trap of poverty and underdevelopment.[102]

As President Correa says, the great challenge we face is to utilize extractivism in order to overcome extractivism. Personally, I believe that the phrase extractivism, like many "isms" in Spanish, has negative connotations and prefer to talk of the need to use resource extraction to overcome extractivism.

Our governments, therefore, need to take steps in the direction of ensuring that the development of our countries depends less and less on extractivism.

The dilemma is not between extracting and not extracting, but rather extracting at rates that maintain a healthy metabolism between humans and nature. This cannot be achieved from one day to the next.

María Fernanda Espinosa, a longtime environmental activist and Ecuador's defense minister, assures us that her government is making an effort to transition from an extractive economy to a service-based economy, but she adds: "This cannot be done by decree, that is, the oil pipelines cannot [be shut off] from one day to the next. . . . So the issue is: how do we, within the realm of the possible, from the government, carry out this transition from a highly oil-dependent extractive economy to a post-oil economy? How can we do this in an organized, planned, and responsible manner?"[103]

Even Alberto Acosta, an Ecuadorian economist who is very critical of extractivism, has made clear that one cannot think of "closing the oil fields currently being exploited, but we must seriously discuss whether it is useful to continue expanding to new oilfields" given the environmentally devastating impacts this would entail.[104]

Approaches Toward an Ecologically Sustainable Society

The environmentalist and American economist Herman E. Daly has established three basic operative criteria that should be applied by an ecologically sustainable society: "1) not to exploit renewable resources at a rate over and above that at which they renovate; 2) do not exploit nonrenewable resources at a rate over and above that at which they can be substituted by renewable resources; 3) do not emit into the air, water and soil an amount or composition of residues over and above the capacity of ecosystems to absorb them."[105] We should add a fourth criterion: respect the biological diversity or biodiversity of different ecosystems.

It is not, then, about saying no to development, but instead "conceiving and making reality genuinely human models of development," or what several authors call "sustainable development" or "ecologically sustainable society." That is, a society that satisfies "in an equal way the necessities of their inhabitants without putting in danger the satisfaction of the necessities of the future generations," a society in which it is the organized people who decide what is produced and how it is produced.[106]

Steps Being Taken

Creating such a society is the direction that our governments should be heading towards, and important steps have been taken in this regard, even if in many cases they have remained at the level of discourse for now. This at least demonstrates an intention to move in this direction.

The fact that this issue has received a lot of attention in the new constitutions is a very important step forward. In all cases, the state is tasked with the responsibility of protecting the environment.

To achieve this, it will be necessary to transition (within a certain timeframe) from a primarily exporting economy to an economy based on services and knowledge, something the Ecuadorian government has embarked upon.

According to the Peruvian scholar and politician Manuel Lajo, the Ecuadorian government "has put an enormous effort into cohering a strategy for the construction of a chain of scientific and technological investigation centers, both public and private, national and international," with the aim of identifying those economic sectors that can, via the intensive use of scientific knowledge and technological innovations, produce for the internal market or for exportation and help achieve this urgently needed change in the productive model.[107]

President Rafael Correa, more than any other Latin American president, has placed emphasis on the role that education must play in training up the future generation of citizens capable of building the future society.

I do not have the space here to detail everything that the government has done in the area of education. Instead, I will simply refer to the government's flagship project, the City of Knowledge, which Daniel Suárez, advisor to the National Secretariat for Higher Education, Science, Technology, and Innovation, describes as "the key project being implemented as part of creating the new knowledge-based Ecuador."[108]

The University of Yachay will be the hub of the city and the first public academic center for higher studies in Ecuador and Latin America. It will focus exclusively on providing courses in science and technology in order to resolve social needs and train creative and innovative professionals.

There will also be eleven public research institutions that will become regional and continental leaders in their respective areas, dedicating their research toward meeting the basic needs of society. Among the areas of research will be development of technologies for increasing production and the generation of safe products for internal consumption and exportation; development of technologies for the industrialization of nonrenewable natural resources (petrochemical and metallurgical); research into alternative materials for low-energy-use housing; research on adapting technologies for efficient, low-energy, and environmentally friendly transport; and research into ways to protect the environment through recycling, waste treatment, and the cleanup of contaminated sites, to name just those that I consider to be the most illustrative of this new research focus.

Another step that our governments can take is to begin the process of restoring ecological systems that have been degraded, damaged, or destroyed. Part of the resources obtained through greater state control over oil extraction in Ecuador has been dedicated to water treatment, for example, which has benefited tens of thousands of families, especially those in the poorest areas.

They are also transforming their energy matrix by reducing dependency on oil and its derivatives. Huge investment is going into hydroelectricity and wind energy.

Steps are also being taken to mitigate the negative environmental consequences of oil extraction through the promotion of prevention and control measures so that the process is no longer as highly contaminating as it was in the 1970s, when Texaco was operating in the country. To achieve this, the government is using revenue it collects from oil extraction to invest in high-level technology.

Among the various precautionary measures and restrictions that have been placed on activities that could lead to the extinction of certain species, the destruction of ecosystems, or the permanent alteration of natural cycles, the government has worked toward restoring and conserving mangrove regions, whose management has been placed in the hands of local communities.

The most important initiative in this regard has been the government's effort to reduce oil exploitation. In 2007, Correa presented to the world an interesting and challenging project, know as Yasuni-ITT.[109] As part of this project, Ecuador would agree to leave under the ground roughly 20 percent of its proven oil reserves, which is located in three oil fields within the Yasuni National Park, in exchange for the international community donating at least $3.6 billion to the project, roughly equivalent to 50 percent of the income Ecuador would receive if it opted to exploit the oil fields. Nevertheless, Correa maintained that if the international community were not willing to contribute to the Yasuni-ITT project, Ecuador would have no alternative but to exploit those oil fields.

Popular Participation in the Defense of the Environment

Given that the challenge is huge and temptations abound, I believe the constitutions of Ecuador and Bolivia propose some very interesting points regarding the role popular participation should play in the protection of the environment. The Ecuadorian constitution says: "The state guarantees the active and permanent participation of people, communities, affected nationalities and peoples, in the planning, implementation and control of all activities that generate environmental impacts."

Article 135 of the Bolivian constitution proposes something similar, but adds that the organized people can and should react via what the constitution calls "popular action" to any violation or threat against a series of rights, including among them those of the environment.

Moreover, the constitution (Articles 187-190) allows for the creation of a tribunal dedicated exclusively to agro-environmental issues. Authorities to this tribunal were elected by the people in unprecedented elections held in October 2011 for the entire judicial system.

Finally, also in Bolivia, on December 21, 2010, the new Law Number 71 dedicated to the rights of Mother Earth came into being, with the purpose of recognizing nature's rights, as well as the obligations and responsibilities of the plurinational state and society in guaranteeing them.

Given everything I have said up till now, I believe that the objectives set out by the aforementioned governments clearly show us a path forward, even if some internal contradictions may exist in the constitutions. Nevertheless, we should recognize that there is still a big gap between theoretical discourse and the practical steps forward being taken by these governments, although I have no doubt that the political will exists to continue pushing toward the goal of *buen vivir*, based on harmony between humans and nature and one of the characteristics of the alternative to capitalism we need to build.

It is equally clear that by using extractive resources to tackle poverty, we are also creating better environmental conditions, because in many cases, poverty is a big contributing factor to environmental degradation. Illegal logging for firewood to use in cooking and to keep warm is one of the clearest examples of this.

Promoting Decentralization and Participatory Regional Planning: the Example of Kerala

Some Latin American nations have put into practice a variety of participatory budget processes, but I know of no experiences like that in Kerala, India, where a massive program of participatory planning was carried out, demonstrating to the world that a Left government can take significant steps in this direction.[110] Using the legal backing of the 1993 constitution, which established three levels of local entities (districts, blocks, and rural villages), the communist government elected in 1996 began a notable and radical experiment in democratic participation, known as the People's Campaign for Decentralized Planning. This program entailed a fundamental change in the role different levels of government played and the emergence of what some people have called local self-governments.

Decentralize All That You Can Decentralize

One of the first decisions made by the new Kerala government was to transfer 35–40 percent of the funds it received from the National Plan toward projects and programs proposed by local entities. In doing so, the government helped stimulate popular participation as people became interested in participating because they saw they had the power to make decisions on concrete and important issues.

During the campaign, they applied the principle of "subsidiarity." That is, anything that an entity at a lower, more local level could do should be done at that level, and only those tasks that needed the intervention of higher levels of administration should be delegated upward.

Given that support for the opposition was close to 40 percent and the government wanted to avoid a scenario in which these sectors could boycott the process, representatives of the opposition were invited to participate both on the high-level national commission as well as in the local commissions. Their opinions were sought when creating a commission with vast powers to investigate any corruption that local governments might get involved in during the exercising of their functions.

Community Assemblies: Mass Bases for Planning

Participatory planning involves the realization of community assemblies (*grama sabhas*) at the level of electoral districts in Kerala, which contain around 1,500 to 2,000 people of voting age, in order to identify what are the most deeply felt needs and problems of the people, and what human and material resources exist in the local area. Once problems and resources have been analyzed, proposals are formulated. I think it is fundamental that they do not simply remain at the level of pointing out problems.

Great importance was attributed to the effective function of the community assemblies as a central component in the creation of a mass base for local planning and assuring transparency in the elaboration and implementation of plans.

Each one of these assemblies elects twenty people to represent it at the level of the rural village or urban municipality, creating what is known as the Council.

More that 1,000 entities were involved in the participatory planning process.

Steps in the Participatory Planning Process

The starting point is identifying the most deeply felt needs of the people. This is done by convening community assemblies and attempting to ensure the maximum level of participation of local residents, especially women and the most marginalized. To facilitate participation, assemblies are convened on non-workdays.

Next, steps are taken to identify not only the problems but also the human and material resources that exist in the locality. Out of this discussion emerge proposals, or what I have termed project-ideas.

Once needs and available resources have been identified, the assemblies begin to develop projects. To make this step a reality, each local entity creates working groups for each project made up of elected representatives, functionaries, experts, and activists.

Based on this set of projects, representatives select those proposals that should be included in the plan. While the lower levels prepare their plans, the higher levels begin to integrate into their plans proposals that emerge from below, evaluating them in technical terms, but without questioning the priorities set by the municipality or village.

Finally, at the district level, a team of functionaries and experts carries out a technical and financial evaluation of the different plans and projects before the District Planning Committee approves them.

These six steps normally took one year to complete and involved three million citizens, tens of thousands of functionaries and experts, numerous mass organizations and other representatives of civil society, and around 100,000 volunteers trained in providing organizational support for the campaign.

Corruption Diminishes Thanks to Measures Adopted

One of the arguments advanced by the opposition against decentralizing resources to local powers was that, given the corruption at the top level of government, decentralizing resources would only shift corruption to the local level. Nevertheless, the opposite occurred: rather than increasing, corruption decreased. This was not achieved spontaneously, however; instead, a series of measures that were effective in tackling this vice were adopted. Transparency was introduced in law. All documents pertaining to the plan, including the selection of people who benefited from programs, accounts, and invoices were considered to be public documents, open and accessible to any citizen.

Whenever a public work was being carried out, a large billboard or wall was constructed, visible for all to see, with all the information relating to the project written on it in the local language. Penalties were imposed if this measure was not enacted. The infamous alliance of contractors, engineers, and politicians was definitively broken in many places.

Regular social audits of community assemblies were carried out, something that was of great help in the fight against corruption.

In consultation with opposition leaders, a seven-member committee was created and granted vast powers to investigate cases of embezzlement that local authorities may have been involved in while exercising their functions.

Monitoring committees made up of ordinary citizens were established to watch over the process of selection, implementation, and evaluation of projects.

10. A Guide to Judging How Much Progress Is Being Made

Thus far I have tried to analyze the characteristics of the processes of building socialism in our subcontinent. I indicated how progress can be made with this project using government power, and said that in order to judge our governments it is more important to look at the direction in which they are going and not the speed with which they are advancing. Now I would like to propose criteria that could allow us to make an objective assessment of the progress made by those governments that have explicitly set themselves the goal of beginning to build 21st century socialism.

Attitude to neoliberalism and capitalism in general. What is the government's attitude toward neoliberalism and capitalism in general? Does it lay bare the logic of capital, does it attack it ideologically, and does it use the state to weaken it?

Attitude to unequal income distribution. Are our governments moving to diminish the gap between the richest and the poorest; are they giving the latter more access to education, health, and housing? Are they taking measures to ensure there is a fairer distribution of wealth between the poorest and richest municipalities?

Attitude towards the institutions our governments inherit. Do they convene constituent processes to change the rules of the institutional game, knowing that the inherited neoliberal state apparatus places huge obstacles in the way of any progress in building a different kind of society? Does the government strive to increase the number of people registered to vote, given that generally the poor are less likely to be on the electoral rolls? Are they taking steps to transform the inherited state apparatus, the manner of governing, the parliament, the judicial system, etc.?

Attitude toward the armed forces. Are steps being taken to transform this institution? Have there been moves to stop training officers at the School of the Americas and end joint training exercises with U.S. armed forces? Has the military been entrusted with social tasks that put it in close contact with the people? Has its education curriculum been changed? Has a new national security doctrine been drawn up? Has the system for the promotion of military officers been changed?

Attitude to economic and human development. Does the government consider the goal of satisfying human needs more important than accumulating capital? Does it understand that human development cannot be achieved with a paternalistic state, one that solves problems by transforming people into beggars? Does the government realize this can only be achieved through practice and creating spaces in which popular protagonism is possible?

Attitude to national sovereignty. Does the government reject foreign military intervention, military bases, humiliating treaties, etc.? Is it recuperating sovereignty over natural resources? Has it made progress in finding solutions to the problem of media hegemony, which until now has been in the hands of conservative forces? Is it promoting the recuperation of national cultural traditions?

Attitude to the role of women. Does the government respect and encourage the protagonism of women?

Attitude toward discrimination of all types. Is the government making progress in eliminating discrimination of all types (sexual orientation, gender, ethnicity, religion, etc.)?

Attitude toward the means of production and producers. Is social ownership of the means of production increasing, and are workers more and more the protagonists in the workplace? Is the division between intellectual and manual labor disappearing? Is workers' capacity for self-management and self-government growing? Is the distance between the countryside and the city diminishing?

Attitude to nature. Are the governments seeking a change in the institutional rules of the game in order to promote environmental protection? Are they making an effort to transition from a largely extractivist model toward a sustainable development model? Have they implemented policies that indicate the country will depend less on extractive industries in the future? Are they dealing with the problem of industrial pollution? Are they ruling out the use of transgenic crops and livestock? Are they implementing educational campaigns to promote environmental protection? Are they encouraging and taking practical measures for recycling rubbish?

Attitude toward the need to place the wealth of society in their own hands. Are the governments taking steps toward a greater decentralization of governmental functions? Are they allowing for citizens' participation in designing national plans? Are they carrying out participatory planning processes at all levels of society?

Attitude to international—especially Latin American—coordination and solidarity. Are the governments looking for ways to integrate with other countries in the region? Are they providing solidarity to countries in the region that need it?

Attitude toward popular protagonism. Do the governments mobilize workers and the people in general to carry out certain measures, and are they contributing to an increase in the people's abilities and power? Do they understand the need for an organized, politicized people, able to exercise the necessary pressure that can weaken the state apparatus and power they inherited and thus drive forward the proposed transformation process? Do they understand that our people must be protagonists and not supporting actors? Do they listen to the people and let them speak? Do they understand that they can rely on the people to fight the errors and deviations that come up along the way? Do they give the people resources and call on them to exercise social control over the process? To sum up, is the government contributing to the creation of a popular subject who is increasingly the protagonist, one who is assuming governmental responsibilities?

PART 3

A New Political Instrument for a New Hegemony

11. Building a New Hegemony

Previously, I specifically focused on the issue of participatory and protagonistic democracy as the fundamental characteristics of the new society we want to build. I also took up the characteristics of the transition in those countries whose governments have decided to advance toward socialism via the peaceful or institutional road. I explored some of the steps these governments could take, pointing out the need not to look at the pace with which they proceed but rather the direction in which they are going, since the pace to a large extent depends on how the obstacles in their path are dealt with.

Now, I would like to briefly focus on how we can achieve the necessary balance of forces in order to advance toward the society we want to build and the society's relationship with the issue of hegemony.

Defining Hegemony

The word *hegemony* is commonly used as a synonym for dominance and to refer to different situations. It can refer to economic hegemony, military hegemony, political hegemony, and cultural hegemony. Here, I use the term to refer to the issue of consciousness, of cultural hegemony.[1]

My starting point, just as it was for Marx, is that the ideas and values that prevail in a determined society, and rationalize and justify the existing order, are the ideas and values of the ruling class. While in previous times these were fundamentally transmitted via the family, the church, and the school system, today they are more and more transmitted via the media, in particular television, whose soap operas have become, as Chilean sociologist Tomás Moulián said, the modern-day opium of the masses, with a strong influence among those sectors of society that are least likely to be armed with critical ideas and thinking.

For me, a class becomes hegemonic when its values, its proposals, its societal project are accepted, looked upon sympathetically, and taken up as their own by broad sections of society. Hegemony is the opposite of imposition by force.

Moreover, we should not confuse the word *hegemony* with domination, because a class can be dominant when its interests are imposed on society by force and can also be dominant when its interests are taken up as their own by the people. Therefore, a class can dominate through terror or dominate through consensus or through a combination of both. Furthermore, hegemony is not something that is achieved once and for all; it can also be lost. It tends to occur that when governments that rule through consensus begin to lose their social base of support, they will increasingly rely on authoritarian methods to maintain their domination. It can therefore be said that there exists a dialectical relationship between the weakening of the capacity to convince and an increase in the need to use force.

When a social class becomes hegemonic, one of its achievements is that it is able to form a social bloc; that is, it can unite a heterogeneous social conglomerate that is normally marked by—in some cases profound—class contradictions. The ideas and proposals of this hegemonic social class serve as a cohering element and help mitigate existing contradiction between different social sectors.

For these proposals to convince and unite others behind them, people must feel that they will help solve their problems. There must exist at least the illusion that measures being adopted will resolve problems, because once people realize this is not the case, hegemony begins to break down.

Bourgeoisie Achieves Popular Approval for Capitalist Order

In a number of countries, bourgeois sectors have been able to embed their values, generate broad acceptance for the capitalist social order, and achieve cultural leadership over society; that is, they are able to govern by consensus rather than by using force. There, propaganda tends to be well refined and is not only able to manufacture artificial necessities but also creates the illusion among important sections of the population that their problems can be resolved by implementing the existing economic model.

Bourgeois Hegemony Begins to Break Down

Nevertheless, the global crisis of capitalism, the incapacity of its neoliberal form to resolve the most acute problems of our peoples, the rapid rise in misery, and the social exclusion of the great majority of the population while fewer and fewer individuals hoard the majority of the wealth have led a growing number of people across the world to reject this model. This was the tipping point that in many countries in Latin America created the condition in which we elected leaders who proposed alternatives to neoliberalism, and that today is the cause of the current mobilizations and popular uprisings occurring in different parts of the world.

The Need for a Political Instrument

This breaking down of bourgeois hegemony does not necessarily mean that a new popular hegemony has emerged in its place. This will not occur spontaneously; we need a political instrument, a political organization to help us construct it.[2]

In recent years, and in increasingly more countries, growing multitudes have rebelled against the existing order and, without a defined leadership, have taken over plazas, streets, highways, towns, and parliaments. But, despite having mobilized hundreds of thousands of people, neither the magnitude of their size nor their combativeness have enabled these multitudes to go beyond simple popular revolts. They have brought down presidents, but they have not been capable of conquering power in order to begin a process of deep social transformation.

The history of successful revolutions ratifies the fact that in order to not waste popular energy and instead transform it into a force capable of bringing about change, a political organization is needed. One that can help overcome the dispersion and atomization of the exploited and oppressed by proposing an alternative national program to serve as a cohering instrument for broad popular sectors. Also needed are strategies and tactics that allow for unity in action to most effectively deal blows at the decisive moment and the decisive place to the powerful enemy that must be confronted in decisive moments and places. This is even more the case today when the potentially revolutionary popular subject—the class of workers and peasants—is so heterogeneous and fragmented in each country.

Solid organizational cohesion not only gives people the objective capacity to act; it also creates an internal climate that facilitates energetic intervention into unfolding events and allow us to make use of opportunities that are available. We must remember that in politics it is not enough to have reason; we must also have time and the necessary force to make it a reality.

A lack of clear ideas as to why we should struggle and the sensation of lacking solid instruments that can help us put into practice the decisions we have made can have a negative impact because of its paralyzing effect.

I recognize that these ideas go against the current trend. There are many who are not even willing to discuss them. They adopt a negative attitude because they associate such ideas with the anti-democratic, authoritarian, bureaucratic, manipulative political practices that have characterized many leftist parties.

I believe it is fundamental that we overcome this subjective blockade and understand that when I speak of a political instrument, I am not talking about just any political instrument. I am talking about a political instrument adapted to the new times, one that we all have to build together.

But to create or remodel the new political instrument, we first have to change the political culture on the left and its vision of politics. This cannot be reduced to institutional political disputes for control of parliament, of local governments, to pass laws or win elections. This form of conceiving politics ignores the people and their struggles. Politics can also not be limited to the art of what is possible.

For the left, politics must be the art of making the impossible possible.[3] This is not some kind of voluntarist statement. What I am talking about is understanding politics as the art of constructing social and political forces that are capable of changing the balance of forces to the benefit of the popular movements, and making possible in the future what today appears to be impossible.

The vision I have of this political instrument is one of an organization that must abandon class reductionism by taking responsibility for defending all social groups that are excluded and discriminated against economically, socially, politically, and culturally. Although it should be concerned with class, its concern must also extend to ethno-cultural, race, gender, sex, and environmental problems. It must bear in mind not only organized workers' struggles but also the struggles of women, First Nations people, people of African descent, young people, children, the elderly, the differently abled, gays, etc.[4]

This must be an organization capable of raising a national project that can bring together all those sectors that are suffering due to the crisis and act as a compass for them.

This must be an organization that directs its efforts toward society, respecting the autonomy of social movements, that refuses to manipulate them.

This must be an orienting and cohering organization at the service of the social movements, and therefore it should not try to gather to its bosom all the legitimate representatives of everyone struggling for emancipation. Instead, it should strive to coordinate the movements' practices into one single political project, by generating meeting spaces so that the assorted social groups can recognize each other and grow in consciousness in the specific struggle that each group has to wage in its own area: the neighborhood, university, school, factory, etc.[5]

This must be an organization that understands politics to be the art of building forces. We have to overcome the old and deeply rooted error of attempting to build political force without building social force.

Political Strategy for current Situation: a Broad Front

We need a political organization that is capable of making use of the depth of the current crisis and the broad-ranging nature of the variety of sectors affected by it. A highly favorable scenario has emerged for overcoming fragmentation and bringing together the growing and diverse social opposition into one single column, in order to form an alternative social bloc. An extremely broad social composition and enormous force means it is sure to continue growing and convoke legions of potential followers.

In cases where a left government exists, the strategic task is to cohere and mobilize all those social sectors interested in defending and deepening the changes that the government has begun to carry out and which are fiercely resisted by those sectors that oppose the changes.

The characteristics of this social bloc—which could unite the immense majority of the population—will vary from country to country. The weight of each social sector, of each ethnic group, etc., will be different in each country. In Latin America, they will include not only traditional groups, such as the urban and rural working class and the poorest and most marginalized sectors, but might also involve impoverished sections of the middle classes, the constellation of small and medium-sized business owners and shopkeepers, informal workers, small and medium-sized agricultural producers, the majority of professionals, the legions of unemployed, cooperative members, retirees, the police, and lower-level military cadres (sub-officers and subordinate cadres).

I also believe that those capitalist sectors whose business dealings have come into objective contradiction with transnational capital could also form part of this social bloc. I am not here referring to those sectors of the bourgeoisie that are able to propose their own project for national development. Rather, I refer to those sectors that, in order to survive in the context of neoliberal globalization, have no other choice but to insert themselves in a national-popular project that can assure them support in the forms of loans and an increased internal market, the product of the social policies of such a government.

And just as neoliberalism impoverished the great majority of the peoples of our countries, not just in the economic sense but also in their subjectivity, their consciousness of themselves as social beings, we should not only talk about economically affected sectors but also all those who are discriminated against and oppressed by the system: women, youth, children, old people, indigenous peoples, Afro-descendants, certain religious groups, those with different sexual orientation, etc.

This bloc should house all those who suffer the consequences of the system and are willing to commit themselves in the struggle, first to put a halt to its advance and, afterward, to reverse its course.

Moreover, in a world in which the exercise of domination is carried out on a global scale, it is more necessary than ever to establish conditions and strategies for struggle at a regional and inter-regional level. The World Social Forums and other gatherings of an international character have enabled notable advances in this sense, although much is still to be done.

What Uruguayan senator Enrique Rubio wrote in 1994 remains as true today as it did then: we need to unite all those who are "excluded, left behind, dominated and exploited at the global scale, including those that live in developed countries. It is necessary . . . to put capitalism in check from the political, both inside and outside the state, whether militant or not, whether pro-party or not, from the social movements, from the scientific-technical complexes, from the cultural and communicational centers where views are molded in a decisive sense, and from self-managed organizations. . . . To put it in a slightly schematic and perhaps confronting fashion, the revolution will be international, democratic, multiple and profound, or it will not be."[6]

I believe that in order to build this bloc, it is necessary for us to be capable of proposing concrete and specific tasks that prioritize points of convergence. We must be able to correctly deal with the contradictions that necessarily will emerge between such diverse sectors of society.

It is important to elaborate a program or platform of accumulation for the political conjuncture, which plays the role of a cohering instrument for all the "losers" of the neoliberal model. This must be a platform that proposes halting the development of the neoliberal project and offers concrete alternatives to the grave problems currently being faced by the people.

This must be a platform drafted with the participation of all those who want to be part of this process. I agree with Rafael Agacino that "the democratic exercise of elaborating policies, of building consensus around popular demands" is very important. "What we are dealing with," he said, "is the opening up of spaces for politics from below, stimulating the most elementary act of communicating face to face, and from there advancing the practice of social processing of diverse interests, congenial minds and willing people around general rights of all those who live off their own labor."[7]

This platform cannot be confused with the program of the political instrument. It must delve more deeply into the goal that is to be achieved and the path to reaching it.

Winning Hearts and Minds of the Immense Majority

Moreover, if our project for an alternative society to capitalism is essentially democratic, we have to be clear that we must win the hearts and minds of the immense majority of the people.[8] We cannot impose our project; we must convince people that this is the best project for them and encourage them to participate in the building of this new society.

What can we do to achieve these objectives?

First, we must understand that it is not enough to lecture people. As President Chávez said, the hearts and minds of the people are won in practice, creating opportunities for the people to understand the nature of the project at the same time as they become its builder.

Second, our call must be broad and not exclude anyone. All good-willed people who want to work for the benefit of the collective, for their well-being, to build solidarity with others, should be included, regardless of their political stripes or religious beliefs.

Third, our attitude must be one where the people feel that their opinions, information, criticisms, reflections, and initiatives are taken into consideration.

This also implies understanding that we cannot govern simply for our own supporters. How many people have we been able to win over to the process because they have seen the government help those who are worse off, regardless of whether they are government supporters or not!

This is why it is fundamental to differentiate between the destructive, conspiratorial opposition and the constructive opposition, and avoid putting all of them in the same basket. I think it could help win over many of those not currently on our side if we show that we are capable of recognizing the positive initiatives of the opposition rather than condemning everything they do. We must combat their erroneous ideas, their mistaken proposals, but we must destroy them with rational and coherent arguments and not with verbal aggression. Perhaps this verbal aggression is well received by the most radicalized popular sectors, but it is rejected by large sections of the middle classes and in many popular sectors. People tend to not feel comfortable with these types of attacks.

We have to ask ourselves, why is it, despite the truth that our project for an alternative society to capitalism is beautiful, profound, and transformational, reflecting the interests of the great majority of the population, that the governments proposing such a project do not count on the support of all those who should be supporting it?

I think that in large part this is because an important part of the population does not know the true nature of our project. The opposition media has entrusted itself with disseminating misinformation, creating false alarms and, on many occasions, terrorizing the people in regard to what the future holds for them. But they are not the only ones responsible for this situation. We have also contributed to it. We tend to have big problems in adequately communicating the nature of our project. We do not dedicate sufficient time, resources, and creativity to this task. And, worse yet, on many occasions the very way we act negates our own project. We propose the creation of a democratic, solidarity-based, transparent, non-corrupt society, and yet we implement authoritarian, clientalist, egotistical, non-transparent practices. Many times there is a wide gap between what we say and what we do, and so what we say becomes less credible.

Thus we should not be surprised that important sections of society do not yet identify with our project and that it is necessary to win them over. We have to work on correcting our errors and overcoming deviations, as only in this manner can we win hegemony over society.

12. A New Political Instrument

Previously, I discussed the necessity of building a new hegemony and why a political instrument is indispensable to achieving this. Now, I want to develop some ideas regarding the kind of instrument we need and the task that this political instrument needs to take up.

Why a Political Instrument Is Necessary

Historical experience shows that the intervention of the state or government to push forward the transition to socialism is crucial. Why is this state intervention necessary? Did this happen with capitalism, too? No, the historical process of capitalist development was very different.

Capitalist relations of production were born in the bosom of pre-capitalist societies, and the only mission of bourgeois revolutions was to conquer political power to then use it to foster the expansion of this mode of production, which has its own logic of development.

The capitalist dynamic is explained by the hunger for profit satiated by exploiting wage labor and the economic laws that govern this process, which is led by an economic logic. The state only intervenes to create the two basic conditions for the existence of the capitalist mode of production: first the complete separation of the producer from his means of production, and second, primitive accumulation of money capital. When this mode of production has established itself, the state intervenes to facilitate or favor the logic of how it functions.

Nevertheless, socialist relations of production are not born spontaneously in the bosom of the preceding society but need the intervention of some kind of political organization that with the support of the people conquers state power—or at least government power. This is because, from that position, they can begin to create the conditions that allow them to move gradually toward establishing socialist relations of production in the various economic spheres of the society. The speed at which this happens depends on the objective conditions in each country.

A Weighty Inherited Culture

However, the people who must be the main protagonists in the construction of the new society do not drop from the sky; they are dragging a weighty cultural heritage behind them. This is why a large process of cultural transformation is needed if socialism is to be built, a process in which the individualist, consumerist, paternalistic culture of every person for him or herself which has created the habit of waiting for the state to solve our problems, is gradually overcome.

A 21st century socialism will only be able to consolidate itself if we manage to impregnate present and future generations with a new humanistic and solidarity-infused ethics, one that respects nature and stresses being rather than having.

What is more, if the goal we are pursuing is the full development of each person, and each person is different from the next, one of the most important characteristics of socialist culture must be respect for difference and fighting sexism and all kinds of discrimination.

Fragmentation of the Revolutionary Subject

Another facet of the reality bequeathed to us is an incredibly fragmented society. Playing upon this fragmentation has been one of the strategies used by the enemy to weaken us. Our transition processes usually get under way with a heterogeneous working class weakened by the processes of labor casualization and subcontracting, and very divided internally, not only because of the objective conditions caused by neoliberalism but also because of ideological differences, personalities, and "*caudillismo*." There are also a large number of social and political organizations that are fighting for their own goals and forget that the most important thing is to make the revolution.

People Have No Experience of Governing

Although the strategic objective aimed for is self-government by the people, in other words that the people govern themselves, that they assume power, this is not something that happens overnight. As Aristóbulo Istúriz says, our people do not have "a culture of participating," they have no "real experience of governing"; they are a people used to "populism, cronyism, to not reasoning politically, to asking for things." It is therefore necessary to govern with the people for a certain length of time so that they can learn to govern themselves.[9]

The Tasks of the Political Instrument

Building socialism entails developing new relations of production, carrying out a real cultural revolution that allows us to go beyond the inherited culture and building a revolutionary subject who is the bedrock of the whole process. It also requires that the people undertake an apprenticeship in forms of self-government. These are not things that come about spontaneously, which is why we need a political instrument.

The following is a list of the most important tasks that this instrument must undertake.

Struggle to transform the people's consciousness by fighting against the harmful cultural heritage of the past. Marx was convinced that decades of "civil wars and national struggles, not only to bring about a change in society but also to change yourselves, and prepare yourselves for the exercise of political power" were required.[10] Through their social practices and their struggles people must leave behind the muck of inherited culture as they begin to discover, experiment with, and incorporate into their lives new values—the values of humanism, of solidarity, of respect for differences, the struggle against sexism and discrimination of all kinds.

However, these practices are not enough. New ideas are needed to go up against the old ideas, otherwise why would Marx have devoted his whole life to writing *Capital*? We need, as Fidel Castro said, to wage a battle of ideas. However, battles don't have a successful outcome if no one is leading them. This explains another of the reasons for having a political instrument.

This political organization must also take on the responsibility for drawing up an educational strategy—based on practice and structured courses—that will make it easier for its members and for the people in general to acquire new knowledge. This kind of knowledge will enable them to have a critical attitude concerning the inherited culture and begin to take on more and more responsibilities related to building the new society.

Design a project for the country we want to build and guide the course the process takes. A political organization is needed because we need a body that sets the scene for the first draft of a proposal, program, or national project that is an alternative to capitalism. This program or project should serve as a map for finding our way, for making sure we don't get lost, for putting the construction of socialism on the right road, for not confusing what has to be done now with what has to be done later, for knowing what steps to take and how to take them. In other words, we need a compass to ensure the ship does not go adrift but reaches its destination safely.

If I have talked about a first draft drawn up by the political organization, it is because I believe we must be very mindful that, as it goes along, this project should be enriched and modified through social practice, with the opinions and suggestions from social actors. As previously stated, socialism cannot be decreed from on high, it has to be built with the people.

Rosa Luxemburg never tired of repeating that the path to socialism was not laid down in advance, nor were there predetermined formulas and blueprints, since the "modern proletarian class does not conduct its struggle according to any blueprint reproduced in a book or a theory; the modern workers' struggle is a part of history, a part of social evolution, and we learn how we should fight in the midst of history, in the midst of evolution, in the midst of the struggle."[11]

This task needs time, research, and knowledge of the national and international situation. It is not something that can be improvised overnight, much less in the complex world in which we live. This project must be set out in a program that serves as a map, which takes the concrete form of a national development plan.

The political instrument must stimulate a constant debate on the big national issues so that this plan, and the more concrete programs that stem from it, are constantly enriched. I agree with Farruco Sesto that these debates cannot be limited to a simple confrontation of ideas but should "lead to the collective construction of ideas and of answers to the problems. . . . Arguments added to or raised against other ideas will allow a shared truth to be created."

The political organization should be, according to Sesto, "a huge workshop for strategic thought, deployed all over the country."[12]

In particular, the political instrument should not only encourage an internal debate but should also endeavour to facilitate active participation in spaces for public debate—such as those previously mentioned—on subjects of more general interest, in which all interested citizens can take part.

For this reason, I find myself once again in agreement with Farruco, that since the party is not something apart from the people but rather has to make "its life within the people," the ideal place for this debate is "in the bosom of the popular movement." Moreover, "if one of the strategic lines of the revolution is to transfer power to the people, that implies transferring not only the ability to take decisions but also that of working out the basis for that decision" because "producing ideas and making clear the road to take is the most important activity in the exercise of power."[13]

Eliminate the social and political fragmentation we have inherited. We need a political body that understands it is not enough to create a huge organization with hundreds of thousands of members; we must go beyond that. We have to create places (cyber or real) where people can meet. We must encourage coordination of the various emancipatory practices that exist by trying to bring together all the actors to discuss goals they have in common: parties, social movements, organizations, and individuals. Our political instruments should be instances for promoting the unity of the people, capable of filling millions of women and men with the enthusiasm to fight for a common goal.

On the other hand, we should strive through our political instruments to construct collective leaderships, and need to understand the positive role that a charismatic leadership can play in the initial stage of the transition process, given the extraordinarily fragmented societies such leaders inherit. Their charisma can contribute vastly to uniting the different sectors of the people. But these leaders should also understand that good leaders are those who create the conditions in which they become less and less indispensable. They should encourage the development of new leaders and the construction of a more collective leadership.

The elements I have outlined here help us understand why several of our presidents have sought to allow and actively promote their reelection to office, a decision forcefully attacked by the opposition, which accuses them of wanting to perpetuate themselves in power.

In this sense it is interesting to note that the *New York Times* has defended the issue of continuous reelection. An October 1, 2008, editorial criticized term limits because it supported the reelection of the mayor of New York City. The newspaper argued that term limits tend to limit elected officials' focus to short-term plans that can be implemented quickly, instead of projects based on a vision for the future that require much more time to be implemented. If a mayor requires more time, we can imagine how much more time will be required by those presidents who seek to radically transform society. We should not be surprised, therefore, that some of our rulers have decided to take measures to allow their reelection to office.

Encourage and facilitate the people's protagonistic participation. Finally, we have the most important task, because without it we will never manage to build socialism. What is needed is a political instrument that encourages popular protagonism in the most varied social and political milieus in the country, one that puts itself at the service of that participation so that it is the people themselves who build the new society. We cannot afford to repeat the Soviet experience, which Kropotkin criticized as one in which the party ended up drowning the creative initiative of popular organizations.[14]

Only thus will we be true to the thesis that revolutionary practice is essential for workers' emancipation and that of the popular movement in general. It is through practice that full human development is reached, this being the most important goal we are aiming for.

To the aforementioned tasks, we need to add two additional ones.

Seek out and recruit new cadres who can breathe new life into and renew the political instrument. All processes dedicated to building socialism are faced with the problem of a scarcity of cadres. Generally there are very few revolutionary cadres available, those politically and technically ready to carry out efficiently the multiple and complex tasks that building socialism entails. This is why all of our left governments have had to rely on the expertise of many professionals and technicians who have worked for previous governments, people not exactly brimming with revolutionary consciousness.

This situation must necessarily change if we really want to push ahead with building socialism. The political instrument should be especially concerned with spotting the new cadres who are coming up in the various spaces for popular participation created by the revolution.

As a temporary measure, perhaps, the revolution could rely on foreign professionals and technicians who are committed to the revolutionary project and whose most important job would be to get underway a process of training the new national cadres.

In addition, new cadres with the new values are needed to revitalize and renew the political instrument.

Give early warning of the weaknesses perceived and the mistakes being made. Lastly, the political instrument should detect in time weaknesses and errors that are made and that have an objective basis, given that our governments will confront limitations such as the following: a) The task of construction must be undertaken with an inherited state structure; b) This state structure will be staffed by professional and technical cadres who do not share our goal; c) The new government has to rely on a people whose political consciousness is far from ideal; d) It will have to experiment on how to go about transforming the relations of production in societies where scarcity and not abundance is king; e) It will often have to contend with parties created to compete in elections that are plagued by opportunists who want to take advantage of their party affiliation to obtain some job or privilege; f) It will temporarily have to accept the fact that top party leaders are also top state officials because of the scarcity of qualified cadres; and finally, h) it will have to confront the permanent danger that even the most revolutionary cadres will become "bureaucratized." The inherited state apparatus has a habit of swallowing up many who, bit by bit, abandon revolutionary logic and begin to operate under an administrative logic, or become corrupt.

In a process with these characteristics it is difficult to avoid mistakes and deviations. That explains the need for a political instrument that acts as the critical conscience of the process, gives early warnings so these errors and deviations can be corrected, and is also highly self-critical.

Characteristics of the Kind of Political Activists We Need

If we revolutionary activists are to contribute to the construction of socialism—the goal of which is full human development through practice—our most important task must be to encourage and facilitate popular protagonism.

However to do that, we have to begin by changing our way of thinking about politics. We cannot reduce politics to the battle to get a job in state institutions, nor want to govern from above because we think we are in possession of the truth.

Let us look at the most important characteristics the members of the new political organization must have.

Way of Life and Activism

One of the difficulties we face when building socialism is the cultural heritage of our peoples, the type of consciousness they have inherited. We have to build socialism without yet having people who have accepted socialist values as their own. However, we cannot build socialism without socialist men and woman. How can we resolve this contradiction? What happens is that there are people who—because of their commitment to earlier struggles—have managed to transform their consciousness and begin to follow socialist values. These are the people who must be the members of the new political instrument.

Those of us who are members must be careful that our own practice does not violate the values of the new society we want to build.

In a world where corruption holds sway and political parties, and politics in general, are losing more and more prestige, it is of the utmost importance that we present a radically different ethical profile, one embodying values we exhibit in our daily lives. We must be democratic, show solidarity, be willing to cooperate with others, practice camaraderie, be honest at all costs, and practice clear-headedness. We must project vitality and *joie de vivre.*

Our practice must be consistent with our political discourse. Octavio Alberola notes: "People turn away from those churches that promise democracy without discrimination for all social classes yet deny their own loyal members basic freedom of expression when they do not blindly accept their slogans. . . . General staff who, on their own, negotiate and make agreements about the welfare of all. . . . Giant [party] machinery that takes away initiative, action, and the right to speak from individual members. . . ."[15]

Since the social revolution's aim "is not only the struggle for survival but also the struggle to transform our way of living," as Orlando Núñez says, "we have to venture into the realm of morality and love in search of a direct, daily transformation of [our] way of living, thinking and feeling."[16]

If we fight for women's social liberation, we should begin right now to change the women-men relationship in the family and eliminate the division of labor in the home and sexist culture. If we believe that young people are the raw material for our work, we must educate them to think for themselves, adopt their own positions, and be capable of defending them, based upon what they feel and think. If we fight against racial discrimination, we must behave in a manner consistent with that in our own lives.

Nonsectarian, Willing to Dialogue and Coordinate

We have to understand that if we are to be victorious, we need the support of the overwhelming majority of the people. To do that we have to create places, spaces where people can meet and exchange ideas, and we must coordinate all revolutionary forces.

All manifestations of sectarianism, each high-handed attitude, will only serve to weaken the march toward socialism. We cannot impose our ideas and our candidates just because we are the majority political organization, even if we are the majority by a long way. A small revolutionary organization can have, proportionally, more cadres ready to assume government tasks than the majority party has. What should count here is quality not quantity and, of course, loyalty to the government program. We must avoid reproducing the harmful practice of the Chilean Popular Unity in which all jobs were shared out on a quota system. When each party had a quota and carried on with its own policies.

We should learn from the new social actors of the twenty-first century. They are particularly sensitive to the topic of democracy. Their fights have generally had as a starting point the fight against oppression and discrimination. They reject being manipulated and demand that their autonomy be respected and that they can participate democratically in the making of decisions. In their organizations they seek consensus, and if this is not possible, they believe decisions should be adopted by a large majority. The Landless Workers' Movement (MST) of Brazil, for example, avoids using narrow majorities to impose its will on those who are in minority. It considers that if it is not the great majority, it doesn't make sense to impose a measure adopted by a narrow majority. It is preferable to wait until people continue to mature and end up being convinced by themselves of the correctness of that measure. Doing so they avoid internal disastrous divisions, so often suffered by movements and left parties, and they avoid big errors that could be made.

On the other hand, we should respect minority positions whenever they are willing to be channeled within the democratic process, remembering that historically there have been minorities who have been right because their analysis of the situation has been more accurate and because they were able to discover the real motivations of given social sectors.

Disciplined

Another characteristic is that our militants should have discipline. The MST considers internal discipline to be a measure of respect for collective decisions. Discipline should be demonstrated for both big decisions and small questions; for example, arriving on time for meetings.

"If there is at least a little discipline, people will respect decisions made at all echelons. . . . This is neither militarism nor authoritarianism; it is only one of the rules of democracy," João Pedro Stédile says. "There is no democracy without rules or regulations to control the behavior of the whole group. The discipline consists of accepting the rules of the game. We have learned this from football and in the Catholic Church, which is one of the oldest organizations in the world. . . . If somebody is in the organization of their free will, they must help to define the rules and respect them, they must be disciplined, respect the collective. Otherwise, the organization will not grow."[17]

Respect for the People's Autonomous Organizations

We must contribute to the autonomous development of the people's autonomous organizations, abandoning any attempt at manipulation. We must have as one of our main tenets that political cadres are not the only ones who have ideas and proposals and that, indeed, the popular movement has a great deal to offer, because through its daily struggles it learns, it discovers ways, finds answers, invents methods that can be very enriching.

Not Cadres with an "I Order—You Obey" Mentality, but Popular Educators

The members and especially the leaders of the new political instrument cannot have an "I order—you obey" cast of mind. We political cadres must be first and foremost popular educators, able to empower all the popular wisdom that exists in the people—both that which comes from their cultural traditions and their traditions of struggle and that which they acquire as they toil every day for subsistence. We must merge this popular wisdom with the more global kind of knowledge that a political organization can contribute. This is why the slogan "Order by obeying" is so wise.

Bureaucratism: the Biggest Scourge

One of the deviations that did most damage to the historical experiences of Soviet socialism was bureaucratism. Why do we say this? Because it destroys the people's energy and creativity, that of the real builders of the new society, and therefore prevents the goal of 21st century socialism from being reached. This goal is that women and men develop themselves completely through revolutionary practice itself.

Due to the disastrous consequences of bureaucratism, I choose to delve deeper into this issue.

The Roots of Bureaucratism

Earlier, when discussing the subject of decentralization, I said that one cannot attribute the existence of bureaucratism in the Soviet state simply to the legacy of the tsarist past. Instead it is more correct to attribute to point to the excessive centralization that existed in that state. However, if excessive centralization inevitably leads to bureaucratism, this phenomenon can also arise in state institutions, in parties and other kinds of public or private institutions.

Moreover, if it were only a matter of red tape and being shunted around, all that would have to be done would be to improve management methods. But that doesn't work.

Where, then, lies the root of this disaster? It is related to the basic question of how management in an institution is conceived of and implemented. Do the top civil servants or cadres make the decisions because they think they are the only ones who have the expertise to do so, or is trust placed in the membership and the organized people, in their energy and creativity?

Civil Servants or Cadres Who Turn Their Backs on the People's Initiatives

It was often said in the Soviet Union that progress could only come about in that country devastated by an imperialist and a civil war if the workers and peasants en masse were committed to work for the country's reconstruction. Nevertheless, when the workers and peasants took these remarks seriously and tried to apply them in real life by taking the initiative on various occasions (by organizing, for example, a people's cafeteria or a day care center to increase female participation in the labor force), their efforts were rejected by the central authorities, both party and government, on various pretexts. The bottom line, however, was that the party could not stand the fact that the people had done things not controlled by them.

Direct Negation of the People's Autonomous Activity

Bureaucratism is the direct negation of autonomous activity. Any independent initiative, any new thought is considered heresy, a violation of party discipline. The center must decide and supervise each and every thing that is done. Nothing can be done if the order didn't come from the center.

Alexandra Kollontai, the feminist Russian revolutionary and leader of the Workers' Opposition, gives an enlightening example: "What would happen if some of the members of the Russian

Communist Party—those, for instance, who are fond of birds—decided to form a society for the preservation of birds? The idea itself seems useful. It does not in any way undermine any state project. But it only seems this way. All of a sudden there would appear some bureaucratic institution that would claim the right to manage this particular undertaking. That particular institution would immediately 'incorporate' the society into the Soviet machine, deadening, thereby, the direct initiative. And instead of direct initiative, there would appear a heap of paper decrees and regulations which would give enough work to hundreds of other officials."[18]

Someone Else Decides for You

Bureaucratism tries to solve problems with formal decisions made by one person or a small group, both in the party and in some state institutions, but the real stakeholders are never consulted. This way of operating not only restricts the initiative of party members but also that of the non-party masses. The essence of bureaucratism is that someone else decides for you.

The Need to Encourage Public Criticism in Order to Save the Party

As discussed previously, a long process of cultural transformation is required to free ourselves of the muck of the inherited culture. According to Marx, this transformation can only be achieved after decades of civil wars and people's struggles, and history has proved him right. It is not only difficult for the common people to change; but this is also true of some of those who are members of the political organization itself.

Even the parties with the most experience in revolutionary struggle, those who led wars of national liberation for many years, such as the Chinese Communist Party or the Vietnamese

Communist Party, have suffered from the scourge of bureaucratism and corruption. In spite of the enormous sacrifices they made during the long years of struggle to liberate their peoples, several of the leaders no longer serve the people, have moved away from them, have become arrogant, treat others in a high-handed authoritarian manner, enjoy privileges, and have become corrupt.

Why Do These Situations Arise?

We must remember that revolutions carry the load of an inherited culture on their shoulders, a culture in which those who held public office always had special considerations and privileges.

Moreover, if their political future does not depend on the people, whom they should serve, but on their superiors, it is natural that these civil servants would be more inclined to satisfy the demands of their superiors than to respond to the people's needs and aspirations. What tends to happen is that because they want to please their superiors or to obtain monetary rewards, they falsify data or obtain the results demanded of them at the cost of the quality of public works. Indeed, it was rather common in socialist countries to inflate production data. However, this is not only negative from a moral point of view but extremely negative from a political point of view, because by falsifying data, they are providing bad information about the situation that really exists, which prevents the party or government from taking the necessary corrective measures.

I should also add that what tends to happen is that those who adulate their bosses tend to be promoted to posts with more responsibility, whereas those who criticize and adopt an independent posture are marginalized in spite of being competent.

Then again, since there is no encouragement for the people to exercise control over the way cadres behave, misappropriation of public resources for personal purposes becomes very tempting.

How to Fight against These Mistakes and Deviations

How can we fight against these errors and deviations? Can we trust the party itself to resolve its problems internally by, for example, creating an ethics committee charged with dealing with these situations? It seems that this is not the solution.

History has shown—especially in one-party regimes or regimes with an obviously hegemonic party that controls the government and often confuses itself with the government—that it is necessary for the party to be controlled from below and be subject to public criticism. That seems to be the only way to prevent cadres from becoming bureaucratized and corrupt and thinking they are the lords of the people's destiny, and accordingly putting the brakes on popular protagonism.

Mao Zedong explained the need for criticism and self-criticism by using the image of a room that needs to be cleaned regularly to prevent it from filling up with dust. His words on this point were: "The only effective way to prevent all kinds of political dust and germs from contaminating the minds of our comrades and the body of our Party" is, among other things, "to fear neither criticism nor self-criticism," "to say all you know and say it without reserve." "Blame not the speaker but be warned by his words" and "correct mistakes if you have committed them and guard against them if you have not."[19]

Criticizing Functionaries to Save the Party

There are some journalists who, when faced with the mistakes and deviations committed by party cadres, try to convince us that any party, or as I prefer to call them, any political instrument, is bad. I think that I have given enough arguments above to substantiate the thesis that we cannot do without a party when building socialism. The point, then, is not to try to do without a political instrument but to find ways of correcting these possible deviations.

Therefore, in the same way that Lenin thought that to save the Soviet state it was necessary to accept the existence of strike movements that fight against bureaucratic deviations, we think today that to save our governments and our political instruments, which are much more than the sum of their leaders, we must allow the organized people to publicly question the mistakes and deviations that some of their cadres may commit.

There is a basic argument for this. We must remember that the political organization is an instrument created so we can achieve the socialist goal of full human development for all people, and therefore it is the people and not the party that is the most important thing. The people have the right to watch over the instrument that will help them to develop themselves and make sure that it fulfills its role, that its cadres really help develop popular protagonism, that they do not try to stifle people's initiatives or disrespect them, and much less use their positions to gain privileges or unjustified rewards.

If we are realists, we cannot think that the very leaders of the party will commit hara-kiri. There is a tendency for leaders to want to protect themselves from criticism by their subordinates and by the people in general. Therefore it is extremely important that it be the people who supervise the actions of government and party leaders. For that reason, the people must be allowed to criticize these leaders' mistakes publicly without being accused of having an "anti-party attitude." The political instrument has to understand that getting rid of these arrogant, corrupt officials who are causing it to lose prestige can only strengthen the party.

It is important that the people's uneasiness over the mistakes or deviations that the leaders make is not suffered in silence, because it can build up inside and explode at any moment. However, if channels for expressing this discontent are established, the defects identified can be corrected in time.

Public Criticism Does Not Weaken the Revolution, It Strengthens It

An argument often used to condemn public criticism is that it is used by enemies to weaken the party and the transformation process. This is the reason why some accuse those who criticize to be anti-party or counterrevolutionaries.

On this point, the remarks Fidel Castro made on criticism and self-criticism are important. He made them after half a century of revolution, in an interview given to Ignacio Ramonet, editor of *Le Monde Diplomatique*. Some days previously, on 17 November 2005, the leader of the Cuban Revolution had said that "a fight to the finish" must be waged against certain evils that existed in Cuba, such as small-scale corruption, theft from the state, and illegal enrichment. He also told Ramonet that they were "inviting the whole country to cooperate in this battle, the battle against all defects, including small theft and massive waste, of any sort and in any place." When Ramonet asked him why the "usual method of recurring to criticism and self-criticism didn't work," Fidel replied:

> We used to trust in criticism and self-criticism, it's true. But this has become almost fossilized. That method, in the way it was being used, no longer really worked because the criticism tended to be inside a small group; broader criticism was never used, criticism in a theatre, for example, with hundreds or thousands of people. . . .
>
> We have to resort to criticism and self-criticism in the classroom, in the workplace and outside the workplace, in the municipality and in the country. . . . We must take advantage of the shame that I am sure people feel.[20]

A little later in the interview, after having admitted to various mistakes made by the revolution, and encouraged by another of Ramonet's questions he said: "I am not afraid of accepting the responsibility I have to accept. . . . We cannot go about being wimpy. Let them attack me, let them criticize me. Yes, many must be hurting a little. . . . We have to take risks, we have to have the courage to tell the truth."

However, what I found the most surprising and the most interesting was what he said next:

> It doesn't matter what those bandits abroad say and the cables that come in tomorrow and the day after tomorrow making ironic comments. He who laughs last laughs loudest. And that is not saying bad things about the revolution. That is saying very good things about the revolution because we are talking about a revolution that can deal with these problems, can take the bull by the horns, better than a Madrid bullfighter. We must have the courage to admit our own mistakes precisely for this reason, because this is the only way to achieve the objective we set out to achieve.[21]

To sum up, public criticism can be used by the enemy to attack the party and the revolution, but it can be better used by revolutionaries to correct mistakes in time and thus strengthen the party and the revolution.

When Will Public Criticism Not Be Necessary?

If the political instrument had an excellent information system that allowed it to quickly identify which of its cadres had fallen into errors or deviations; and if, moreover, it took immediate measures against those cadres, there would be no need for public criticism. Nor would there be any need for it if this information were provided from outside the party or from its own grassroots members and the party had time to process the information and adopt the relevant sanctions.

However, if these conditions do not exist, and the mistakes and deviation that occur every day are in full view of everyone, including the opposition, my opinion is that there is no other option but to denounce them publicly so as to appeal, as Fidel says, to the shame of those who are destroying the political instrument with their attitude.

Is it not better to ask the people, those who have firsthand experience of the cadres' defects, to watch over their behavior and denounce the mistakes and deviations they commit, and do so constructively? Is that not better than having our enemies, filled with rage and the desire to destroy our revolutionary project, denounce them?

How Can We Avoid Anarchic Criticism?

However, stressing the need for public criticism does not mean swallowing any old public criticism. We must avoid anarchic, destructive, ill-founded criticism. Criticism must be filled with the desire to solve problems, not to increase their number.

To do that, it is necessary that a) criticism and denunciations be well-founded; b) strong sanctions exist for those who make unfounded criticisms or denunciations; c) criticisms are accompanied by proposals for solutions; d) an effort is made to get criticisms to the party first; and if they are not answered after a short space of time, then they can be made public.

The ideal situation is for the party to take the initiative and open up public spaces so all those interested can make known their opinions on how the party and state cadres in a given locality are operating.

Conclusion

These reflections about the political instrument needed to build 21st century socialism are intended to show how we imagine the horizon toward which a growing number of Latin American governments are moving.

However, so that this task may be successfully carried out, we need a new left culture: a tolerant and pluralist culture that gives the most important place to everything that unites and a secondary place to that which divides; that promotes unity around values such as solidarity, humanism, respect for difference, and protection of the environment; and that turns its back on the hunger for profit and the laws of the market as the principles that guide human activity.

We need a left that begins to realize that being radical does not consist of raising the most radical slogan or in carrying out the most radical actions—which only a few agree with and which scare off the majority—but is instead about being capable of creating spaces for bringing together the broadest possible sectors where minds can meet and join in struggle. Realizing that there are many of us who are in the same struggle is what makes us strong; it is what radicalizes us.

We need a left that understands we must obtain hegemony; that is to say, we need to convince rather than impose.

We need a left that understands that more important than what we have done in the past is what we do together in the future to win our sovereignty and build a society that makes possible the full development of human beings: the socialist society of the 21st century.

Bibliography

Agacino, Rafael. "Movilizaciones sociales: coyuntura y aperturas políticas del período," *Plataforma Nexos*, May, 2012, http://www.plataforma-nexos.cl/index.php?option=com_contentandview=articleandid=137:movilizaciones-sociales-coyuntura-y-aperturas-politicas-del-periodoandcatid=35:plataformaandItemid=32.

Aharonian, Aram. "Latin America Today," paper presented at International Situation and Twenty-First Century Socialism conference, Centro Internacional Miranda, Caracas, September 30, 2009.

Alberola, Octavio. "Etica y revolución," *El Viejo Topo* 19 (April 1978).

Ambrogi, Thomas E. "Jubileo 2000: La campaña para la cancelación de la deuda," *Revista del Sur*, September 1999, http://old.redtercermundo.org.uy/revista_del_sur/texto_completo.php?id=735.

Balibar, Etienne. "Sur la dialectique historique (Quelques remarques critiques a propos de Lire le capital)," in *Cinq études sur le materialismo historique* (Paris: Maspero, 1974).

de la Barra, Ximena. "Miradas hacia el futuro: el papel del nuevo dialogo sureño," in *Diálogo Sudamericano: Otra Integración es Posible,* ed. R. A. Dello Buono (Santiago de Chile: Editorial Bolivariana, 2007).

———. "Estructuras legales transformadoras en América latina en el siglo XXI," *Revista Sociedad y Equidad* 1 (January 2011).

de la Barra, Ximena, and R. A. Dello Buono. "From ALBA to CELAC: Toward 'Another Integration'?," *NACLA Report on the Americas* 45/12 (Summer 2012).

Bellamy Foster, John. *Marx's Ecology: Materialism and Nature* (New York: Monthly Review Press, 2000).

Biardeau, Javier. "El nuevo socialismo del siglo XXI. Una breve guía de referencia," April 5, 2009, http://saberescontrahegemonicos.blogspot.com.au/2008/02/el-nuevo-socialismo-del-siglo-xxi-una.html.

Britto García, Luis. "Tegucigolpes," July 12, 2009, http://luisbrittogarcia.blogspot.com.au/2009/07/tegucigolpes.html.

BuciGlucksmann, Christine. *Gramsci y el Estado: Hacia una teoría materialista de la filosofía* (Madrid: Siglo XXI, 1978).

Burbach, Roger, Michael Fox, and Federico Fuentes. *Latin America's Turbulent Transitions: The Future of Twenty-First-Century Socialism* (London: Zed Books, 2013).

Castro, Fidel. Speech given on the occasion of the 10th anniversary of the Committee for the Defense of the Revolution, September 28, 1970.

Castro, Raul. Speech given at a seminar for the delegates of the Matanzas Popular Power Assembly, August 22, 1974.

Ceceña, Ana Esther. "Honduras y la ocupación del Continente," *Alai*, August 17, 2009 http://alainet.org/active/32415.

———. "Procesos emancipatorios y militarización de nuestra América en el siglo XXI," *Línea Sur* (Ministerio de Relaciones Exteriores, Comercio e Integración, Ecuador, No. 4, 2013).

Chávez Frías, Hugo. *Discurso de la unidad* (Caracas: Ediciones socialismo del siglo XXI, 2007).

Chomsky, Noam. "El control de los medios de comunicación," in Noam Chomsky and Ignacio Ramonet Miguez, *Como nos venden la moto. Información, poder y concentración de medio* (Barcelona: Ed. Icaria 1996).

Devine, Pat. *Democracy and Economic Planning: The Political Economy of a Self-Governing Society* (Cambridge: Polity Press, 1988).

———. "Social Ownership and Democratic Planning," in *Feelbad Britain: How to Make It Better*, ed. Pat Devine, Andrew Pearmain, and David Purdy (London: Lawrence and Wishart, 2009).

Dos Santos, Theotonio. "Las lecciones de Honduras," July 6, 2009, http://theotoniodossantos.blogspot.com.au/2009/07/las-lecciones-de-honduras.html.

Drago, Tito. "América latina con los ojos puestos en China," November 27, 2012, http://www.titodrago.com/index.php?option=com_contentandview=articleandid=1489:america-latina-con-los-ojos-puestos-en-chinaandcatid=4:politica-internacionalandItemid=14.

Engels, Frederich. "Principles of Communism," in Karl Marx and Frederick Engels, *Collected Works*, vol.6 (New York: International Publishers, 1976).

———. Engels to C. Schmidt, August 5, 1890, in Karl Marx and Frederick Engels, *Selected Correspondence* (Moscow: Progress Publishers, 1965).

Fukuyama, Francis, "The End of History?, " *The National Interest*, Summer 1989.

Gallardo, Helio. "Globalización neoliberal y alternativas populares," *Surda* 12 (June 1997).

García Linera, Álvaro. "Estado plurinacional," in *La transformación pluralista del estado*, ed. García Linera, Luis Tapia Mealla, and Raúl Prada Alcoresa (La Paz: Muela del Diablo, 2007).

———. Concluding remarks at press conference during the 6th International Forum on Philosophy, Maracaibo, Venezuela, 2012.

García Brigos, Jesús P. "Cinco tesis sobre los consejos populares," *Revista Cubana de Ciencias Sociales* 31 (2000).

González, Fernando, Dario Machado, Juan Luis Martín, and Emilio Sánchez. "Notas para un debate acerca del hombre nuevo," *Ponencias Centrales. Seminario El socialismo y el hombre en Cuba* (Havana: 1988).

Gruppi, Luciano. *El concepto de Hegemonía en Gramsci* (Mexico: Ediciones de Cultura Popular, 1978).

Harnecker, Marta. *Cuba: Dictatorship or Democracy?* (Westport, CT: Lawrence Hill, 1979).

———. *Reflexiones acerca del problema de la transición al socialism* (Managua: Nueva Nicaragua, 1986).

———. *Vanguardia y crisis actual o Izquierda y crisis actual* (Madrid: Siglo XXI, 1990).

———. *Forjando la esperanza* (Santiago de Chile: LOM ediciones, 1995).

———. *La Izquierda en el umbral del Siglo XXI: Haciendo posible el imposible* (Madrid: Siglo XXI 2000).

———. *La izquierda después de Seattle* (Santiago de Chile: Surda Ediciones, 2002).

———. "Forging a Union of the Party Left and the Social Left," *Studies in Political Economy* 69 (Autumn 2002).

———. *Militares junto al pueblo* (Caracas: Vadell Hermanos, 2003).

———. *Landless People: Building a Social Movement* (Sao Paulo: Editora Expressão Popular, 2003).

———. *Haciendo camino al andar* (Caracas: Monte Ávila, 2005).

———. *Los desafíos de cogestión (las experiences de Cadafe y Cadela)* (Caracas: La Burbuja Editorial, 2005).

———. "La lucha de un pueblo sin armas," Rebelion, September 10, 2006, http://www.rebelión.org/docs/95161.pdf.

———. *Rebuilding the Left* (London: Zed Books 2007).

———. *Los conceptos elementales del materialismo histórico* (Mexico: Siglo XXI, 2010).

———. "De los consejos comunales a las comunas," *Rebelión*, February 22, 2010, http://www.rebelion.org/docs/97085.pdf.

———. "Latin America and Twentyfirst Century Socialism: Inventing to Avoid Mistakes," *Monthly Review* 62/3 (July–August 2010).

———. "Tiempos políticos y procesos democráticos: Entrevista con Alberto Acosta," *Rebelion*, September 21, 2010, http://www.rebelion.org/docs/113474.pdf.

———. "Ecuador: Los gabinetes itinerantes: una forma de acercar el gobierno al pueblo," *Rebelión*, December 1, 2010, http://www.rebelion.org/docs/117764.pdf.

———. "Hacia la construcción de una nueva hegemonía anticapitalista: Tareas de nuestros gobiernos y de la organización popular," speech given at UCA, El Salvador, October 21, 2011.

———. "Five reflections About 21st Century Socialism," *Solidarity Economy*, June 18, 2012, http://www.solidarityeconomy.net/2012/06/18/five-reflections-about-21st-century-socialism/.

———. "Conquering a New Popular Hegemony," *Links*, September 21, 2012, http://links.org.au/node/3038.

———. "Entrevista colectiva a dirigentes estudiantiles de la FECH, " Santiago de Chile, November 25, 2012, unpublished.

———, ed. "La descentralización ¿fortalece o debilita el estado nacional?," *Rebelión*, May 14, 2009, http://www.rebelion.org/docs/97088.pdf.

Harnecker, Marta, with Federico de Fuentes. *Ecuador: Una nueva izquierda en busca de la vida en plenitud* (Caracas: Monte Avila 2013).

———. *MAS-IPSP: Instrumento político que surge de los movimientos sociales,* (Caracas: CIM, Monte Ávila Editores, 2008).

Herman, Edward S., and Noam Chomsky. *Manufacturing Consent: The Political Economy of the Mass Media* (New York: Pantheon Books 1988).

Hernández, Gustavo. "Banco del ALBA y el Financiamiento al Desarrollo," SELA, Caracas, Venezuela, 2008, http://www.sela.org/DB/ricsela/EDOCS/SRed/2008/06/T023600002884-0-Banco_del_ALBA_y_el_financiamiento_al_desarrollo.pdf.

Hinkelammert, Franz. *Cultura de la esperanza y sociedad sin exclusión* (Costa Rica: DEI 1995).

Hobsbawm, Eric. *La historia del siglo XX (1914-1991)* (Barcelona: Crítica, 1995).

Isaac, Thomas, and Richard Franke. *Local Democracy and Development .The Kerala's People Campaign for Descentralized Planning,* (Boulder, CO: Rowman and Littlefield, 2002).

Jiménez Guillén, Raúl, Elizabeth Rosa Zamora et al. *El desarrollo hoy en América Latina* (Mexico City: Colegio de Tlaxcala, 2008).

Kollontai, Alexandra. "The Workers' Opposition," *Marxist Internet Archives* https://www.marxists.org/archive/kollonta/1921/workers-opposition/index.htm.

Kropotkin, Peter. Letter to V. Lenin, March 4, 1920, http://dwardmac.pitzer.edu/Anarchist_Archives/kropotkin/kropotlenindec203.html.

Lebowitz, Michael A. *Build It Now: Socialism for the Twenty-first Century* (New York: Monthly Review Press, 2006).

———. "Venezuela: A Good Example of the Bad Left," *Monthly Review* 59/3 (July–August 2007).

———. *The Path to Human Development: Capitalism or Socialism?* (Toronto: Socialist Project, 2009).

———. *The Socialist Alternative: Real Human Development* (New York: Monthly Review Press, 2010).

———. "A Path to Socialism: Building Upon the Foundations Begun by Hugo Chávez," *Links*, March 2014 http://links.org.au/node/3741.

Lenin, Vladimir I. "Resolution on the Current Situation," *Collected Works*, vol. 24 (Moscow: Progress Publishers, 1977).

———. "The Impending Catastrophe and how to Combat It," *Collected Works*, vol. 25, (Moscow: Progress Publishers, 1977).

———. "Report on the Activities of the Council of People's Commissars," *Collected Works*, vol. 26 (Moscow: Progress Publishers, 1977).
———. "The Immediate Tasks of the Soviet Government," *Collected Works*, vol. *27* (Moscow: Progress Publishers, 1972).
———. "The Proletarian Revolution and the Renegade Kautsky," *Collected Works*, vol. 28 (Moscow: Progress Publishers, 1974).
———. "10th Congress of the RCP(B)," *Collected Works*, vol. 32 (Moscow: Progress Publishers, 1965).
———. "Our Revolution," *Collected Works*, vol. 33 (Moscow: Progress Publishers, 1980).
———. "How Should We Reorganize the Workers' and Peasants' Inspection," *Collected Works*, vol. 33 (Moscow: Progress Publishers, 1965).
———. "On the Role and Functions of the Trade Unions in the New Economic Policy," *Collected Works*, vol. 33 (Moscow: Progress Publishers, 1965).
———. "The Question of Nationalities or 'Autonomization,'" in *Lenin's Last Fight* (New York: Pathfinder Press, 2006).
Llancaqueo, Víctor Toledo. *Pueblo mapuche: Derechos colectivos y territorio: Desafíos para la sustentabilidad democrática* (Santiago de Chile: LOM, 2006).
Luxemburg, Rosa. "The Mass Strike, the Political Party and the Trade Unions," *Marxist Internet Archive*, http://www.marxists.org/archive/luxemburg/1906/mass-strike/.
Maneiro, Alfredo. *Ideas políticas para el debate actual, Selección de Marta Harnecker* (Caracas: Ministerio del Poder Popular para la Cultura, 2007).
Marx, Karl. Letter to F. A. Sorge, September 27, 1877, in Marx and Engels, *Selected Correspondence* (Moscow: Progress Publishers, 1965).
———. *Critique of the Gotha Program* (Moscow: Progress Publishers, 1971).
———. "Economic and Philosophic Manuscripts of 1844" in Marx and Engels, *Collected Works*, vol. 3 (New York: International Publishers, 1975).
———. "Revelations Concerning the Communist Trial in Cologne 1853," in Marx and Engels, *Collected Works*, vol. 11 (New York: International Publishers, 1975).
———. *Capital*, vol. 1 (New York: Vintage Books, 1976).
———. *Capital*, vol. 3 (New York: Vintage Books, 1976).
———. "The Civil War in France," in Marx and Engels, *Selected Works*, vol. 2 (Moscow: Progress Publishers, 1977).
Matus, Carlos. *El líder sin estado mayor* **(La Paz:** Fundación ALTADIR, 1997).
Mészáros, István. *Beyond Capital* (New York: Monthly Review Press, 1995).
Montero Mejía, Álvaro. "Honduras: las trampas de la mediación," *Alai*, July 10, 2009, http://alainet.org/active/31597andlang=es.
Moulián, Tomás. *Chile actual, anatomía de un mito* (Santiago de Chile: Ed. Arcis/LOM, 1997).
———. *Socialismo del Siglo XXI: La Quinta Vía* (Santiago de Chile: LOM Ediciones, 2000).

Núñez, Orlando. *La insurrección de la conciencia* (Managua: Editorial Escuela de Sociología de la Universidad Centroamericana, 1988).

Ospina, Hernando Calvo. "Siguen las tensiones entre Colombia y Ecuador," *Le Monde Diplomatique*, June 29, 2009

Partido Socialista de Chile, "Elementos a considerar para la política de participación de los trabajadores en la empresa industrial," unpublished document from 1971.

Pérez, Justino Martínez. "Triple grito por dignidad, justicia y vida," *Red Ciudadana por la Abolición de la Deuda Externa*, http://www.rcade.org/deuda/articulos/consultabrasil.doc.

Petras, James. "Latin America—Four Competing Blocs of Power," April 17, 2007, http://petras.lahaine.org/?p=1700.

Pomar, Valter. "La línea del Ecuador," *Rebelión*, October 12, 2008, http://www.rebelion.org/noticia.php?id=77280.

———. "Las diferentes estrategias de la izquierda latinoamericana," in *América Latina hoy ¿reforma o revolución?*, ed. German Rodas (Mexico City: Ocean Sur, 2009).

———. "10 anos de PT no governo e o desafío de uma esquerda socialista de massas: Entrevista especial com Valter Pomar," *HIU Online*, March 30, 2013, http://www.ihu.unisinos.br/entrevistas/518837-10-anos-de-pt-no-governo-e-uma-esquerda-socialista-de-massas-entrevista-especial-com-valter-pomar.

Raby, Diana. *Democracy and Revolution: Latin America and Socialism Today* (London: Pluto Press 2006).

Ramonet, Ignacio. *Cien Horas con Fidel* (Havana: Oficina de Publicaciones del Consejo de Estado, 2006), 677.

Rauber, Isabel. "Los pies, la cabeza y el corazón de Evo Morales," *Rebelión*, January 3, 2011, http://www.rebelion.org/noticia.php?id=119661.

Regalado, Roberto. "Introduction," in *América latina hoy ¿reforma o revolución?* ed. German Rodas (Mexico City: Ocean Sur, 2009).

———. "Es necesario construir una contrahegemonía popular," *Rebelión*, October 19, 2009, http://www.rebelion.org/noticia.php?id=93265.

Rubio, Enrique, and Marcelo Pereira. *Utopía y estrategia, democracia y socialismo* (Montevideo, Ed. Trilce, 1994).

Sader, Emir. "La crisis hegemónica en América Latina," in *El desarrollo hoy en América Latina*, ed. Raúl Jiménez Guillén, Elizabeth Rosa Zamora et al. (Mexico City: Colegio de Tlaxcala, 2008).

Sallari, Andrés. "Honduras: ¿Un golpe de estado contra Barak Obama?," 9 July 2009, http://andressallari.blogspot.com.au/2009/07/honduras-un-golpe-de-estado-contra.html.

Sánchez Ancochea, Diego. "China's Impact on Latin America," *Observatory on Chinese Society and Economy* 11 (June 2009).

Sesto, Farruco. ¡Que viva el debate! (Caracas: Editorial Pentagráfica, 2009).

Shanin, Teodor. *Late Marx and the Russian Road: Marx and "The Peripheries of Capitalism"* (New York: Monthly Review Press, 1983).

Stolowicz, Beatriz. *Gobiernos de izquierda en América Latina: Un balance politico* (Bogota: Ediciones Aurora 2007).

———. "El debate actual: Posliberalismo o anticapitalismo" in *América Latina hoy ¿reforma o revolución?*, ed. German Rodas (Mexico City: Ocean Sur, 2009)

Tapia Mealla, Luis. "Gobierno multicultural y democracia directa nacional," in *La transformación pluralista del estado*, ed. Álvaro García Linera, Tapia Mealla, and Raúl Prada Alcoresa (La Paz: Muela del Diablo, 2007).

Tello, Enric. "Economía y ecología en el camino hacia ciudades sostenibles," *Papeles de la FIM N°8 (Alternativas al desarrollo)* (Madrid: FIM, 1997).

Toussaint, Eric. "Venezuela, Equateur et Bolivie: la roue de l'histoire en marche," *CADTM*, November 2, 2009, http://cadtm.org/Venezuela-Equateur-et-Bolivie-la.

Ugarteche, Oscar. "El Banco del Sur y la arquitectura financiera regional," *Alai*, December 12, 2007, http://alainet.org/active/23083andlang=es.

U.S. Embassy, Asuncion. "Paraguayan pols plot parliamentary putsch," March 28, 2009, http://wikileaks.org/cable/2009/03/09ASUNCION189.html.

Vicent, Mauricio "La OEA levanta la sanción que excluye a Cuba desde 1962," *El País*, June 4, 2009, http://elpais.com/diario/2009/06/04/internacional/1244066410_850215.html.

Vivas, Esther. *La lucha contra la deuda externa, campañas internacionales y en el Estado español* (Madrid: El Viejo Topo, 2007).

Zecevic, Miodrag. *The Delegate System* (Belgrade: Jugoslovenska stvarnost, 1977).

Zedong, Mao. "On Coalition Government," 24 April 1945, *Marxist Internet Archives*, http://www.marxists.org/reference/archive/mao/selected-works/volume-3/mswv3_25.htm.

Author's Interviews

Francisco Figueroa, FECH vice president, November 2011.

Álvaro García Linera, May 2010.

Notes

Introduction

1. Marta Harnecker, "Five Reflections About 21st Century Socialism," *Solidarity Economy*, June 18, 2012; Marta Harnecker, "Conquering a New Popular Hegemony," *Links*, September 21, 2012.

Part 1: Latin America Advances

1. The first part of this book has benefited from the valuable contributions of Chilean investigator Ximena de la Barra and Mexican investigator Ana Esther Ceceña, who provided me with valuable suggestions and new elements for consideration after reading an earlier draft.
2. In total, Chávez won four presidential elections (1998, 2000, 2006, and 2012) and a recall referendum (2004).
3. Roberto Regalado, Introduction to *América latina hoy ¿reforma o revolución?* (Mexico: Ocean Sur, 2009), ix.
4. According to Eric Toussaint: "Cuba [played] a pioneering role. It attempted to promote the creation of an international front for the non-payment of foreign debt, but unfortunately was not able to win the support of other governments." In Preface to Esther Vivas, *La lucha contra la deuda externa, campañas internacionales y en el Estado español* (Madrid: El Viejo Topo, 2007). This campaign "garnered support from a number of important peasant organizations, trade unions, parties . . . in Brazil, Argentina, Peru, Ecuador and Mexico. It was a massive and popular campaign that included street mobilizations and the publication of books and informational materials. Despite this, Latin American governments in the end opted against building a united front for non-payment."
5. Speech at event to commemorate the 24th anniversary of the Caracazo, February 2, 2013, available at http://www.youtube.com/watch?v=W7vIIC9fgVg.

6. The exact death toll was never known. The government officially recognized 372 deaths, but some human rights organizations put the figure at around 5,000.
7. Marta Harnecker, *La izquierda después de Seattle* (Madrid: Siglo XXI, 2002), in particular "Primera Parte, Capítulo V. Ecuador: Movimiento indígena encabeza la lucha"; and Marta Harnecker, *Ecuador: Una nueva izquierda en busca de la vida en plenitud* (Caracas: Monte Avila, 2013).
8. Víctor Toledo Llancaqueo, *Pueblo mapuche: Derechos colectivos y territorio, Desafíos para la sustentabilidad democrática* (Santiago de Chile: LOM ediciones, 2006) 103.
9. Ibid., 104–5, 107.
10. This repression has been denounced by, among others, UN Special Rapporteur for Indigenous Peoples Rodolfo Stavenhagen and Pedro Cayuqueo, the editor of the Mapuche newspaper *Azkintuwe.*
11. Marta Harnecker, *Forjando la esperanza* (Santiago de Chile: LOM ediciones, 1995).
12. Ibid., 177–78.
13. Harnecker, *La izquierda después de Seattle.*
14. Founded in 1984, the MST unites sharecroppers, tenants, rural workers, occupants, and small farmers. It is estimated that out of the 800,000 families that have been given access to land since the end of the military dictatorship until now, some 450,000 follow the MST, and another 80,000–100,000 are in occupation camps demanding land.
15. Marta Harnecker, *Sin Tierra: Construyendo movimiento social* (Madrid: Siglo XXI, 2002)
16. Marta Harnecker and Federico Fuentes, *MAS-IPSP: Instrumento político que surge de los movimientos sociales* (Caracas: CIM-Monte Ávila Editores, 2008), in particular chapter 1 of Part 2, "Explosiones sociales y ciclos de lucha."
17. Ana Esther Ceceña, "Procesos emancipatorios y militarización de nuestra América en el siglo XXI," *Línea Sur* 4 (Ministerio de Relaciones Exteriores, Comercio e Integración, Ecuador) 2013: 86.
18. Thomas E. Ambrogi, "Jubileo 2000: La campaña para la cancelación de la deuda," *Revista del Sur,* September 1999, http://old.redtercermundo.org.uy/revista_del_sur/texto_completo.php?id=735.
19. Justino Martínez Pérez, "Triple *grito* por dignidad, justicia y vida," *Red Ciudadana por la Abolición de la Deuda Externa.*
20. Ceceña, "Procesos emancipatorios y militarización de nuestra América en el siglo XXI," 89.
21. Gabriel Boric, ex-president of FECH in 2011, interviewed in Marta Harnecker, "Entrevista colectiva a dirigentes estudiantiles de la FECH," Santiago de Chile, November 25, 2012, unpublished manuscript.
22. Ibid.
23. Author's interview with Francisco Figueroa, FECH vice president, November 2011.

24. Tomás Moulián, *Chile actual, anatomía de un mito* (Santiago de Chile: Ed. Arcis/LOM ediciones, 1997), 102–14.
25. Harnecker, "Entrevista colectiva a dirigentes estudiantiles de la FECH."
26. Andrés Fielbaum, in ibid.
27. Gabriel Boric, in ibid.
28. Ceceña, "Procesos emancipatorios y militarización de nuestra América en el siglo XXI," 89.
29. *Forajidos* was the name that Lucio Gutiérrez gave to the protestors; it was later appropriated by the movement that overthrew him.
30. "One section of the elites saw Lucio as a *cholo* (half-caste) who could not be president of Ecuador," said Osvaldo León in an interview I did with him for my book *Ecuador: Una nueva izquierda en busca de la vida en plenitud.*
31. Ximena de la Barra, "Estructuras legales transformadoras en América latina en el siglo XXI," *Revista Sociedad y Equidad* 1 (January 2011).
32. Francis Fukuyama, "The End of History?" *The National Interest* (Summer 1989).
33. Emir Sader, "La crisis hegemónica en América Latina," in Raúl Jiménez Guillén, Elizabeth Rosa Zamora, et al., *El desarrollo hoy en América Latina* (Mexico City: Colegio de Tlaxcala, 2008), 18.
34. Latinobarómetro Report 2008 is available at http://www.latinobarometro.org/latContents.jsp.
35. Latinobarómetro Report 2011 is available at http://www.latinobarometro.org/latContents.jsp.
36. Valter Pomar, "10 anos de PT no governo e o desafío de uma esquerda socialista de massas: Entrevista especial con Valter Pomar," *HIU On-Line*, March 30, 2013.
37. The Alianza Bolivariana para los Pueblos de Nuestra América—Tratado de Comercio de los Pueblos (Bolivarian Alliance for the Americas–People's Trade Treaty, ALBA-TCP), more commonly known simply as ALBA, the acronym of its original name Alternativa Bolivariana para los Pueblos de Nuestra América (Bolivarian Alternative for the Americas), is a platform for the integration of Latin American and Caribbean countries that emphasizes the struggle against poverty and social exclusion, and is inspired by leftist ideals.
38. Ximena de la Barra, "Miradas hacia el futuro: el papel del nuevo dialogo sureño," in R.A. Dello Buono, ed., *Diálogo Sudamericano: Otra Integración es Posible* (Santiago de Chile: Editorial Bolivariana, 2007).
39. Hernando Calvo Ospina, "Siguen las tensiones entre Colombia y Ecuador," *Le Monde Diplomatique*.
40. Mauricio Vicent, "La OEA levanta la sanción que excluye a Cuba desde 1962," *El País*, June 4, 2009.
41. Aram Aharonian, "Latin America Today," paper presented at the International Situation and 21st Century Socialism conference at the Centro Internacional Miranda, Caracas, September 30, 2009.
42. Oscar Ugarteche, "El Banco del Sur y la arquitectura financiera regional," *Alai*, December 12, 2007.

43. Gustavo Hernández, "Banco del ALBA y el Financiamiento al Desarrollo," SELA, Caracas, 2008.
44. Ximena de la Barra and R. A. Dello Buono, "From ALBA to CELAC: Toward "Another Integration?" *NACLA Report on the Americas* 45/2 (Summer 2012).
45. Tito Drago, "América latina con los ojos puestos en China," November 27, 2012, http://www.titodrago.com/index.php?option=com_content&view=article&id=1489%3Aamerica-latina-con-los-ojos-puestos-en-china&Itemid=13.
46. "In 2004 for example 83 percent of Latin American exports to China were of primary products or of industrial goods based on natural resources: in contrast, 89 percent of imports from China were manufactured goods not based on natural resources." Diego Sánchez Ancochea, "China's Impact on Latin America," *Observatory on Chinese Society and Economy* 11 (June 2009).
47. Eric Toussaint, "Venezuela, Equateur et Bolivie: la roue de l'histoire en marche," *CADTM*, November 2, 2009.
48. Ana Esther Ceceña, "Honduras y la ocupación del Continente," *Alai*, September 17, 2009, http://alainet.org/active/32415
49. Theotonio Dos Santos, "Las lecciones de Honduras," July 6, 2009, http://theotoniodossantos.blogspot.com/2009/07/las-lecciones-de-honduras.html.
50. Álvaro Montero Mejía, "Honduras: las trampas de la mediación," *Alai*, July 10, 2009.
51. Andrés Sallari, "Honduras: ¿Un golpe de estado contra Barak Obama?," 9 July 2009.
52. Quoted in Luis Britto García, "Tegucigolpes," July 12, 2009, see http://cubasilorraine.over-blog.org/article-tegucigolpes-luis-britto-garcia-45786041.html.
53. Ceceña, "Honduras y la ocupación del Continente."
54. Ospina, "Siguen las tensiones entre Colombia y Ecuador."
55. U.S. Embassy, Asuncion, "Paraguayan pols plot parliamentary putsch," March 28, 2009.
56. Aharonian, "Latin America Today."
57. Roberto Regalado, "Es necesario construir una contrahegemonía popular," *Rebelión*, October 19, 2009.
58. Ibid.
59. Aharonian, "Latin America Today."
60. Regalado, "Es necesario construir una contrahegemonía popular."
61. James Petras, "Latin America—Four Competing Blocs of Power," April 17, 2007, http://petras.lahaine.org/?p=1700.
62. Beatriz Stolowicz, "El debate actual: Posliberalismo o anticapitalismo," in German Rodas, ed. *América Latina hoy ¿reforma o revolución?* (Mexico: Ocean Sur, 2009), 99.
63. Beatriz Stolowicz, *Gobiernos de izquierda en América Latina: Un balance politico* (Bogota: Ediciones Aurora, 2007), 15.

64. Marta Harnecker, *La Izquierda en el umbral del Siglo XXI: Haciendo posible el imposible* (Madrid: Siglo XXI, 2000)
65. Franz Hinkelammert, *Cultura de la esperanza y sociedad sin exclusión* (Costa Rica: DEI 1995), 145.
66. Hinkelammert, *Cultura de la esperanza y sociedad sin exclusión*, 147.
67. Stolowicz, "El debate actual: Posliberalismo o anticapitalismo," 87–88.
68. The democratic regimes that arose after the dictatorships in the Southern Cone and expanded throughout the subcontinent are what some authors have called "restricted or wardship" democracies. Hinkelammert, *Cultura de la esperanza y sociedad sin exclusión*, 147.
69. For a fuller discussion of this topic, see Harnecker, *La Izquierda en el umbral del Siglo XXI*, 183–90.
70. Noam Chomsky, "El control de los medios de comunicación," in Noam Chomsky and Ignacio Ramonet Miguez, *Como nos venden la moto. Información, poder y concentración de medio* (Barcelona: Ed. Icaria, 1996), 16. See also Edward S. Herman and Noam Chomsky, *Manufacturing Consent: The Political Economy of the Mass Media* (New York: Pantheon Books, 1988).
71. Toussaint, "Venezuela, Equateur et Bolivie: La roue de l'histoire en marche."
72. Valter Pomar, "Las diferentes estrategias de la izquierda latinoamericana," in Rodas, *América Latina hoy ¿reforma o revolución?*, 246.
73. Pomar, "10 anos de PT no governo e o desafío de uma esquerda socialista de massas."
74. Valter Pomar, "La línea del Ecuador," *Rebelión*, October 12, 2008.
75. Michael A. Lebowitz, "Venezuela: A Good Example of the Bad Left," *Monthly Review* 59/3 (July–August 2007).

Part 2: Where Are We Going? Twenty-First Century Socialism

1. Hugo Chávez Frías, *Discurso de la unidad* (Caracas: Ediciones socialismo del siglo XXI, 2007), 41.
2. An empanada is a typical Chilean food.
3. Diana Raby, *Democracy and Revolution. Latin America and Socialism Today* (London: Pluto Press, 2006), 33.
4. Some authors, such as Michael Lebowitz, prefer to call it "socialism for the 21st century."
5. Tomás Moulián, *Socialismo del Siglo XXI: La Quinta Vía* (Santiago de Chile: LOM Ediciones, 2000). On the debate over who first used the term, see Javier Biardeau, "El nuevo socialismo del siglo XXI. Una breve guía de referencia," April 5, 2009.
6. Chávez Frías, *Discurso de la unidad*, 37.
7. Ibid., 37–39, 44.
8. Ibid., 47.
9. Álvaro García Linera identifies four civilizing regimes in Bolivia. "The first is the modern, mercantile, industrial regime, the second is economy and culture organised around simple domestic type mercantile activity, either

craft or peasant (this activity accounts for 68 percent of urban employment), the third is communal civilization and the fourth and final is Amazonian civilization based on the itinerant character of its productive activity, technology based on individual knowledge and industriousness and the absence of a state." Altogether, two-thirds of the country's inhabitants are in the last three "civilizing or societal bands." Furthermore, most of the Bolivian population "is submerged in economic, cognitive and cultural structures that are non-industrial and, in addition, are carriers of other cultural and linguistic identities and other political habits and techniques that stem from their own technical and material life: placing collective identity above individuality, deliberative practice above elections, normative coercion as a form of behavior that is rewarded above free acceptance and compliance, the depersonalisation of power, its consensual revocability, rotation of positions etc., are forms of behavior that speak of political cultures different from liberal and party representative political cultures." Álvaro García Linera, "Estado plurinacional," in Álvaro García Linera, Luis Tapia Mealla, and Raúl Prada Alcoresa, *La transformación pluralista del estado* (La Paz: Muela del Diablo, 2007), 46.

10. Chávez Frías, *Discurso de la unidad*, 44.
11. In his *Critique of the Gotha Program*, Karl Marx spoke of the "all round development of the individual" (Moscow: Progress Publishers, 1971), 18.
12. See Michael A. Lebowitz, *Build It Now: Socialism for the Twenty-first Century* (New York: Monthly Review Press, 2006); Michael A. Lebowitz, *The Path to Human Development: Capitalism or Socialism?* (Toronto: The Socialist Project, 2009); and Michael A. Lebowitz, *The Socialist Alternative: Real Human Development* (New York: Monthly Review Press, 2010).
13. "Above all we must avoid postulating "society" again as an abstraction vis-à-vis the individual. The individual is the social being. His manifestations of life—even if they may not appear in the direct form of communal manifestations of life carried out in association with others—are therefore an expression and confirmation of social life. Man's individual and species-life are not different, however much—and this is inevitable—the mode of existence of the individual is a more particular or more general mode of the life of the species, or the life of the species is a more particular or more general individual life." Karl Marx, "Economic and Philosophic Manuscripts of 1844," in Karl Marx and Frederick Engels, *Collected Works*, vol. 3, (New York: International Publishers, 1975), 299.
14. Miodrag Zecevic, *The Delegate System* (Belgrade: Jugoslovenska stvarnost, 1977).
15. Marx, *Critique of the Gotha Program*, 17–18.
16. I have borrowed this idea from Michael Lebowitz. He writes: "Read *Capital* with the purpose of identifying the inversions and distortions that produce truncated human beings in capitalism and we can get a sense of Marx's idea of what is 'peculiar to and characteristic of' production in the 'inverse situation,' socialism." *The Socialist Alternative, Real Human Development*, 56–57.

17. Karl Marx, *Capital,* vol. 1 (New York: Vintage Books, 1976), 283; and Karl Marx, *Capital,* vol. 3 (New York: Vintage Books, 1976), 949.
18. Marx, *Capital,* vol. 3, 959.
19. Frederick Engels, "Principles of Communism," in Marx and Engels, *Collected Works,* vol. 6 (New York: International Publishers, 1976), 353.
20. Regarding the influence of Liebig on Marx, see John Bellamy Foster, *Marx's Ecology: Materialism and Nature* (New York: Monthly Review Press, 2000), 149–56.
21. Ibid., 142.
22. Marx, *Capital,* vol. 1, 637–38.
23. Frederick Engels, *Socialism: Utopian and Scientific* (Sydney: Resistance Books, 1999), 90.
24. Alfredo Maneiro, *Ideas políticas para el debate actual, Selección de Marta Harnecker* (Caracas: Ministerio del Poder Popular para la Cultura, 2007), 35–36.
25. Personal comments sent to the author on a previous version of this text.
26. In Venezuela, municipalities are divided into parishes.
27. Lebowitz, *The Path to Human Development: Capitalism or Socialism?*, 27
28. The letter goes on to say: "At present, it is the party committees, not the soviets, who rule in Russia. And their organization suffers from the defects of bureaucratic organization. To move away from the current disorder, Russia must return to the creative genius of local forces." Peter Kropotkin to V. Lenin, March 4, 1920.
29. Marta Harnecker, "De los consejos comunales a las comunas," *Rebelión,* February 22, 2010.
30. "What they are electing," says Tapia, "is a person that will substitute for the citizens, for a period of time, in carrying out executive or legislative tasks within the state, be that at a municipal or national level. What the representative does after being elected may have no relation to what the citizens that voted for them want, in the sense that there is no space for citizens to participate and feed through their political opinions to the supposed representative." Luis Tapia Mealla, "Gobierno multicultural y democracia directa nacional," in García Linera, Tapia Mealla, and Prada Alcoresa, *La transformación pluralista del estado* (La Paz: Muela del Diablo, 2007), 126–27.
31. Álvaro García Linera, concluding remarks at a press conference in Maracaibo, Venezuela, during the VI International Forum on Philosophy.
32. Karl Marx, "The Civil War in France," in Karl Marx and Frederick Engels, *Selected Works,* vol. 2 (Moscow: Progress Publishers, 1977), 222.
33. István Mészáros, *Beyond Capital* (New York: Monthly Review Press, 1995), 906. According to Mészáros, the positive reference made by Lenin in *The State and Revolution* "to the experience of the Paris Commune (as the *direct* involvement of *all* the poor, exploited sections of the population in the exercise of power) disappeared from his speeches and writings and the accent was laid on 'the need for a central authority.'' A little further on, he

says, "The ideal of autonomous working class action had been replaced by the advocacy of the greatest possible centralisation.'"

34. Vladimir I. Lenin, "10th Congress of the RCP(B)," *Collected Works,* vol. 32 (Moscow: Progress Publishers, 1965), 165–271.
35. Vladimir I. Lenin, "How Should We Reorganize the Workers' and Peasants' Inspection," *Collected Works,* vol. 33 (Moscow: Progress Publishers, 1965), 481–86.
36. Vladimir I. Lenin, "The Question of Nationalities or 'Autonomization,'" in *Lenin's Last Fight* (New York: Pathfinder Press, 2006), 194.
37. Vladimir I. Lenin, "On the Role and Functions of the Trade Unions in the New Economic Policy," *Collected Works,* vol. 33, 188–96.
38. Most of what follows has been taken from the introduction to Marta Harnecker, *Cuba: Dictatorship or Democracy?* (Westport, CT: Lawrence Hill, 1979).
39. Fidel Castro, speech given on September 28, 1970, on the occasion of the 10th anniversary of the Committees for the Defense of the Revolution.
40. Raúl Castro, speech given at a seminar for the delegates of the Matanzas Popular Power Assembly, August 22, 1974.
41. Jesús P. García Brigos, "Cinco tesis sobre los consejos populares," *Revista Cubana de Ciencias Sociales* 31 (2000).
42. Marx, "The Civil War in France," in Marx and Engels, Selected Works, vol. 2 (Moscow: Progress Publishers, 1977), 221.
43. In particular, Articles 16, 157, 158, 85, and 269.
44. Marta Harnecker, "La descentralización ¿fortalece o debilita el estado nacional?" *Rebelión*, May 14, 2009.
45. Lebowitz, *The Socialist Alternative*, 85–89.
46. See Pat Devine, *Democracy and Economic Planning: The Political Economy of a Self-Governing Society* (Cambridge: Polity Press, 1988).
47. On the concept of property and real appropriation, see Marta Harnecker, *Los conceptos elementales del materialismo histórico* (Mexico: Siglo XXI, 2010), esp. chaps. 2 and 9.
48. Devine, *Democracy and Economic Planning*, 123.
49. Partido Socialista de Chile, "Elementos a considerar para la política de participación de los trabajadores en la empresa industrial," unpublished document, 1971.
50. I have borrowed the principal ideas that I develop here from Lebowitz, *The Socialist Alternative*, 154–61.
51. Ibid., 144–49.
52. Lebowitz, *Build It Now: Socialism for the Twenty-First Century*, 73–84.
53. Fernando González, Darío Machado, Juan Luis Martín, and Emilio Sánchez, "Notas para un debate acerca del hombre nuevo," *Ponencias Centrales: Seminario El socialismo y el hombre en Cuba* (Havana: 1988).
54. Lebowitz, *Build It Now: Socialism for the Twenty-First Century*, 73–84.
55. Marta Harnecker, *Los desafíos de cogestión (Cadafe y Cadela)* (Caracas: La Burbuja Editorial, 2005).

56. Frederick Engels to C. Schmidt, August 5, 1890, in Karl Marx and Frederick Engels, *Selected Correspondence* (Moscow: Progress Publishers, 1965), 415.
57. Lebowitz, *The Socialist Alternative*, 31–45.
58. Another example of separation between juridical and real ownership is when the state intervenes in a company. The capitalist continues to be the owner from the legal point of view, but the state-appointed managers decide how the means of production are to be used and what is to be produced.
59. Engels, *Socialism: Utopian and Scientific*, 90.
60. "Social ownership is best defined as ownership by those affected by decisions over the use of the assets involved, in proportion to the extent to which they are affected. It has much in common with the green concept of stakeholding. Following the principle of subsidiarity which underpins, at least in theory, the multi-layered governance structure of the European Community, the social owners will differ according to the degree of generality, the reach, of the decisions to be made. Decisions made at higher levels of generality will involve more assets and affect a wider range of people and interests than those made at lower levels. At each level, the social owners need to negotiate with one another to agree on the use of the assets that will further their collective social interest, as defined by them. This multi-layered process of negotiated coordination is what is meant by participatory planning." Pat Devine, "Social Ownership and Democratic Planning," in *Feelbad Britain: How to Make It Better*, ed. Pat Devine, Andrew Pearmain, and David Purdy (London: Lawrence and Wishart, 2009).
61. Karl Marx to F. A. Sorge, September 27, 1877, in Marx and Engels, *Selected Correspondence*, 308.
62. Teodor Shanin, *Late Marx and the Russian Road: Marx and 'The Peripheries of Capitalism'"* (New York: Monthly Review Press, 1983).
63. Vladimir I. Lenin, "Resolution on the Current Situation," *Collected Works*, vol. 24 (Moscow: Progress Publishers, 1977), 310.
64. Marta Harnecker, *Reflexiones acerca del problema de la transición al socialism* (Managua: Nueva Nicaragua, 1986), 23–35.
65. Vladimir I. Lenin, "The Proletarian Revolution and the Renegade Kautsky," *Collected Works*, vol. 28 (Moscow: Progress Publishers, 1974), 227–325.
66. Vladimir I. Lenin, "The Impending Catastrophe and How to Combat It," *Collected Works*, vol. 25 (Moscow: Progress Publishers, 1977), 323–69.
67. Vladimir I. Lenin, "Our revolution," *Collected Works*, vol. 33 (Moscow: Progress Publishers, 1980), 478.
68. Ibid., 480.
69. Vladimir I. Lenin, "Report on the Activities of the Council of People's Commissars," *Collected Works*, vol. 26 (Moscow: Progress Publishers, 1977), 460.
70. Marta Harnecker, "La lucha de un pueblo sin armas," *Rebelión*, September 10, 2006.
71. Engels, *Socialism: Utopian and Scientific*, 92.

72. Pomar, "Las diferentes estrategias de la izquierda latinoamericana," 246.
73. Ibid., 247.
74. Lebowitz, *Build It Now,* 67.
75. Vladimir I. Lenin, "The Immediate Tasks of the Soviet Government," *Collected Works*, vol. 27 (Moscow: Progress Publishers, 1972), 235–77.
76. Harnecker, *Los conceptos elementales del materialismo histórico*, 215; Etienne Balibar, "Sur la dialectique historique (Quelques remarques critiques a propos de Lire le capital)," in *Cinq études sur le materialismo historique* (Paris: Maspero, 1974), 243.
77. Harnecker, with Fuentes, *Ecuador: Una nueva izquierda en busca de la vida en plenitud*, 261–68.
78. Carlos Matus, *El líder sin estado mayor* (La Paz: Fundación ALTADIR, 1997), 27.
79. Much of this information has been taken from Roger Burbach, Michael Fox, and Federico Fuentes, *Latin America's Turbulent Transitions: The Future of Twenty-First-Century Socialism* (London: Zed Books, 2013), 78–97.
80. The current and following paragraphs are based on personal comments sent to the author by Magdalena León, April 8, 2013.
81. Michael A. Lebowitz, "A Path to Socialism—Building Upon the Foundations Begun by Hugo Chávez," *Links*, March 2014.
82. Marta Harnecker, "Ecuador: Los gabinetes itinerantes: una forma de acercar el gobierno al pueblo," *Rebelión*, December 1, 2010.
83. Harnecker, with Fuentes, *Ecuador: Una nueva izquierda en busca de la vida en plenitud*, 277.
84. Ibid., 280.
85. Ibid., 282–83.
86. Isabel Rauber, "Los pies, la cabeza y el corazón de Evo Morales," *Rebelión*, January 3, 2011.
87. Ibid.
88. Personal comments sent to author.
89. He is referring to the Center of Studies that Sassone runs in the National Assembly of Venezuela.
90. Tapia Mealla, "Gobierno multicultural y democracia directa nacional," 128.
91. Ibid., 129.
92. Ibid., 132–37, 180–82.
93. Ibid., 134.
94. Ibid., 181.
95. Lebowitz, *The Socialist Alternative*, 152.
96. Marta Harnecker, *Militares junto al pueblo* (Caracas: Vadell Hermanos, 2003).
97. Interview with Álvaro García Linera, May 2010.
98. Ibid.

99. Ibid.
100. Eric Hobsbawm, *La historia del siglo XX (1914–1991)*, (Barcelona: Crítica, 1995), 561.
101. Constitution of the Republic of Ecuador, Article 71: "Nature or Pachamama, where life is reproduced and exists, has the right to exist, persist, maintain and regenerate its vital cycles, structure, functions and its processes in evolution. Every person, people, community or nationality, will be able to demand the recognitions of rights for nature before the public organisms. The application and interpretation of these rights will follow the related principles established in the Constitution. The State will motivate natural and juridical persons as well as collectives to protect nature; it will promote respect toward all the elements that form an ecosystem."
102. Marta Harnecker, "Tiempos políticos y procesos democráticos: Entrevista con Alberto Acosta," *Rebelión*, September 21, 2010.
103. Harnecker, with Fuentes, *Ecuador: Una nueva izquierda en busca de la vida en plenitud*, 334.
104. Harnecker, "Tiempos políticos y procesos democráticos."
105. Quoted in Enric Tello, "Economía y ecología en el camino hacia ciudades sostenibles," in *Papeles de la FIM N°8 (Alternativas al desarrollo)*, (Madrid: FIM, 1997), 136.
106. Tello "Economía y ecología en el camino hacia ciudades sostenibles," 135.
107. Personal comments sent to author.
108. Ibid.
109. The initials ITT come from Ishpingo, Tambocoha, and Tiputini, the three oil fields that exist in the park, which contain 846 million barrels of oil.
110. Thomas Isaac and Richard Franke, *Local Democracy and Development: The Kerala People's Campaign for Decentralized Planning* (Boulder, CO: Rowman and Littlefield, 2002).

Part 3: A New Political Instrument for a New Hegemony

1. Here I have borrowed ideas from Gramsci and two researchers who have closely studied this Italian philosopher: Christine Buci-Glucksmann, *Gramsci y el Estado: hacia una teoría materialista de la filosofía* (Madrid: Siglo XXI, 1978); and Luciano Gruppi, *El concepto de Hegemonía en Gramsci* (Mexico: Ediciones de Cultura Popular, 1978).
2. The following paragraphs are largely based on sections of Marta Harnecker, *Ideas for Struggle* (Toronto: Socialist Project, 2010). I also touch on some of the ideas in Marta Harnecker, "Forging a Union of the Party Left and the Social Left," *Studies in Political Economy* 69 (Autumn 2002); Harnecker, *Rebuilding the Left*; Marta Harnecker, *La izquierda después de Seattle* (Santiago de Chile: Surda Ediciones, 2002); Harnecker, *La izquierda en el umbral del Siglo XXI*; and Marta Harnecker, *Vanguardia y crisis actual o Izquierda y crisis actual* (Madrid: Siglo XXI, 1990).
3. Harnecker, *Rebuilding the Left*, 66–72.

4. Ibid., 90.
5. Ibid., 91. See also Enrique Rubio and Marcelo Pereira, *Utopía y estrategia, democracia y socialismo* (Montevideo: Ed. Trilce, 1994), 151; and Helio Gallardo, "Globalización neoliberal y alternativas populares," *Surda* 12 (June 1997): 13.
6. Rubio and Pereira, *Utopía y estrategia*, 149–50.
7. Rafael Agacino, "Movilizaciones sociales: coyuntura y aperturas políticas del período," *Plataforma Nexos*, May 2012.
8. I further expanded on this idea in Marta Harnecker, "Hacia la construcción de una nueva hegemonía anticapitalista. Tareas de nuestros gobiernos y de la organización popular," speech given at the University of Central America (UCA) San Salvador, October 21, 2011.
9. Marta Harnecker, *Haciendo camino al andar* (Caracas: Monte Ávila, 2005), 334–35.
10. Karl Marx, "Revelations Concerning the Communist Trial in Cologne 1853," in Karl Marx and Frederick Engels, *Collected Works*, vol. 11 (New York: International Publishers, 1975), 399.
11. Rosa Luxemburg, "The Mass Strike, the Political Party and the Trade Unions," *Marxist Internet Archives*, http://www.marxists.org/archive/luxemburg/1906/mass-strike/.
12. Farruco Sesto, *¡Que viva el debate!* (Caracas: Editorial Pentagráfica, 2009), 10–11.
13. Sesto, *¡Que viva el debate!*, 27–28. The following statement by Alexandra Kollontai is along similar lines: "Fear of criticism and of freedom of thought, combined with bureaucratic deviations frequently produces harmful results. There can be no self-activity without freedom of thought and opinion since self-activity manifests itself not only in initiative, action and work but also in independent thought." Alexandra Kollontai, "The Workers' Opposition," *Marxist Internet Archives*, https://www.marxists.org/archive/kollonta/1921/workers-opposition/index.htm.
14. Peter Kropotkin to V. Lenin, 21 December 1920, http://dwardmac.pitzer.edu/Anarchist_Archives/kropotkin/kropotlenindec20.html.
15. Octavio Alberola, "Etica y revolución," *El Viejo Topo* 19 (April 1978): 35.
16. Orlando Núñez, *La insurrección de la conciencia* (Managua: Editorial Escuela de Sociología de la Universidad Centroamericana, 1988), 29, 60.
17. Marta Harnecker, *Landless People: Building a Social Movement* (Sao Paulo: Editora Expressão Popular, 2003), 231–32.
18. Kollontai, "The Workers' Opposition."
19. Mao Zedong, "On Coalition Government," 24 April 1945, *Marxist Internet Archive*, http://www.marxists.org/reference/archive/mao/selected-works/volume-3/mswv3_25.htm
20. Ignacio Ramonet, *Cien Horas con Fidel* (Havana: Oficina de Publicaciones del Consejo de Estado, 2006), 677.
21. Ibid., 682–83.

Index

Acosta, Alberto, 110, 149
agriculture: communes for, 91; Marx on, 66; ownership of land used for, 95
Aharonian, Aram, 33, 47
ALBA, *see* Bolivarian Alternative for the Peoples of Our Americas
Alberola, Octavio, 182
Alianza Bolivariana para los Pueblos de Nuestra América, *see* Bolivarian Alternative for the Peoples of Our Americas
Alianza del Pacífico (Pacific Alliance), 31
Allende, Salvador, 17, 85; overthrow of, 104; on socialism, 58–59
Amin, Samir, 107
Andrés Bello Plan (Venezuela), 144
Antigua and Barbuda, 31
Anzalone, Pablo, 69
Argentina: gas subsidy is, 128–29; neoliberalism in, 47; popularity of democracy in, 28; popular movements in, 22
armed forces: attitudes of governments toward, 159; in transformations, 141–47
Asamblea Popular de los Pueblos de Oaxaca (Popular Assembly of the Peoples of Oaxaca, APPO; Mexico), 24
Astorga, Armando, 32

Bachelet, Michelle, 14
banks: Banco del Sur (Bank of the South), 34–35; Banco de Venezuela, 116; communal, 137–38
Bermudez, Jaime, 43
Bolívar, Simón, 113
Bolivarian Alternative for the Peoples of Our Americas (ALBA), 31, 5–36, 207*n*37
Bolivarian constitution (Venezuela), 70, 114; respect for environment in, 152–53
Bolivia: in ALBA, 31; armed forces of, 142, 143, 145–46; attempted coup in, 40; changing policies in, 128; García Linera on, 209–10*n*9; nationalizations in, 116–17; national sovereignty of, 146–47; neoliberalism opposed by, 47; networks of direct democracy in, 131–32; new constitution for, 114;

respect for environment in constitution of, 153; U.S.-supported movements in, 39; Water War in, 20–21
Boric, Gabriel, 23
Borja, Rodrigo, 16
bourgeois democracy, 27–29, 74; media in, 52; participatory and protagonistic democracy distinguished from, 68–69
bourgeoisie, 165
Brazil: Bank of the Americas and, 35; foreign debt of, 21–22; French military equipment bought by, 33; Lula in, 54–55; MST in, 91–92; neoliberalism in, 19–20, 47
Brownfield, William, 43
Bucaram, Abdalá, 16
bureaucratism, 78–80, 185–88

cadres, 180–85; criticizing, 189–93
capitalism, 49–51; alternatives to, 172; attitudes of governments toward, 158; dull instruments of, 92–93; Marx on, 64–65; state in development of, 173–74; transition to socialism from, 98–108
capitalist companies, 121–22
Castañeda, Jorge, 47
Castro, Fidel, 15, 88, 176; on bureaucracy, 79–80; on criticism and self-criticism, 191–93
Castro, Raúl, 80–81
Cayuqueo, Pedro, 206*n*10
Ceceña, Ana Esther, 20–21, 39, 42
Central America, 47
Central America Free Trade Agreement (CAFTA), 31
Chávez, Hugo, 40, 54–55; Allende distinguished from, 104; armed forces under, 143; attempted coup against, 141; Banco del Sur proposed by, 34; on communal councils, 133; on communes, 134; in election of 1998, 13; in election of 2012, 14; on FARC arms, 53; on inherited culture, 140; on popular protagonism, 71; radio programs of, 127–28; recall of, 114–15; socialism of, 7–9, 58–61; on winning hearts and minds, 171
Chile: under Allende, 85; Allende overthrown in, 104; education in, 22–24; Mapuhe movement in, 17–18; multinational corporations in, 86–87; neoliberalism in, 13, 47; socialism in, 58; social movements in, 28
Chilean Popular Unity, 183
China, 37–38, 208*n*46
Chinese Communist Party, 188
Chomsky, Noam, 52
City of Knowledge (Ecuador), 150–51
Clinton, Hilary, 41
Cochabamba (Bolivia), 20–21
collectivism, 63–64
Colom, Álvaro, 14
Colombia: neoliberalism supported in, 47; U.S. military aid to, 39; U.S. military bases in, 42–43
Comites de Tierra Urbana (Urban Land Committees, CTU; Venezuela), 72
communal councils, 72–74, 133
communes, 134–38
communism, Marx on, 64
Communist Parties: criticizing functionaries in, 189–93; public criticisms of, 187–89; *see also* political organizations
communitarian socialism, 61
communities, 134
Comunidad de Estados Latinoamericanos y Caribeños (Community of Latin American and Caribbean States, CELAC), 36–37
CONAIE (Ecuador), 16

consciousness, 88–93; cultural hegemony and, 163–65; cultural heritage and, 176; socialism and, 182
Consejo de Todas las Tierras (Council of All the Lands; Chile), 17
Constituent Assembly (Venezuela), 142
constitutions, 142; respect for environment in, 147–48, 152–53, 215*n*101
cooperatives, 120–21
Coordinadora por el NO (NO Coalition; Ecuador), 16
Correa, Rafael, 14, 31; attempted coup against, 43–44; on education, 150; itinerant cabinets created by, 124–26; media analyzed by, 126–27; on oil exploitation, 152; on use of natural resources, 148
Cuba: in ALBA, 31; armed forces of, 144–46; bureaucracy in, 79–80; in CELAC, 37; decentralization in, 80–81; foreign debts of, 205*n*4; joins Rio Group, 32; OAS sanctions lifted against, 32–33
cultural hegemony, 163–65
culture, inherited, 140, 174, 176

Daly, Herman E., 149
debts: Brazil's, 21–22; Cuba's, 205*n*4
decentralization, 78–83; in Kerala, 153–57
Defense Council of UNASUR, 146
de la Barra, Ximena, 31
delegated democracy, 73–78
democracy, 27–29; participatory and delegated, 73–78; participatory and protagonistic, 68–71; in political organizations, 183–84; restricted, 209*n*68
development, *see* economic development
Devine, Pat, 85, 96, 97, 213*n*60
direct democracy: delegated democracy and, 74–78; limits of, 73–74; networks for, 130–33
discipline, 184
discrimination, 160
distribution, 92
division of labor, 65; women in, 182
Dominica, 31
Dominican Republic–Central America Free Trade Agreement (CAFTA), 31
dos Santos, Theotonio, 41
Drago, Tito, 37
Duarte Frutos, Nicanor, 44

Economic Commission for Latin America and the Caribbean (ECLAC), 37
economic development, 67; attitudes of governments towards, 159; respecting nature, 147–53
Ecuador: accountability of officials in, 126–27; in ALBA, 31; attempted coup in, 43–44; elections delayed in, 110; "los forajidos" in, 24–25; itinerant cabinets in, 124–26; natural resources of, 149; neoliberalism opposed by, 47; new constitution for, 114; new state institutions created in, 124; popular movements in, 15–17; respect for environment in constitution of, 147–48, 150, 215*n*101; state capitalism in, 117–19; U.S. attack on, 39; U.S. military base closed in, 31–32; U.S.-supported movements in, 39
education: for armed forces, 143–44; in Chile, 22–24; in Ecuador, 150–51
efficiency, 86–88
Ejército Zapatista de Liberación Nacional (Zapatista National Liberation Army, EZLN; Mexico), 19
elections, 211*n*30; electoral cycle of, 109; postponements of, 110; term limits for, 179; in Venezuela, 77–78

El Salvador, 41, 130
energy, 151
Engels, Friedrich, 62–67; on distribution, 92; on state, 105; on state ownership of property, 95–96
Espinosa, María Fernanda, 149

Falconí, Fander, 33
Fernández, Cristina, 14
Fielbaum, Andrés, 23
los forajidos (the outlaws; Ecuador), 24–25, 207*n*29
Foster, John Bellamy, 66
France, 33
Franco, Federico, 44
Free Trade of the Americas Agreement (FTAA): in Brazil, 20–22; defeat of, 30–31
Frei, Eduardo, 17
Frente Amplio (Broad Front; Uruguay), 18–19
Frente Farabundo Martí para la Liberación Nacional (Farabundo Marti National Liberation Front, FMLN; El Salvador), 130
Frente Patriótico (Patriotic Front; Ecuador), 16
Frente Unitario de los Trabajadores (United Front of Workers, FUT; Ecuador), 15–16
Fuerzas Armadas Revolucionarias de Colombia (Revolutionary Armed Forces of Colombia, FARC), 32, 48, 53
Fukuyama, Francis, 26
Funes, Mauricio, 14

gabinetes itinerantes (itinerant cabinets), 124–26
García Linera, Álvaro, 61, 76, 145–46, 209–10*n*9
globalization, 51
González Casanova, Pablo, 43
government, *see* state
Gramsci, Antonio, 140
Gran Misión AgroVenezuela, 123
Gran Misión En Amor Mayor (Venezuela), 123
Gran Misión Hijos e Hijas de Venezuela, 123
Gran Misión Saber y Trabajo (Venezuela), 123
Gran Misión Vivienda Venezuela, 123
Gran Nacional Minera Mariscal Sucre (Grand National Mining Company Mariscal Sucre), 118
Gutiérrez, Lucio, 24, 44, 207*n*29, 207*n*30

hegemony: breaking down of, 165–68; definitions of, 163–65; political strategy for alternative to, 168–72
Hinkelammert, Franz, 50
Honduras: in ALBA, 31; coup in, 40–42
Humala, Ollanta, 14

indigenous peoples: in Bolivia, 21; in Chile, 17–18; in Ecuador, 15–17; socialism of, 61; symbols and traditions of, 146
infrastructure, 144–45
inherited culture, 140, 174, 176
Intellectuals, politicians and, 110–11
International Monetary Fund (IMF), demands placed on Venezuela by, 15
Internet, 119
itinerant cabinets *(gabinetes itinerantes),* 124–26

Kerala (India), 153–57
Kirchner, Néstor, 14
Kollontai, Alexandra, 187, 216*n*13
Kropotkin, Peter, 71, 179, 211*n*28

Lagos, Ricardo, 14
Lajo, Manuel, 150

Landless Workers Movement (Movimento dos Trabalhadores Rurais Sem Terra, MST; Brazil), 19-20, 91–92, 183, 184, 206*n*14
Latin America: ALBA Alliance in, 31; Chávez's impact on, 7; coordination and solidarity within, 160–61; neoliberalism in, 13; neoliberalism loses legitimacy in, 26–29; regional integration in, 113; socialism in, 57–59; trade between China and, 37–38, 208*n*46; typology of governments in, 46–48
Latinobarómetro, 27–28
Lebowitz, Michael: on twenty-first century socialism, 63, 83; on efficiency under socialism, 87; on Marx, 210*n*16; on productive relations, 119; on revolutionary democracy, 70–71; on socialist conditionality, 121; on state companies, 120; on state during transition period, 139; on transition to socialism, 106
Lefebvre, Henri, 63
left governments: after coming to power, 51–53; definition of, 49–51; forces in opposition to, 53–55
Lenin, Vladimir I., 190; on bureaucratic ulcer, 78–79; Kropotkin's letter to, 71, 211*n*28; on Russian Revolution, 100–102; on state property and socialization, 84
León, Agdalena, 118
León, Osvaldo, 207*n*30
Llancaqueo, Víctor Toledo, 17
Lugo, Fernando, 14, 33–34; coup against, 44
Lula da Silva, Luiz Ignácio, 14, 33, 54–55
Luxemburg, Rosa, 177

Machado, Darío, 88–89
Mahuad, Jamil, 16
Maneiro, Alfredo, 69
Manta (Ecuador), 31–32
Mapuhe movement (Chile), 17–18
Mariátegui, José Carlos, 8, 61
Marx, Karl, 62–67; on consciousness, 176; on cultural hegemony, 164; on decentralization, 81–82; on ownership of means of production, 94–95; on state, 78; on time needed for transformation, 187; on transition to socialism, 99
Matus, Carlos, 110–11
means of production, 93–94; attitudes of governments toward, 160; ownership of, 94–95; participatory planning for, 96–97; social ownership of, 84–86
media: Chávez's use of, 127–28; Correa's analyses of articles in, 126–27; in countries with left governments, 52–53; values transmitted through, 164
Mészáros, István, 78, 211–12*n*33
Mexico: NAFTA in, 19; neoliberalism supported in, 47; Oaxaca rebellion in, 24
military: spending on, 52–53; transforming, 141–47
Misión Barrio Adentro (Venezuela), 122–24
Misión Cultura (Venezuela), 123
Misión Guiacaipuro (Venezuela), 123
Misión Manuela Espejo (Ecuador), 124
Misión Mercal (Venezuela), 123
Misión Milagro (Venezuela), 123
Misión Negra Hipólita (Venezuela), 123
Montero, Álvaro, 41
Morales, Evo, 14, 40, 128
Moreno, Lenín, 124
Moulián, Tomás, 23, 60, 164
Movimento dos Trabalhadores Rurais Sem Terra (Movement of Rural

Landless Workers, MST; Brazil), 19–20, 91–92, 183, 184, 206*n*14
Mujica, José, 14

natural resources, 148–49
nature, 65–66; attitudes of governments toward, 160; development respecting, 147–53
neoliberalism, 7; attitudes of governments toward, 158; in Bolivia, 20–21; in Brazil, 19–20; in Chile, 22–24; in Ecuador, 16; governments opposing, 47–48; governments supporting, 46; in Latin America, 13; loses legitimacy in Latin America, 26–29; program of alternatives to, 170; rightist attacks on, 51; in Uruguay, 18–19; in Venezuela, 15
New Left, 49
Nicaragua: in ALBA, 31; neoliberalism opposed by, 47
North American Free Trade Agreement (NAFTA), 19
Núñez, Orlando, 182

Oaxaca (Mexico), 24
Obama, Barack, 41, 45
oil industry, in Ecuador, 151–52
Organización Nacional de Jubilados (National Organization of Retired Workers; Uruguay), 19
Organization of American States (OAS): CELAC alternative to, 36–37; defeat of FTAA in, 31; sanctions against Cuba lifted by, 32–33
Ortega, Daniel, 14, 36–37
Oviedo, Lino, 44
ownership, 94–95; social, 213*n*60

Pacific Alliance (Alianza del Pacífico), 31
Pando (Bolivia), 40, 147
Paraguay: coup in, 44; U.S. military presence in, 33–34
Paris Commune: Lenin on, 211–12*n*33; Marx on, 82
parliaments: for communes, 136; transformation of, 129–33
participatory democracy, 68–71; delegated democracy and, 73–78
participatory planning, 93–97, 155–56
Partido de los Trabajadores (Workers' Party, PT; Brazil), 54
Patiño, Ricardo, 126
PDVSA (Venezuelan oil company), 115
Penguin Rebellion (Chile), 22–23
People's Campaign for Decentralized Planning (Kerala, India), 154
People's Council (Cuba), 81
Pérez, Carlos Andrés, 15, 115
Petras, James, 48
Piñera, Sebastián, 18
Plan Bolívar 2000 (Venezuela), 143
planning: for communes, 137; in Kerala, 153–57; participatory, 93–97
political activists, 181–85
political democracy, 68–69
political organizations (instruments), 165–68; activists needed for, 181–85; bureaucratism in, 185–87; criticizing, 190; necessity of, 173–75; public criticism of, 189–93; strategy for, 168–72; tasks of, 175–81; *see also* Communist Parties
political parties, 27
politicians, Intellectuals and, 110–11
politics, 167
Pomar, Valter, 30, 54, 55, 105–6
popular movements, 14–26
popular protagonism: attitudes of governments toward, 161; decentralization for, 78–83; *see also* protagonistic democracy
privatization: in Ecuador, 117–18; in Uruguay, 18–19
productive relations, *see* relations of production

propaganda, 52
property, owned by state, 95–96, 213*n*58
protagonistic democracy, 68–71, 179; attitudes of governments toward, 161; decentralization for, 78–83; in workplace, 89–91

radio, 127–28
Ramonet, Ignacio, 15, 191
Rangel, José Vicente, 41
Regalado, Roberto, 14, 47, 48
relations of production, 119; capitalist companies in, 121–22; cooperatives in, 120–21; state companies in, 119–20
Reyes, Raúl, 32
Rio Group, 32
Rojas, Jesús, 130
Rousseff, Dilma, 14
Rubio, Enrique, 170
Russian Revolution, 100–102

Sachs, Jeffrey, 20
Sader, Emir, 27
Saint Vincent and the Grenadines, 31
Sánchez Ancochea, Diego, 38, 208*n*46
Sarkozy, Nicolas, 33
Sassone, Pedro, 129–30
School of the Americas, 141, 143, 159
Second Africa-South America Summit (2009), 34
sectarianism, 183–84
Sesto, Farruco, 177, 178, 216*n*13
social class, hegemony by, 164
social democracy, 68–69
Social Democrats, 101
socialism: characteristics of, 83–84; Chávez's, 7–9, 58–61; consciousness for, 182; cultural transformation needed for, 174; decentralization in, 83; dull instruments of capitalism and, 92–93; efficiency under, 86–88; as goal of left governments, 49–50; incentives in construction of, 88–93; in Latin America, 57–59; of Marx and Engels, 62–67, 210*n*13; participatory planning in, 93–97; social ownership under, 84–85, 97; transition to, 98–108
socialist conditionality, 121, 122
social left, 49
social movements, 25–26
social property, 85
Sorge, Friedrich Adolph, 99
South America: U.S. military bases in, 38; *see also* Latin America
South American Community of Nations, 34
South American Summit, 34
sovereignty: attitudes of governments towards, 159; of Bolivia, 146–47
Soviet Union, 62; bureaucratism in, 78–79, 185–86; centralization in, 78; Chávez on, 59; incentives for efficiency in, 88–89; Kropotkin on, 71, 179, 211*n*28; lack of democracy in, 68; means of production in, 84–85
state, 103; accountability of officials in, 126–27; built from below, 105–6; bureaucratism in, 78–79; Chávez on, 9, 104; for communes, 135–39; created from below, 133–41; Marx and Engels on, 67, 78, 82; means of production owned by, 84–85; new institutions created within, 122–24; paternalism by, 69; during period of transition, 139; property owned by, 95–96, 213*n*58; transforming central government's management, 124–29; transforming Parliaments in, 129–33; in transition to socialism, 173–74; working class control of, 72
state capitalism, 84–85; in Ecuador, 117–19
state companies, 119–20

state institutions, new, 122–24
Stavenhagen, Rodolfo, 206*n*10
Stédile, João Pedro, 184
Stiglitz, Joseph, 148
Stolowicz, Beatriz, 50, 51
student movements, in Chile, 22–24
Suárez, Daniel, 150–51
subsidiarity, 154
sucre (currency), 36
Sullivan, Max, 32
Sweden, 53

Tapia Maella, Luis, 130–33, 211*n*30
term limits, 179
Thatcher, Margaret, 13
Tito, 89
Toussaint, Eric, 205*n*4
transition to socialism: in advanced countries, 98–99; in backward countries, 99–102; in countries where government as been conquered, 102–6; intervention of state in, 173–74; specific to each country, 106–8; state during, 139; time needed for, 187
Troncoso, Patricia, 18
twenty-first century socialism, *see* socialism

Ugarteche, Oscar, 35
Union of South American Nations (UNASUR), 34; Defense Council of, 146
United Kingdom, 13
United States: decline in power of, 38–45; FTAA and, 30–31; limits on power of, 30; military base in Ecuador of, 31–32; School of the Americas of, 141, 143, 159
Uruguay: ALBA and, 31; neoliberalism in, 47; popularity of democracy in, 28; privatization in, 18–19

Vallejo, Camila, 23
Vázquez, Tabaré, 14
Venezuela: in ALBA, 31; armed forces of, 141, 145; Bolivarian constitution in, 114; Chávez elected in, 13; communal councils in, 72–74; elections in, 77–78; media in, 52–53; nationalization of resources of, 115–16; neoliberalism in, 15; neoliberalism opposed by, 47; new constitution for, 142; new state institutions created in, 122–24; popularity of democracy in, 27, 28; respect for environment in constitution of, 152–53; social parliamentarianism in, 129–30; trade between China and, 37–38; U.S.-supported movements in, 39; workers' co-management in, 89–90
Vietnamese Communist Party, 188
voceria (delegations), 74, 76–77
voting, 74, 211*n*30; electoral cycle for, 109; in Venezuela, 77–78

Water War (Bolivia), 20–21
Whipala (people), 146
women, 160; in division of labor, 182
World Meeting of Intellectuals and Artists in Defense of Humanity (Caracas, 2004), 59
World Social Forums, 169

Yachay, University of (Ecuador), 151
Yasuni-ITT project (Ecuador), 152
YPFB (firm; Venezuela), 117
Yugoslavia, 89

Zapatista National Liberation Army (EZLN; Mexico), 19
Zapatistas, 75
Zecevic, Miodrag, 63
Zelaya, Manuel, 40–42, 114

THE CHAOTIC ORDER

An Unknown Teacher's Pedagogic Travelogue

Avijit Pathak

AAKAR

The Chaotic Order: An Unknown Teacher's Pedagogic Travelogue
Avijit Pathak

First Published 2015
Reprinted 2018
Reprinted 2025

ISBN 978-93-5002-350-1 (Pb)

Published by
AAKAR BOOKS
28 E Pocket IV, Mayur Vihar Phase I
Delhi 110 091, India
www.aakarbooks.com

Printed at
D.K. Fine Art Press, Delhi

To my daughter who, I believe, has realized that her father is primarily a child trying to be a teacher.

Preface

Here is a book on education, on pedagogy, on teaching, and on the ethos of the university as a centre for higher learning. But then, it is not like what professional sociologists of education would like to regard as an appropriate 'text' with theoretical as well as empirical chapters, with references and bibliography. In fact, here is a book which has no chapter in its standardized format; there is no structural design; instead, there are twenty reflexive narratives—not necessarily always arranged in a chronological order—through which I have sought to communicate with my readers. And the language I have used is not of the kind professional journals adhere to; instead, it flows like a river with its metaphors, symbols and poetic imagination.

In a way, the book is about what I do. I am a university professor. And as a researcher (yes, research is an integral part of the university life) I am expected to write on a spectrum of issues: modernity, culture, religion, politics, nationalism, globalization, ethnicity and identity. It is not that I escape from these professional obligations. However, I am also a teacher. And this aspect of my role in the university is no less important. In fact, it gives a distinctive identity to us; we are not just researchers; we are engaged in an act of communion with young learners. Have I ever bothered to reflect on what I do every morning as I enter the university—the practice of teaching, my engagement with my students, my pedagogic experiments? Is it possible for me to see my own practice as a text, read it, reflect on it, and write about it? In this book I have tried to do so; I have allowed myself to be contemplative and inner-directed; I have reflected on my own journey—what it means to exist primarily and fundamentally as a teacher, what it means to grow with students, and what it means to experiment, and rethink the very meaning of the university as a centre for higher learning.

A book of this kind, needlessly to add, cannot claim 'objectivity'. Because it is about my experience; it is about my context—my location in a leading central university that is not yet indifferent to the possibility of creative exploration; it is about my journey—my modes of learning and unlearning, my success and failure. Yet, the fact that I have chosen to publish it indicates that even though its fragrance is biographical, it has a story to tell that is likely to excite all those who reflect on education and pedagogy, the vocation of teaching, its deeper meanings, and the ethos of the university. It is not an egotistic venture (if my readers find the trace of my 'ego' in the text, I would consider it as my failure); it is all about connectivity and shared concerns.

Here is a book that emerges out of love and trust. My students have loved me. They have enabled me to evolve as a teacher, and reaffirm my conviction that to teach—and teach in silence—is an immensely graceful act. My protectors—my parents and my wife who have been constantly looking at me from the mysterious stars; my sisters and brothers; my loved ones; and above all, my daughter: I am eternally indebted to all of them. I trust Mr. Saxena—my publisher. I am grateful to him. And how elevated I would feel if my readers find a meaning in an unknown teacher's pedagogic travelogue, in this chaotic order!

Jawaharlal Nehru University **Avijit Pathak**
New Delhi
May 4, 2015

1

I look at them. They surprise me. Even an examination, far from being oppressive, can be a celebration. My mind is filled with joy. I get my reward.

How elevated I feel as I narrate this incident! I have just come out from the examination hall. My students are writing their end semester examination. Some senior students are waiting in my room. They are eager to see the question paper that I have designed for my MA students. They see it; they smile; and one of them expresses his feelings with absolute joy: 'It is beautiful. It takes me to the realm of imagination.' How do I respond? A current of emotions overflows my being. I begin to tell him about my engagement, my way of seeing my work. I find myself in a communicative space. Time becomes magical, and it leads me to invoke my wife. True, she left her physical body; yet, the energy she carried envelops my consciousness. And the miracle is that at that very moment I find myself near the majestic Taj Mahal at Agra. My wife looks at a brick with great wonder, and whispers: 'See this small piece of brick. How beautifully designed it is; so much labour and hard work! Nothing is trivial. Every element has been taken care of. And that is why, the Taj Mahal as a whole is extraordinarily illuminating.' I continue to hear that voice, that language of wisdom. And I tell my student... I have enjoyed—enjoyed immensely—the act of formulating this question paper. I have celebrated it. I have moved around, seen peacocks and butterflies, looked at the sky, read books, and waited and waited. And then suddenly ideas embrace me—the way God appears in silence. I receive the message, and formulate my question paper.

Does my celebration have a meaning in the hard/pragmatic world of academics? Why should a professor spend so much time and energy in designing a question paper? As it is believed, it is just a matter of five minutes. Work on your computer, think for a while about the syllabus you have covered, and type five straightforward questions—define... explain... elaborate.... That's all. A professor is supposed to do great things: writing a scholarly paper, publishing a book, attending a conference, conducting a project, visiting institutions abroad for international collaboration. A professor spending a considerable amount of time and energy in formulating a question paper for the end semester examination, and feeling excited about it—possibly it looks absurd and strange! But then, I deny this rationale because my wife whispers: 'Recall that brick of the Taj Mahal. Nothing is trivial.' Yes, every small thing—even this question paper, I tell my student, is important. And when you do something that does not have a very concrete and tangible recognition—an award for publications, a position in the academic bureaucracy, a membership in the selection committee, a prime time television appearance, and applause and clapping for a speech in a conference hall—and do it with absolute joy, creativity and seriousness, you find God. Because God is that small thing; God is that ordinary event; God is that naturalness; God is simple. My student, I wish to tell you—everything I do, be it writing a book, or attending a conference or formulating a question paper, is equally important; I do not hierarchize; I see it as a celebration. And that is the way I feel the completeness of my academic life.

Time passes. The examination is over. As I start collecting their papers, a student approaches me. 'Sir, may I say something?' 'Why not?' I ask her to continue. 'Sir, I do not know whether I am brilliant, whether my answers are sufficiently academic and intellectually sound. But Sir, I have allowed my heart to take hold of my pen. For the first time in my life, I am writing an examination in which my heart has played such an important role'. And here is yet another student articulating her experience with great enthusiasm: 'Sir, thank you very much. You asked a question—what does it to mean to share Rassundari Devi's *Amar Jiban* with one's grandfather? Sir, believe me, I really wanted to share that extraordinary life story—a woman's struggles and aspirations in a patriarchal society—with my grandfather, and feel what it would have meant to him had my own grandmother been a Rassundari Devi.'

I look at them. They surprise me. Even an examination, far from being oppressive, can be a celebration. My mind is filled with joy. I get my reward. I invoke my wife. And this time I whisper in her ears: 'You are right. Nothing is insignificant. Even formulating a question paper is as creative as discovering the law of gravitation!' I come back to my residence, make a cup of tea, open the answer scripts. How wonderful it is to read the experiential writings of these young/vibrant minds:

> If I had narrated Rassundari Devi to my grandfather the first reaction of his would be of discomfort because my grandfather as I know him is a man of authority and dominance. A man who would never tolerate anything or anyone that would challenge his authority so to speak...My reading of *Amar Jiban*would also make him realize the fact that his wife that is my grandmother, might also have undergone the same agony, disappointment and despair as Rassundari Devi. And I think there I would feel successful for at least making my grandfather realize that my grandmother too in some way

> or the other had certain expectations from her husband which my grandfather failed to meet because he was busy meeting the expectations of the society which is essentially patriarchal in nature. Maybe towards the end of the narration when the text would be over and only my grandfather and I would be there, there would be an ambience of silence because we might both be lost in the process of critically reflecting on the text. I would be thinking about my grandmother whose absence would then become the real presence and for my grandfather the same silence would be working as a haunting experience but he would be chased by a guilty conscience for failing to acknowledge what his wife did to her on a regular basis.

Yes, I tell myself, I have succeeded in arousing their imagination. And I feel like whispering in their ears: 'Dear students, you are like those beautiful bricks I need to construct my own Taj Mahal—the Utopia that a teacher loves to visualize.'

2

You should never try to compel someone (because you happen to be a teacher, a supervisor) to read your book; you should not even persuade. If it happens...let it happen naturally, spontaneously, easily—the way a bird comes to a tree.

Visit our Centre. You find a huge board displaying the publications of the faculty: the cover pages of the books written by our professors, reviewed by the well-known experts in the field, and brought out by the publication houses that charm the academic circle. As a matter of fact, it all began with a need to showcase the achievements of our Centre before the UGC committee: how its teachers as dynamic researchers are perpetually contributing to the domain of knowledge, and taking the Centre as well as the university to a great height. The committee came, saw it, and, needless to add, sanctioned the grants.... Yet, the board remains. In fact, with the passage of time new additions make the display more and more attractive. But I ask myself: After the departure of the UGC committee, who are the ones seeing this grand display of our academic creations? Are they our students? It is possible that every morning as they come to the Centre they look at this display, and feel how great their teachers are; they are indeed privileged to be taught by them! Or, is it altogether impossible that we ourselves see our own creations, feel happy, and gratify the irresistible instinct of egotistic pride?

Yes, my books too have been displaced. Something is happening deep inside my consciousness. I am not feeling particularly easy and comfortable. I have a sense of embarrassment. Quite often, as I enter the Centre, my eyes invariably take me near the board, and I begin to feel immensely uneasy. I recall my father who had nothing to do with the high culture of academics. With his characteristic simplicity he used to tell me: 'Never advertise your own achievements. Never display your knowledge as a product. Never talk about yourself.' Have I forgotten my father? Am I seeing him as old-fashioned— a naïve semi-urban gentle man with no idea of how the academic world functions? My discomfort, my uneasiness, my guilt: I feel condemned.

Time passes. The board of display does not seem to have any space left. Possibly in the coming days the Centre has to think of arranging yet another board for showcasing the publications of its professors. After all, our colleagues are dynamic; they write ceaselessly; and big publishers wait for their manuscripts.

But then, one day I acquire the courage. I come to the Centre; I ask a student of mine who, as I feel, understands my dilemma, to accomplish the final act in silence: removing the cover pages of my books from that grand display. Nobody sees it; nor do I inform anybody. I feel relieved. I feel: 'From the clouds my father must have seen this act, blessed me, and my student.' Am I preaching? Am I sounding like an orthodox/puritan idealist? I do not know. But then, dear students, I wish to tell you something: something very deep that has become part of my looking at my work. True, books are needed; books are desirable; good ideas, good thoughts, good research findings—we must communicate, write books and publish. I too write books; I read books; I love their smell, their touch. But once you write your book, don't advertise it, don't speak too much about it; don't display, commodify, showcase. Your books are in bookshops; your books are in libraries; your books have reached the relevant journals for reviews. You need not bother. Let your books be read, liked, disliked, loved, hated by your readers. Let your publishers do what they feel important to take your books to your potential readers. You create; and then, you forget. Don't hold on. Don't possess. Don't get excessively attached to it. Learn to forget, and laugh at yourself.

Is it the reason that I am becoming increasingly sceptical about book release functions? Is it the reason that I do not include my own books in the reading list for the courses I teach? Is it the reason that in a seminar/ conference while delivering a lecture I do not refer to my own book? Or, is it the reason that I share the experiences of the books I write only with my loved ones: those who understand me and make me grow? Possibly my way of writing or looking at a book does not always fall in line with the way the academic establishment sees it. When I write a book, it becomes my child, my beloved. The entire experience is deeply sacred. Yes, it has its reason, its empiricism, its theories, its discourses, its hard facts, its bibliography, its notes, its indexing, its appendix; yet, for me, the experience remains intimate and aesthetically fulfilling; it refuses to be categorized as just technical and professional. The experience is essentially that of a mother conceiving her child—deeply maternal, feminine and sacred. And if the sacred becomes a product, if it becomes a tool for ego boosting, if it becomes a medium through which I engage in 'networking' and enhance my social capital, it gets profaned; and that is indeed a great loss.

It is of course true that when one reads your book, and communicates that experience with you, you feel good. This feeling is very pure; it is a bond; it is a sense of humility; it is filled with sacred tears. But then, it happens....It cannot be enforced. You should never try to compel someone (because you happen to be a teacher, a supervisor) to read your book; you should not even persuade. If it happens...let it happen naturally, spontaneously, easily—the way a bird comes to a tree, and converses with it. This means waiting...waiting in silence... waiting with grace...waiting without even being aware that one is waiting. And then, suddenly one fine morning someone gives you a call: 'I have just read your book. It makes me think and feel. I wish to meet you.' That is the moment when that bond takes place, when a writer and a reader communicate, embrace each other. That is a pure moment. That is eternity. Is the culture of waiting disappearing in the world of high academics? Publish, get instant recognition, or perish—that seems to be the mantra driving us to showcase our achievements. Facebook, book release functions, or, for that matter, the display at our Centre—we do not wish to miss any opportunity. We are restless. If our books are not quoted, we feel unhappy. We grow crazy if our PhD students do not include our books in their impressive bibliographies. It seems everything is a theatric play: you are what you present yourself to be, you are your uniform, your mask, your stage performance! You are your book; the more it is talked about the more real you are!

Dear students, I tell you all this because I pray, I pray for you. I want you to write books—

enchanting books. But I do not want you to reduce your creations into products; even academic products, believe me, are nothing but products. I want you to feel easy with your creations, not to get heavily burdened with the baggage of 'name' and 'fame'. And now may I request you to come with me, my dear. See this garden. How beautiful this tiny blue flower is. It attracts you. Its fragrance enters your being. It becomes your soul. It does not promote itself. It does not speak the language of narcissism. It does not have a price tag. It is not conscious of its beauty. And that is why, it is so beautiful. Let the book you write be like this flower. Remember the day when I wrote a brief comment in your classroom diary: 'You are destined to bloom like a flower'.

3

The wonder and mystery of life is that, despite my grey hair, and the constant enquiry about the date of my retirement, my intimate friends are my students. Their fragrance purifies me; their laughter makes me alive; their brilliant questions arouse and stimulate my thoughts; their pain, their aspirations, their dreams, their moments of fall and despair take me to the core of a relationship.

'You are always surrounded by a group of students. I wonder whether they are your chelas: a bunch of sycophants', a fresh MA student once told me. I value his frankness, his clear statement, his wonder, his doubt, his question. In fact, at times, I myself reflect on this relationship. And I realize that I need not justify or defend it. As a matter of fact, I feel good when I am with them; there is so much beauty, laughter, joy and pain in this relationship. Let me narrate what happened the other day. It was a lazy afternoon, and I received a call: 'Sir, may I come to see you for just five minutes?' 'Why not? Please come', I replied. And then he arrived—always pleasant, filled with laughter and joy. 'Here is a gift for you, Sir. Please open it and see it', he persuaded me. I obeyed. Oh, what a wonderful gift! My student, after a long...long search, finally managed to find a poster of *Deewar*—the famous Amitabh Bachchan film I often talk about it in the class. We began to laugh. We cracked jokes. We merged. That is it. My student does not fear me, nor does he retain a distance. He knows—and how often I myself have shared it—that his 'Sir' grew up in the 1970s with Amitabh Bachchan films; he loved *Deewar*, loved Bachchan's intensity in the film, his anger, his deep pain, his longing for his mother. He knows that his 'Sir' does not have any hesitation in admitting his love for some of these Bollywood films. True, I love Ray and Chaplin, Ghatak and Benegal; but this longing for the aesthetics of good and meaningful cinema has never caused heaviness in my being. I have never allowed it to burden me with some sort of cultural capital in my persona. I have my lighter moments. I laugh; I crack jokes; I recite the dialogues of popular Bachchan films. My student knows that. And that is why, the gift makes me feel the lightness of being. A professor becomes a friend; a student becomes an intimate companion. Amitabh Bachchan to Walt Whitman, Herman Hesse to Antonio Gramsci: how beautifully, gracefully we share everything.

Here is the tale of yet another student. Who says that beauty does not exist in the world? Who says that everything about our everydayness is instrumental and calculative? This student of mine loves flowers; he carries their fragrance. Almost every alternative day he arrives with flowers; and in the freshness of the morning his flowers enter my soul. As he arranges these flowers with absolute patience and aesthetics, I realize the meaning of an action filled with love and creativity. God sends me to the kitchen; I make a cup of tea for him. We talk, laugh and share feelings, experiences and readings. Who is he? A sycophant? Or, a flower? An object in a 'network' society? Or, a fountain of love and care? A research scholar 'serving' his professor? Or, an upward flame of the illuminating light? It is sad that in a cynical environment we feel tempted to see these relationships as calculative and instrumental—a teacher with his 'resources' using his student, or a student 'pleasing' his teacher to gain some profit: a teaching job, a fellowship abroad, a recommendation letter, a good grade! It is equally sad that there are teachers who feel that it is 'distance' that makes them powerful; this distance is legitimated in the name of 'professionalism'. 'Send me an e-mail. Seek an appointment. And the exact date and timing will be communicated to you'—it is not difficult to find professors speaking this language, and erecting a wall separating them from their students. It is really sad that they feel that if they retain a distance, evoke fear, avoid intimacy, they are powerful, they are productive, they are perfect managers of their valuable time. You know me, my dear. My transparent self is before you. If my students fear me, I would see it as my defeat, my ultimate failure as a teacher. Fear separates; love unites. Distance brings a wall; dialogue brings the souls together. The power of separation causes an illusion of efficiency; Love brings about real work, real efficiency, real dynamism. Love is friendship; love is reverence; love is trust; love is the real power of powerlessness! And one has to feel it. This bond does not trivialize the role of a teacher. Instead, it is the true colour of grace and gratitude. So I give you a call. You will find your answer. My door is open—for you, for everybody. Come. Join the celebration. Have a cup of coffee with me. Share a book, a painting, a story of your being. Who is preventing you, my dear?

'How do you spend time? Who are your friends?' I am often asked this question. My friends are indeed many. I am in touch with my school friends. Suddenly a telephonic conversation—boundless laughter, and recalling the poem a common friend once wrote for his imaginary beloved! My friends are in diverse vocations—in teaching, in administration, in social activism. But the wonder and mystery of life is that, despite my grey hair, and the constant enquiry about the date of my retirement, my intimate friends are my students. Their fragrance purifies me; their laughter makes me alive; their brilliant questions arouse and stimulate my thoughts; their pain, their aspirations, their dreams, their moments of fall and despair take me to the core of a relationship. 'Don't worry, Sir. My doctors are hopeful. I am recovering from cancer'—a student of mine assures me, and I realize what it means to be a teacher. Dear student, possibly you too are going to become a teacher. Celebrate it, celebrate it every moment. Your true power is your love; your real strength is your transparent self; your authentic religiosity is your symmetry with your students. Teaching, believe me, is a deeply spiritual act.

Imagine the magical night at Ranikhet where with some of my students I went for a rhythmic workshop. The post-dinner walk made us see and feel what a seeker strives for—the garland of mountains looking like Sufi mystics, the whisper of those tall pine/oak trees, the curved road, and the vastness of the sky with the radiant moon. We all sat on the road; we remained silent. And then something happened. Since eternity, I felt, we have been walking, walking together. Dear student, do you understand the meaning of this miraculous soundless sound? Feel it, and you will realize what the teacher-taught relationship is all about.

4

The dialogue goes on; you do not stop; you continue your journey; you see with your own eyes; you learn, you unlearn; you fill your minds with all sorts of information; yet, you know how to empty yourself; you exist as a very real, very alive, unique person, despite their books, their fame, their awards. Because you realize that this sunrise is yours, this sunset is your poem, this moon is your magic, this child is your innocence. You are no less important than the books you read.

There is indeed a deep-rooted fear prevailing over the academic culture: the fear of plagiarism. Yes, professors fear that their students are deceiving them; they are not original in their writings, assignments, theses; they are simply copying and engaging in the act of plagiarism. And in the age of mistrust and suspicion it is feared that even some known intellectuals/professors are not altogether free from this vice. So, it is asked, who is blaming whom? Possibly, as a cynic tends to answer, it is a game of mutual deception. I often reflect on this issue. Why is it that in our times this fear/doubt is all-pervasive? Is it because we find ourselves—thanks to the Internet—in the world of abundance—abundance of information, abundance of reading material, abundance of commentaries and reviews, and as a result, we are tempted to borrow and project these ideas as our own? Or, is it because in a recklessly competitive culture we are asked to produce ceaselessly, and write and publish without any limit, and as a consequence, the act of borrowing emerges as an instant solution to the unnatural target that we have posed before ourselves? Yes, all these are possibly true. However, there is something deep about this malice which is not generally talked about. It is in this context that I wish to narrate a story. I remember an incident that happened when I was doing my postgraduation. A professor taught us a course on social stratification. And I studied—and studied reasonably carefully—what the professor wanted us to read: Dumont, Srinivas, Beteille.... Then, one day I asked him: 'Sir, in my term paper is it possible for me to write my own experiential account—the way in the process of growing up in a small town in West Bengal I saw the presence/absence of caste?' 'No, you can't. You are not M.N. Srinivas', my professor reminded me of the 'absurdity' of my wish. I was young and vulnerable. I could not say anything to my professor. Instead, I wrote a 'technically perfect' term paper: nothing original, but full of appropriate quotes and references. And I got a satisfactory grade. However, my professor's remarks continued to haunt me. Today let me share with you—my students—what I wanted to tell my professor. 'Yes, I am not M.N. Srinivas. Why should I be M.N. Srinivas? Or, for that matter, why should I at all try to be M.N.

Srinivas? I am what I am with all my follies and mistakes. Yet, I wish to be an eager learner whose eyes are open, whose mind is alert, who seeks to observe, analyse and interpret the world—not just through the ideas given by celebrity social scientists (even though he adores their scholarship and learns from them), but also through his own experience. I am not dead. Yes, I have tried to read all that you wanted me to read. But then, this reading should not bind me. I ought to have my freedom to learn and unlearn. Why should I be deprived of my right to make mistakes, and yet rise each time I fall? Is everybody in the world—from Srinivas to Beteille—important except my own mind, my own eyes, my own reasoning, my own intuition, my own sensibilities?'

See the deep-rooted malice. As professors we are asking our students to produce 'technically perfect' products. And what is the ideal type of a technically perfect term paper or a dissertation? References... references... references. How frightening it has become! You are compelled to quote. You are not supposed to write anything that cannot be 'substantiated' through the writings of others. See its pathology. 'The sunset is beautiful'—it is not possible to write even this experiential truth without quoting somebody. To quote, it seems, has become your compulsion. You are required to use appropriate vocabulary, give a glossary, and follow a standardized style: say, the style of a reputed refereed journal. But one thing is certain. You need not bother much about your own thoughts, feelings and experiences. As every student of social science would admit, to write about discipline and power is to refer to Michel Foucault; to write about education is to refer to Bernstein and Bourdieu; to write about nationalism is to refer to Partha Chatterjee and Sudipta Kaviraj; and to write about the Dalit issue is to refer to Gail Omvedt and Kancha Illiah. There is no escape. You are almost compelled to do so. It does not matter whether these references emerge out of your genuine conviction and understanding. Your soul is dead. And you just follow an academic ritual, and your professor as a priest of the discipline is evaluating you on the basis of the perfection of this ritual. What, therefore, emerges is a ritually perfect term paper or a dissertation, but devoid of the fragrance of originality, daring spirit, creativity and those 'mistakes' that make it more real and authentic.

What is this academic product, my dear? Is it original? Or, is it an act of plagiarism, even when not seen as such? The difference, we must be honest enough to accept, is that those who are naïve copy and borrow without acknowledging; and the intelligent ones do the same, but they are perfectly trained in the science of referencing. And what about your professors? You can take a simple test. Ask them to write ten pages—say, on caste, gender, religion or power—without any reference, without footnotes, without quotes. Ask them to imagine for these ten minutes that no Foucaults, no Marxs, no Durkheims, no Hegels had ever existed in the world. Ask them to imagine that they are discovering everything once again with absolute innocence. Believe me, many of us would not pass this test. The fact is that our words, because of a very inauthentic academic practice, have become ornamental; our ideas are borrowed, and our writings are pretentious. We have lost the courage to remain fresh. One sort of plagiarism is punished; but then, most of our academic practices are nothing but 'legitimate' articulations of plagiarism.

I do not wish to be misunderstood. It is by no means my contention to suggest: 'Don't read.' I am suggesting something deeper. Read, and read intensely and meaningfully. Have a conversation with great writers and researchers. Let your reading be an act of dialogue. As a fellow traveller you are talking to those who too have travelled. You are conversing with Marx while exploring the world produced by capitalism. You are talking to Gandhi and Fanon while you are making sense of the spirit of decolonization. You are sharing great moments with Herbert Marcuse and Walter Benjamin while you are looking at cotemporary mass culture. This dialogue enriches you, it does not restrict you, confine you, burden you, make you a prisoner. The dialogue goes on; you do not stop; you continue your journey; you see with your own eyes; you learn, you unlearn; you fill your minds with all sorts of information; yet, you know how to empty yourself; you exist as a very real, very alive, unique person, despite their books, their fame, their awards. Because you realize that this sunrise is yours, this sunset is your poem, this moon is your magic, this child is your innocence. You are no less important than the books you read.

There is yet another question that confronts me. As a professor, if I always fear that my students can copy, or borrow words, ideas and even sentences from others, is it altogether impossible for me to give them a different kind of assignment that cannot be copied, that cannot be written even if you give them the entire library—an assignment that demands their own imagination, an assignment that requires authenticity, not cleverness? In fact, this constant fear that our students are expert in plagiarism also reflects our own failure, our poverty of imagination, our inability to intervene meaningfully in the existing pedagogic process. Schools give projects that parents or hired experts do; university professors give assignments (say, an essay on the types of suicide Durkheim talked about; or, a note on Marx's notion of class conflict; or, a review of Foucault's *Madness and Civilization*) that the Internet can do. How tragic it is. Believe it, as teachers we have failed. Yet, I dream. None can deprive me of the joy of dreaming and experimenting. That is my own intimate space, and I value it as a teacher. I am teaching a course entitled *Methods of Social Sciences*. Yes, my students have read a great deal about 'observation'—about Malinowski and Margaret Mead, about their modes of observation, the nuances implicit in the process of observation, the meaning of the observer being observed. But then, I do not feel like asking them to write yet another term paper on 'social anthropology and participant observation'. I know they can write a technically perfect term paper with appropriate notes, quotes and references. But a work of this kind is replaceable. I, therefore, choose to give them an assignment like this:

> Location: Bhikaji Cama Place Crossing. Remain silent and observe—at least for ninety minutes—the continual flow of traffic, the hoardings all around, and above all, the street children engaged in diverse activities. And then, write a sociological essay on 'observation'—its complexities, its multiple layers.

It is simply impossible to copy, to borrow, to impress the professor with big names and their latest publications; the Internet is of no use. What matters is the arousal of creative imagination—the spirit of honest work. And yes, my students realize themselves as creative thinkers; they begin to trust themselves, rather than the Internet or the quotes from Ruth Benedict and Clifford Geertz (even when they have read and understood their texts). My students, I am convinced, you can make a new beginning. If a challenge is given to you, you feel encouraged to unfold your creativity. And hence I appeal to you to read, and read with great joy. Let books, for you, be enabling, not constraining. Write what you yourself have seen, felt, understood, realized and arrived at. References as such are not bad; there is no harm in quoting others. However, you should quote not to impress, but to have a meaningful conversation with a fellow traveller. And always believe that you matter, you exist, you are unique. Your style is your style. There is no standardized style. There is no *EPW*/OUP style! You create your own style. Have the courage to fail, to fall down, to make mistakes. Yet, trust yourself. I know that you can make it. You can prove that it is possible to create a culture of learning refreshingly free from the fear of plagiarism. After all, how can I forget that it is you, dear students, who have made me realize that even a theory class, far from being a bombardment of names and loaded concepts, can become as rhythmic as a piece of Mozart music?

5

Something happens. An invisible force enters my body, my soul. Words, ideas, concepts, analogies and illustrations begin to flow. I have surrendered. I am possessed.

I have taught; I have delivered a lecture—an introductory lecture on the methods of social sciences; I have come back to my chamber; and I see an extraordinarily sacred gift lying on my table—a beautiful picture and a poetic sentence: 'Sir, what a wonderful lecture...poems, Whitman, Satyajit Ray, Weber, Nisbet, science, sociology, Blake...! Isn't methodology becoming engaging and closer to one's reality?' With tears in my eyes, I feel that this morning is truly revealing, and it is through this beautiful gift that God has come to me, and made me realize that I am nothing, my ego is false; I just happen to be a medium through which everybody, every particle spoke, taught, delivered a lecture. It is not this discrete ego—a superficial sense of 'I' with a title/position, with a bio-data, with books and projects—that is teaching; it is essentially the enchanting inspiration nurtured and sustained by God that is teaching. This feeling relaxes me, makes me free; a sense of lightness and joy fills my heart. I begin to see everything.

I see my father taking me to a local school at a small town in West Bengal for admission. I see his eyes: the eyes that see a potential tree in a seed. I see my mother continually encouraging me, and coming to the railway station to see me off as I board the train for Delhi for higher studies. I see her tears of joy. I see my elder brother protecting me, encouraging me to expand, to do meaningful things. I see my friends, their light, their sharpness. I feel their faith, their concern, their positive vibrations. My wife—are you listening? Your physical body might have returned to the earth; but you remain. You remain as a song, you remain as a Himalayan peak, and you remain as the tales that continue to be lived. Are you listening? You possess me as I enter the class. 'Papa, you have to deliver a good lecture', my daughter reminds me as I prepare for the class. She enters my being; I feel God is accompanying me.

Who am I? Who is teaching? Yes, the official record—the record that the university bureaucracy produces every year—would state that Professor Pathak has taught this particular course. But my inner world knows how superficial it is. Because it does not realize that everything happens because of love and connectedness; one carries everybody within oneself. No, I am not teaching; it is through me that all of them are teaching. I wake up quite early in the morning; I see the sun in the eastern horizon; I am inspired. I start for the Centre; I see peacocks and butterflies, they come to me, and enter my being. I go for a walk; a tree whispers; I look above; the radiant moon smiles; ideas begin to strike my imagination; I feel elevated. I read books, listen to music, talk to my daughter, and invoke my wife, my parents. They come and make it possible. My lecture is ready. I come to the class. A foggy morning, shivering cold, 9 am class—yet, all of them are present. They are my flowers; I feel them; their curious eyes, their patience, their penetrating questions and reflections keep me alive. Something happens. An invisible force enters my body, my soul. Words, ideas, concepts, analogies and illustrations begin to flow. I have surrendered. I am possessed. Who is teaching, my dear? This professor is empty, and his emptiness receives you, receives every particle. It is this love that teaches, that delivers a lecture, that communicates, narrates, shares, philosophizes, visualizes.

It happens like this. One day I come back from the class, enter my room; and then, a student of mine arrives, gives me a gift: a literary masterpiece. I begin to value the beauty of studentship—the depths in the relationship between the teacher and the taught. With deep gratitude I open the book, and I see a beautiful passage my student has written in it: 'Sir, you are my father; you are my Gurudev; you are my philosopher, my guide, my friend.' Tears...only tears; God has knocked on my door. What an intensity in this trust, in this offering, in this prayer! Believe me, I am ordinary, simply ordinary. It is the all-pervading energy—my divine inspiration, my teacher, my bird, my tree, my mountains, my rivers—who make it possible. With deep gratitude and longing I keep the book, hold it softly, and begin to prepare for the next lecture.

6

My students—I am immensely grateful to you. With deep gratitude I recall your gift. A guitar, a melodious voice, a simple, yet profound poem—the song makes me see life. I evolve with it. My sociology evolves; my lecture finds its soul; my romance, my love and my revolution, despite the continual movement of clock time, do not disappear.

How fondly I recall the gift. It was 1992—a group of students gave me a wonderful gift. 'Sir, here is a music cassette for you. We are sure you would love these songs.' With their warmth and assurance I took the gift, and as I started listening to Kabir Suman's extraordinarily beautiful songs, I realized the sensitivity of my students and the worth of a gift. What a magical play of poetic sensibilities and deep feelings emanating from the depths of the inner world! And especially, one of the songs—*Prathomato Tomake Chai*—entered my being, my soul. What a prayer: poetic and political, temporal and transcendental, secular and spiritual! First, I want you. Second, I want you. Third, I want you. Till the end I want you. I want you when I am happy. I want you when I am unhappy. I want you after a long...long walk. I want you when I am tired. I want you in revolutions, in music, in all that is meaningful. Kabir Suman's (who in a way altered the landscape of contemporary Bengali music) enchanting voice, the poetry in his music, its soul, its everydayness, yet its realm of transcendence: everything touched me. I evolved a relationship with the song.

And it seems that there is something eternal about this relationship. I love its romanticism. I love its religiosity. I love its nuanced narratives of everyday life. I love its ability to transcend the duality of politics and prayer. It gives me a call; it inspires; it enhances my longing; it makes my tears deeply sacred. In a way this song has become my biography. Did my students have the third eye to see it? I felt this song at every moment—after reading a good book, after delivering a lecture, after seeing a beautiful film, after smelling the fragrance of early morning in the high altitudes of Uttarakhand, after sharing a cup of tea with my loved ones, after experiencing a flowing river, after pain, after anxiety, after revelation.... It kept my wonder, my romance alive. I could feel. I could love. I could cry. I was indeed enchanted. But then, one day things turned upside down....

Yet, the song remained as my intimate companion. Because at a deeper level nothing that is eternal disappears; forms change, but the essence remains. The singer's 'You' became my song, my flower, my mountain peak, my cherished utopia, my living history, my occultism, my faded manuscript, my books, my lectures, my kitchen, my smell. My students—I am immensely grateful to you. With deep gratitude I recall your gift. A guitar, a melodious voice, a simple, yet profound poem—the song makes me see life; I evolve with it. My sociology evolves; my lecture finds its soul; my romance, my love and my revolution, despite the continual movement of clock time, do not disappear.

2013: I am with yet another group of students. We are concluding the course which I have taught in the monsoon semester with a cultural programme. And see the miracle. As the programme is about to end, they play the same song. Tears in my eyes. What else do I do? The singer is not separated from me. He utters my voice, communicates my melody. Yes, I want you. I want you all the time. I want that feeling, that assurance, that intensity, that religiosity, that touch, that love. And at this very moment I want you—in this room where my students are organizing the cultural programme. In all my creations, in all my aspirations I want you. Do my students understand it? Who knows? It is a miracle. 1992-2013: one miracle leads to another.

My students who gave me the gift in 1992 have grown up; they are well-settled; they are scattered in different parts of the world. And after twenty- two years I am engaging with yet another group of students. Yet, the song remains, love remains. How can something that is eternal die? With this song I keep moving; my journey continues; I see places, read books, write ideas, meet people, discover the oceans in the eyes of my students, encounter difficulties, pain and struggle. But that 'You'—the mystery of the divine interplay of time and timelessness, form and formlessness, historical and mythical, earthly and heavenly—accompanies me. Yes, I want you. I want you at every moment. How can I exist without you?

January, 2014. I have just returned to my residence after a long evening walk. The cold wave, its mystery and the rhythm of my footsteps: Kabir Suman whispers in my ears. I begin to breathe the song. I want you. I want you. I want you. Where are you—my mother, my wife, my God, my flower, my soul, my Himalayan peaks, my mythology, my epic? I look at the sky. The moon has just begun to arrive. I have found you. I feel that I will continue to find you. My love has not dried up. My romance has not disappeared. Dear students, can a teacher exist without the abundance of love and romance?

7

There is an element of indeterminacy in life. That is the wonder, the surprise. That makes life mysterious. And that is why, there are limits to 'methods'. Learn methods. But at the same time, be aware of their limitations. That makes you humble. That transforms you—from a technically efficient scientific observer with a carefully drafted 'research design' to a humble wanderer.

It was quite an unusual class. It was 9 am—a foggy winter morning. Its implicit mysticism created an ambience that led us to assemble at the Partha Sarathy Rock—a beautiful space inside the university campus surrounded by rocks, an open air theatre, and above all, an expanded horizon. We thought that we would feel the space, smell the fragrance of cold breeze, look at the vast sky—the play of the dark clouds, and discuss all that we were studying in a course relating to the methods of social sciences. Yes, the abundance of nature touched us. Limits were transcended; the culture of learning was acquiring a poetic vision; the mundane nature of everydayness was becoming sacred.

The class began. Rocks, trees, birds, clouds were witnessing. But then, something happened. It started raining.... Should we then run, run faster, go back to the normal classroom: the sanitized 250 sq ft space with its four walls, neon light, television screen and air conditioner? 'No', suggested a student. 'There is a room behind the open air theatre. Sir, let's move there', he added. We followed him. It was a small room—not very clean. Yet, at that moment our inner cleanliness was more than sufficient to take that room which, despite its darkness and cave like structure, emerged as our dialogic space. We began.... It was a discussion class: a discussion on a methodological riddle on which I had already delivered a lecture. It was about 'structure', 'structuralism', and 'structuration'. To put it in simple words, while travelling through the ideas of the luminaries like Emile Durkheim, Louis Althusser, Levi Strauss, Alfred Schultz and Anthony Giddens we were enquiring whether our actions were determined by something called 'social structure'—its institutionalized pattern, its orderly arrangement of 'status' and 'role', its codified principles, laws and sanctions; or whether, irrespective of differences in cultural manifestations, there was an underlying 'structure' in our mind (continually operating in terms of the play of binary opposites like 'raw' and 'cooked', 'hot' and 'cold', 'up' and 'down') 'explaining' all our deeds; or whether, despite the prevalence of 'structure', we too—as creative/reflexive beings— could give meanings to our actions leading to the process of 'structuration': a creative and dialectical interplay of 'structure' and 'agency'.

My students were ready to comment, to converse, to make their observations. They were looking at their notes, referring to Durkheim and Giddens, summarizing their arguments, and adding new insights. Meanwhile, rains...more rains... thunderstorm: the room was getting darker. Yet, there was light in the darkness—the light emanating from all these young/vibrant students. A student began with an interesting observation. 'Sir, see how the 'structure' operates. Tuesday 9 am. As the time-table—the codified rule of the university—suggests, you are required to take the class, and as students we are compelled to attend it. That is the way the 'structure' has defined us. And see the weather. It is severely cold; it is raining. Yet, we can't escape the overwhelming power of the 'structure'. You have to take the class. And we have to attend it.' What a beautiful point. An example emanating from the experiential domain of this very moment—not a high sounding quote from a book mechanically recited. Theory became experiential; philosophy touched the being; learning became an inner awakening.

She inspired. I could see the smiling faces. They began to speak. I allowed myself to listen, listen carefully. And then I spoke: 'Yes, my student. How right you are. There is indeed a 'structure' that has arranged us—teachers and students—in a manner that is institutionalized, codified; it is almost like a 'thing' existing out there with its time-table, course-instructor, registered students, assignments, credit system, evaluation, grading and official certification. Our freedom, you are right, is not that of a bird flying in the sky. As historically located actors, we are bounded. I agree with you—my student. The rains, the thunderstorm, the shivering cold are not yet powerful enough to alter the 'script' (as a teacher, I teach; as a student, you attend my class) that the 'structure' of the university as a 'social system' has already written for us. Yet, I wish you to see something more. We are redefining the script. Isn't it? True, we are within the 'structure'; yet, from within we are altering, changing and modulating it. The class is not taking place in the allotted lecture hall sanctified by the 'official' time-table. The venue of this class is what the 'structure' has never dared to imagine. And hence we too are emerging as creators, skilled performers; we are not just passive role-performers. Yes, it is a theatre with a director, a script, an allocation of roles; yet, it is an alive theatre that innovates itself every moment, that perpetually negotiates with the script, with the director—a theatre that is a process, a continual process. And what else is 'structuration',my dear?'

Their eyes were filled with wonder and curiosity. Durkheim and Giddens were coming out of thick books, term paper footnotes, and fashionable bibliographies. They were merging with the rains, with the rocks, with the sky. My students were learning; learning was becoming a celebration. It was 11 am. The rains had already stopped. A song, a poem by Rlike, and then, we all moved towards our 'official' location.

It was quite late in the afternoon. I was discussing with a group of students in my office room. One of them asked: 'Sir, this morning was beautiful. But tell me Sir, how do you explain the sudden rainfall?' The question filled my mind with joy. And I replied: 'I am happy that you have asked this question. You see I feel the sudden rainfall as a messenger through which God has sent his message: Be aware of your planning. There are limits to our planning. We thought that we would take the class under the open sky. We did not predict the rains. But then, the rains turned our plan upside down. We had to seek refuge inside a tiny room. So please realize that there are limits to planning; there is an element of indeterminacy in life. That is the wonder, the surprise. That makes life mysterious. And that is why, there are limits to 'methods'. Learn methods. But at the same time, be aware of their limitations. That makes you humble. That transforms you—from a technically efficient scientific researcher with a carefully drafted 'research design' to a humble wanderer. And believe me, only when you are a humble wanderer you see and experience the deeper reality.'

The discussion was over. As I was coming

back to my residence, a strange thought came to my mind. I felt like shouting: 'Mr. Vice-Chancellor. The choice is yours. You can suspend me for bringing the analogy of rains, thunderstorm, sky, clouds, music, poetry in an academic lecture, and that too in a discussion on 'methods'. Or, you can join me, join my students, celebrate the rains, look at the sky, and feel what every educationist needs to realize: Nature is our best tutor!'

8

You find the nuances of social reality—not necessarily always by following 'methods'; you find it at moments when your research design has failed, your structured questionnaire has become incapable of going deeper, and something unexpected happens—an outburst of laughter, a joke, some intense moments of silence, tears in reddish eyes, an accident, a death, a traumatic memory. Be prepared for these surprises.

Yes, in my class I dare to recite a poem and tell a ghost story, even when I am acutely aware of the fact that my students are young researchers pursuing a course on the methods of social sciences, and many of them will eventually emerge as professional sociologists, forget poetry, abhor the romance of innocence, and with their 'adult like maturity' love to speak a heavily loaded language taking its vocabulary from the likes of Bourdieu, Rorty and Derrida. Yet, I dare. And I feel immensely happy that my academics have not yet been able to diminish what William Blake would have categorized as 'songs of innocence'. I teach methods. I teach all that the high culture of academics wants me to do: how to think 'rationally'; how to see the epistemological roots of 'induction' and 'deduction' in Francis Bacon and Rene Descartes respectively; how to get enriched by Karl Popper's theory of refutability, or Thomas Kuhn's path-breaking ideas on 'normal science', 'paradigm' and 'puzzle solving'; how to construct a hypothesis for validation; how to formulate a questionnaire and an interview schedule; how to conduct a 'focus group interview'; how to engage in the act of sampling, select respondents and informants, and use statistical techniques for measuring, tabulating and quantifying empirical data; how to experience the science of hermeneutics—from Dilthey to Gadamer, and interpret the cultural domain of symbols, meanings and texts; or how to go through ethnography, and learn the lessons of 'field work' from Malinowski and Evans Pritchard, Clifford Geertz and M.N. Srinivas.

Yet, I dare. And hence I ought to reflect on the poetic vision which is seldom found in the language of academics, in its obsession with 'methods'—with its belief that there is a road to truth, and if you learn to read the map of the road, you can surely arrive; the belief that if you know the grammar of English you can invariably write like Blake and Whitman; the belief that truth knocks on your door only when you are prepared with your tools and techniques of research. But the poet said something else. The entire day, as the poet began, we made beautiful arrangements, we made appropriate plans, we prepared ourselves. Yet, He didn't arrive. All our thoughts, designs and structures failed. We gave up. If He didn't arrive in day light, if He didn't arrive when we were prepared, how could He arrive at this odd hour, in this silence of dark night? Then, suddenly a knock at the door, a sound of footsteps...; we didn't bother; we felt that it was the wind, the thunderstorm.... We didn't realize that He had actually arrived.

What a great poem! I wanted my students to feel it. I wanted them to realize that there are limits to 'methods', there are limits to our research designs, there are limits to the methodological certainty that professors seek to inject in their minds: 'Be scientific. Overcome your biases. Choose the proper site—your 'field'. Decide your 'primary' and 'secondary' sources. Use right techniques. And you are bound to get it.' No, it doesn't happen like this. You find the nuances of social reality—not necessarily always by following 'methods'; you find it at moments when your research design has failed, your structured questionnaire has become incapable of going deeper, and something unexpected happens—an outburst of laughter, a joke, some intense moments of silence, tears in reddish eyes, an accident, a death, a traumatic memory. Be prepared for these surprises. Yes, the poem gave me the language to articulate this point. Sorry, my colleagues, I love to recite poems in the methodology class.

And then one day as my lecture gained its momentum, I began to tell them a ghost story.

Was it superstitious? Was I insulting the rationality of intelligent JNU researchers? I don't know. But let me narrate how it happened. I was delivering a lecture on diverse modes of engagement between the knower and the known in sociological research. While referring to the writings of Emile Durkheim, Max Weber and Alvin W. Gouldner, I was trying to make them see the three possible modes of engagement often discussed and talked about. First, it is said that a sociologist as a 'value-neutral' professional ought to retain a distance from his/her respondents; this 'distance', it is argued, helps to objectify the social reality, see it as hard data, and retain the rigour of 'scientific explanation'. Second, there is yet another argument. Yes, distance is needed; it helps one to see facts as facts; yet, it should not be forgotten that social facts are not just 'things'; there are deep meanings and experiences implicit in these facts; and it is, therefore, important to cultivate the skill of 'empathy' so that the sociologist can imagine himself/herself in the position of the actor, and understand the meaning intended by him or her. And third, it is argued that the sociologist's 'self' too should play a creative role in research, in this engagement with the field; 'reflexivity' breaks 'methodological dualism', and enables the researcher to realize that to know the world is to know oneself. Knowledge is not just information; it is also an awakening.

My lecture was gaining its momentum, and I was about to conclude. And then, I felt that I must end with a ghost story. I began to narrate.... I was engaging with a group of children and their parents dislocated from Jharkhand, Chhattisgarh and Bihar, earning their livelihood as construction workers, and living in poorly constructed/unhygienic huts inside the campus. Yes, 'distance' and my 'professional gaze' were more than sufficient to gather some hard facts and data, and place them in neatly devised sociological categories: urbanity, migration, displacement, daily wages, and malnourished children somehow managing to attend poor quality government schools. But then, something happened. Looking at these children I felt that I too was a child, and as a child I always waited for someone—maybe my elder sister, my father, my mother—to tell me a ghost story; I wanted to experience the thrill of fear and joy. Are these children different simply because they are the children of construction workers? Are they just my empirical 'data'? My question took me to the domain of reflexivity, and then everything changed. It was a foggy winter night and we were shivering. An ideal moment for a ghost story, and I rediscovered myself as a story teller. What a joy! All these children who, till now, were mere data, began to come closer; they touched me, and in that touch I experienced their thrill mixed with fear and joy, belief and unbelief. 'Pathakji, you have to tell another story. Please...please come again', I received my gift. Distance was broken. With empathy and reflexivity I began to enter their world; I began to understand; I began to feel yet another engagement between the knower and the known.

I could not resist the temptation. I narrated the entire incident and repeated the same ghost story in my class. Boundless joy and laughter in the class. Yes, it was laughter, pure laughter. Sorry, sorry all the authors of the 'prescribed' textbooks of research methodology—you didn't teach me how to tell a ghost story, or recite a poem. Yet, it happened, and acted as a miracle. So, my students—come, come near me; hold my hand; let us begin yet another poem, another ghost story...

9

I wake up. 9 am class. I acquire the courage to come to our garden, smell the fragrance of a flower, pluck it, take it with me, walk towards the university, enter the lecture hall, see my students, feel the light, and give them the flower—my gift, my Universe.

I know that there are many occasions when I have failed, failed as a teacher, as a friend, as an elderly comrade. And these moments of failure make me pass through a dark tunnel. I experience many emotions: anger, fear, pessimism, a sense of defeat and withdrawal. I cease to inspire. No, I need not pretend; I need not deny; I acknowledge this fall, this failure. And possibly this failure is a reminder: 'Never think that you have achieved. You have your limitations, your weaknesses. True, you are a teacher; but even for a second don't think that you have ceased to become a student.' I receive the message, and I begin to pray: 'Let the sun rise once again and illumine my being after this terrible darkness.'

Binsar—a Himalayan hamlet in Uttarakhand—is a narrative of extraordinary illumination. With a group of students I move around Binsar. High altitude, dense forest, snow peaks, whisper of trees, stars in the revealing sky, infinite void, and deep...deep silence—nature heals, nature teaches, nature evokes poetry. And we are at Binsar to feel the mountains, to experience the trees, to merge with this soundless sound, and to reflect on poetry: not just as the rhythm of written words, but the poetry of the inner world—our intense moments of love, longing, pain, solitude and prayer. We are at Binsar to realize our innate potential—to give and hence to receive, to communicate, to nurture one another. Not as insulated/atomized/egocentric individuals burdened with all sorts of complexity and negativity, but as humble wanderers, as fellow travellers holding one another's hands, understanding, communicating, receiving, giving, loving and radiating the waves of sublime poetry—our journey begins with this aspiration.

Yes, we are finding, finding what a seeker strives for—the sun kissing, and kissing with such tenderness, the snowy peaks, a rhythmic walk through the woods, the melancholy of the sunset, the play of colours in the sky, its music; and we find our poems: some intimate/pure moments in our biographies; we eat together—reading and sharing our diaries, and feeling the ecstasy of togetherness. Yet, amidst all these positive vibrations, something has begun to happen. From the peak we fall down; from our inner beauty we come back to what society regards as our 'normal' selves—negative talk, gossip, internal rivalry, miscommunication, indifference, symbolic violence. A flower has just begun to bloom; but it is sad that we are destroying it. We have just begun to realize that God is this abundance, this extraordinary beauty, this silence, this depth; but it is unfortunate that we cannot bear it any more; we do not believe our own eyes, we condemn ourselves, we become limited, fragmented, divisive, negative.

It is happening. I feel it. I have already experienced many ventures of this kind—largely with a great degree of fulfilment and satisfaction. This possibly made me proud. But now God is teaching me the lesson: 'Your pride is false. Your vanity is the reason for your fall. You have overestimated yourself.' Yes, I fall down. I lose my temper. I tell my students: 'Forgive me. This is my last venture. I am withdrawing. I can't bear it any more.' Something happens. My fall shocks them, surprises them. Possibly they thought that somehow their 'Sir' would be able to retain his calm, manage things and restore order. But something else is happening. Like a dejected/ defeated being I am sinking, negativity is enveloping me, I am thinking that it is not possible to work in a group because we are essentially selfish and wicked. I crumble. I am almost dead. At this juncture, things begin to take a different turn. They all come to my room.

They cry. They apologize. And a reversal of roles takes place. They become my tutors, my guardians. My eyes are closed. Their words reach my ears: 'Sir, you have brought us together. You are the connecting link. You are our source of inspiration. It is you who have told us that we can fall down, but our divinity lies in our ability to rise once again.'

I try. I fail. I start walking through the woods. And then I happen to see two of my students. A leaf has just fallen from a huge tree. They take the leaf, and give it to me. Their gift touches my being. They become my mothers. I become their child. I cannot control myself. I begin to cry—tears of joy, tears of longing. There is lightness in my being; I now see the snowy peaks once again. We come back. Discussion, reflection, sharing—it continues. For some, the mind is still heavy; the wound does not heal easily. For some, the healing process has begun. And what about my own state of consciousness? I know it is not easy. I become alert. However, there are three reminders that convey a deep message to me. First, as human forms we are deeply ambiguous: a constant battle is taking place between our limitedness and our innate potential for experiencing the infinite, between our egotistic self-centredness and our urge to love and melt, between despair and the glimpse of light. The battle does not end. But then, there is no reason to give up. It is this epic battle, it is this struggle for rising, for unfolding our goodness, our innate potential that gives a meaning to our existence. Second, the moment you emerge from your shell, begin your journey, it evokes reactions. You are liked; you are disliked. You are praised; you are condemned. We tend to get paralyzed by someone's negative remarks, harsh words. This negativity provokes us, and we too become negative. But then, this is a trap. We allow ourselves to be caught in this vicious circle. At this juncture, I begin to feel that we must continue to walk, remain dialogic, and do what our conscience permits. We should not be unduly affected by praises or condemnations. Third, there seems to be no other way than love. We all wish to be loved, healed and nurtured. So if I want love, why should I not give it to others? Yes, there is always a fear—if you care, if you love, if you spread out, if you melt, if you do not show your 'power' you are likely to be exploited. But who would exploit whom? When I hate someone, when I generate negativity around me, I exploit myself because I do not allow myself to evolve, to elevate; instead, I sink, I degenerate. Moreover, if I love you, what will you deprive me of? My wealth, my possession, my power, my ego? In fact, when love overflows, wealth, power, possession, ego—everything becomes secondary, meaningless. Take everything from a lover; yet, a lover gives because to love is to experience the infinite.

All these flashes of truth strike me. I seek to rise. And then comes yet another sunrise, another morning. I find an envelope. I open it. What a wonderful gift! A student of mine has written a letter, articulated her dilemmas, struggles, confusions, yet her constant urge to see the golden light. And she concludes the letter with a beautiful poem:

Yes, my child, go out into the world; walk slow
And silent, comprehending all, and by and by
Your soul, the Universe, will know
Itself: the Eternal I.

I wake up. 9 am class. I acquire the courage to come to our garden, smell the fragrance of a flower, pluck it, take it with me, walk towards the university, enter the lecture hall, see my students, feel the light, and give them the flower—my gift, my Universe.

10

True, in this ongoing play of interpretation there is no absolute truth, no objective/foundational knowledge; but then, what emerges is no less beautiful; it is a journey: an artist with colours shaping, changing, adding, deleting, altering the landscape she is painting. It is not perfect mathematics; but it is nearer to life because life too evolves, grows, waits for surprises.

As I teach a course entitled *Methods of Social Sciences*, I am obliged to deliver a series of lectures on what is known as the *hermeneutic* method—a process of understanding and interpreting meanings, actions, symbols and texts. In a way, it is what my profession demands; I ought to tell my students how and why this mode of interpretation and understanding gained importance—how it makes us aware of the fundamental distinction between natural sciences and cultural sciences, why law-like generalizations and explanations that characterize natural sciences are not necessarily always applicable to the study of cultural life because humans are subjective/reflexive, they attach meanings to their world, they create symbols, languages and mythologies that require a deeper understanding, not a ruthlessly homogenized process of scientific reductionism. Yes, I prepare myself; I orient myself; I familiarize myself with the genealogy of the entire tradition; I tell them about Dilthey, Heidegger and Gadamer; I make them see how the art of understanding is immensely interesting, yet a complex process, how it begins to shake our belief in certainty, in objective/foundational knowledge, how it creates a world filled with the plurality of interpretations generating a possibility of relativism and indeterminacy. The debate goes on; students read, argue, write their assignments.

Yet, something happens. I keep asking myself: Is it only an academic question? Is it only about the methods of social sciences? The question disturbs me. And then slowly I begin to realize that this urge to understand, or this need to understand, or this aesthetic play of understanding is essentially about life—not just the preoccupation of professional social scientists. For some time I allow myself to remove these texts from my sight; I seek to unlearn; I wish to regain that simplicity, that curiosity, that intuitive flash through which I understand why a flower is looking at me and smiling, I understand the stories hidden inside the eyes of my daughter, I understand the act of my student when she comes with a book, and says 'Sir, I read parts of this book and I loved it; I felt like sharing this book with you.' I understand; indeed, I understand. Who bothers about theory? I understand; that's all. Is my understanding a 'right' understanding? At this moment, that is not my question. I feel I understand, and this understanding leads me to an act of deep communion. The flower talks to me; my daughter's eyes make me pray for her spiritual elevation; my student's act makes my hand touch her head with deep love and blessing. Life becomes oceanic.

My urge to understand does not end. How can it end? To live is to expand, to meet people, to come across historical characters, to experience literary narratives, artistic creations and symbols. Do I succeed? Do I always understand? I do not know. But the play goes on; it has its own beauty, mystery and thrill. I move. I come across a historical character like Mohandas Karamchand Gandhi. Through my historical imagination I see him in his prayer meetings; I hear his voice, his cross-religious dialogue. Do I understand? Or do I see it as just a fact, a hard archival fact, a soulless information? History, for me, is not a chronicle of facts and events; instead, history whispers, history sings, history touches, history acquires a soul. I seek to understand. I am not Gandhi; my upbringing is different from that of Gandhi. I live in a different time; I feel tempted to speak a language that is 'rational' and 'secular'. Does it then mean that I can never understand Gandhi? Does it then mean that, instead of understanding, I can only impose my categories on him? No, I don't do that. I become humble and alert. I familiarize myself with Gandhi's biography; I try to feel the turbulent history Gandhi was passing through; and then with the power of my imagination I enter his prayer meeting. I listen. I receive. I do not impose. And then possibly an act of communion begins to take place. I understand why, for him, man's inner world is important; why, for him, the purification of the soul leads to compassion; why, for him, religiosity is not a sectarian dogma, but an ethical quest that characterizes all great religious leaders, be it Krishna or Christ, the Prophet or Nanak. I understand why at that painful time of religious/communal divide, Gandhi's prayer meeting was like the much desired raindrop in a deserted land; I feel the healing touch.

Life moves... From history I come back to my everydayness. I meet people—friends, relatives, strangers. They seek to understand me. I try to understand them—not necessarily always consciously—their gestures, their experiences, their symbols, their narratives. I am in a super-speciality hospital. My student is struggling in the Intensive Care Unit; she is about to die. I see her husband. I see her daughter, their only child. She is not talking; there is immense silence, pain, depth in her being, in her eyes. Do I understand her? My lived experiences take me back to 2009. My wife was in yet another hospital—her last moments, her departure, and our only daughter's pain, silence and hidden tears. Everything becomes one. I understand—believe me, I understand—what my student's daughter is passing through.

But then, do I understand those things about which I have no lived experience? I am not a woman; I am not a Muslim. As an upper caste/ Hindu man I have never experienced what my student passes through every day. Yes, society looks at her 'Muslim' identity; she is subject to some sort of surveillance. She covers her head; and the security person at the metro station would invariably give her a suspicious look, search her belongings, and scrutinize her thoroughly, whereas others who look 'normal' would not pass through the similar experience. She is not 'normal'; she is a stereotype; a potential threat to the nation! She narrates her experiences, the story of her humiliation. Can I understand it? Even though I do not have a lived experience of it, I move, I expand; my empathy, my intuition make me somewhat nearer to her experience. I see it as a human possibility. I see it as the ultimate human strength that enables us to see beyond our limited horizons, and feel what happens elsewhere. In fact, it was she who once told me: 'Sir, see the amazing power of Rabindranath Tagore. It seems he has experienced all sorts of emotions; it appears he has lived the lives of every character he has created.' Yes, she is right. An artist carries that strength so deeply. Tagore understands the spiritual churning of Gora;

Premchand understands the agony of Dukhi, and Marx understands the pain of an alienated worker. Each of us is a potential artist. To understand, to feel, to relate, to touch, to expand is to cultivate the quality of an artist implicit in each of us. Understanding is indeed a process of artistic play.

Does understanding necessarily mean acceptance of one's act? Not really. I understand you—your historicity, your context, your psychic experience, your compulsion, your aspirations; but it does not necessarily mean that I accept what you do. Let me begin with an example. My destiny makes me engage with a builder who is expected to deliver me a small cottage in a beautiful Himalayan hamlet. I pay him, give him the instalments in advance with the hope that he will deliver the cottage in due time. However, things take a different turn. He breaks promises after promises; he invents excuses; he lies; and eventually, he refuses to accept my phone call; he does not reply to my mail. Yes, I grow angry; I feel cheated; I begin to feel that he is taking advantage of my 'softness'; he has taken me for granted; he is exploiting me. I feel like becoming hard, taking legal action. Yet, there are moments when, despite my anger, my definition of the builder as a liar, I ask myself: Why is it that he is behaving like this? I seek to understand him. And I keep imagining: possibly he does not take my call because he feels ashamed, because he does not have the courage to face me; or possibly he has suffered a severe financial loss which happens to businessmen quite frequently because of their never-ending greed, or he has invested the money collected from people like us somewhere else, and hence he is not in a position to complete the construction work and deliver the cottage. I begin to see him through his eyes. That does not mean that I give my consent to his act. But then, this very act of understanding, under these heavily hostile/ unpleasant circumstances, begins to teach me a couple of lessons. I do not know what happens to the builder; but something happens to me. I realize that I ought to have patience; I ought to have some control over my anger, and I ought to try once more to convey a message to him: 'Mr. Builder, you can discuss your difficulties freely. I am willing to give you some time and space before I decide to take legal action. But please don't hide, don't lie, don't give yet another excuse, don't run away. Trust your higher self. You can fulfil the promise, no matter how difficult your circumstances are.' And I also realize—through my own experience of being cheated—how important it is to keep the trust alive in life. My understanding of the builder does not lead me to accept his act; but this very urge to understand enriches me as a human being.

Life poses these challenges time and again. For example, I do not approve of terrorism; but

I seek to understand the situation of a terrorist. What is it that compels a young man (who too like many other young people must have fascination for love, beauty, sexuality, art and sports) to take up guns and bombs and play with death? I do not approve of the act of a rapist. But I seek to understand: What is it that makes him incapable of experiencing love as a gift of reciprocity, as a poetic rhythm, as tenderness, as a divine touch, as the union of bodies and souls producing enchanting *ragas*? Why is it that for him a woman is only flesh, an object of gross pleasure? Why is it that someone's pain and humiliation fulfils his masculinist ego? As I begin to understand—even though I condemn his act, something happens. I realize that the aggression of a rapist or the nihilism of a terrorist is not something that exists out there; it might lie within me, and my psychic/spiritual evolution lies in my ability to overcome this negativity, and realize my oceanic love. In other words, understanding others is always self-understanding.

It is this act of understanding that makes me sensitive to the possibility of plurality of interpretations. How often it happens. I watch a film, read a poem, listen to a song; I find my own meaning; my interpretation is something that is very intimate to me. But then, as I share my interpretation with my friends and colleagues, I see that their interpretations do not necessarily always converge with mine. While

I do not undervalue my own interpretation, I become aware that it is not proper to absolutize my position. I can engage; I can debate; I can learn; I can unlearn. In other words, my interpretation is not something static; it evolves and grows; it is a continual process. True, in this ongoing play of interpretation there is no absolute truth, no objective/foundational knowledge; but then, what emerges is no less beautiful; it is a journey: an artist with colours shaping, changing, adding, deleting, altering the landscape she is painting. It is not perfect mathematics; but it is nearer to life because life too evolves, grows, waits for surprises. Another thing happens. I interpret a poem, a painting, a religious text; but my interpretation need not resemble what the poet or the painter or the author intended. Does it then mean that my interpretation has no validity? It is not like that. The text transcends its author; it is now subject to multiple readings and interpretations. And who knows that at times the author herself might get enlightened by the reader's interpretation? Not solely that. The fact that I can have my engagement with, say, a William Blake, or a Rabindranath Tagore, or the *Bhagavad Gita* frees me from the tyranny of 'experts'. My Tagore is my Tagore; even though I am always willing to grow, I do not wish to be dictated by a literary critic, a Tagore expert, or a professor of literature. I do not bother about the 'correct' interpretation. I find my Tagore at the moment of my pain, my deep longing, my love, my ecstasy, my solitude, my darkness. I value it. I do not know whether I am legitimating relativism. But I wish to believe that I too exist.

There is always a possibility of what we regard as 'misunderstanding'. Everyone seeks to be understood and listened to. However, we often realize that we are not understood; instead, we are judged, evaluated and condemned. I am seeing the mountain peaks; I wish to be alone; I wish to be in a deep communion with these peaks. But my friend grows angry. He complains: 'You are avoiding me. You are showing an attitude.' I feel bad. Why is it that my friend is not understanding me? I am not self-centred; I am not avoiding him; instead, being alone for some time is my deep existential need, my prayer; it arouses all that is beautiful in me that, I believe, would also illumine my friend. But my friend, I am afraid, does not understand me. I am unhappy, sad. For me, it is misunderstanding. We live with this rapture, this gap, this broken communication. Do we understand ourselves? How often we realize that we are ignorant of our own actions. The fact is that this actor/performer/doer in me is not always a concretely defined, stable, coherent agent. There are many layers inside us—partly known , partly unknown. We surprise ourselves: 'Oh, it is me. Even I could do that.' That surprise or that mystery or that inexplicable occurrence makes life a poem, not a mathematical theorem.

Yes, my students, I know you are reading. You are reading how Durkheim interpreted the totemic symbol, how Weber interpreted the Calvinist doctrine of predestination, how Clifford Geertz interpreted the Balinese cock fight. You are reading about Dilthey's 'transposition', Gadamer's 'fusion of horizons'. But then, never forget that it is not a technique, not just a methodological skill; understanding is life itself. Live life. Feel life. Touch life. Wonder. Love. Fail. Rise. Make the metamorphosis possible—from technique to poetry, from information to illumination. Your life, believe it, is the embodiment of hermeneutics.

11

Yes, my eyes look at the treasure of printed words stored in *The German Ideology, Economic and Philosophic Manuscripts of 1844* and *Capital*; my brain cognizes, analyzes and dissects this huge bundle of information; my pen creates essays that need the certification of scholarship. But I do something more. With love and pain, with laughter and humour, with dream and aspiration, with sunrise and sunset I engage with Marx. I de-Brahminize Marx.

We—university scholars—are known for our rigorous critique of Brahminism: the way it hierarchizes human faculties and society, its story of degradation of manual labour, its central emphasis on intellectual cognition and abstract knowledge rather than love and action, the way it sanctifies select texts as the ultimate source of knowledge and wisdom, and sees that these texts remain confined to the select elite, and do not get disseminated among people. This critique is immensely significant and powerful. However, I ask myself: What are we doing? Isn't it that we too are practising yet another form of Brahminism—possibly secular, but nevertheless equally hierarchical, textual, esoteric and cognitive? I cannot deny this anxiety; every moment it confronts me. I wish to face it, and maybe this acknowledgement leads to a new awakening and practice.

To begin with, let me reflect on the way we

have grown up in a modern university, the way it has socialized us, trained us and shaped our consciousness. We strive for knowledge, for some sort of abstract theorization to make sense of the world. Disembodied intellect, pure cognition, discursive reasoning, abstract thought—these are some of our distinctive markers. We think. We theorize. We philosophize. We debunk. We critique. But seldom do we engage ourselves in practice; it is like erecting a wall: the abstraction/purity of thought should by no means be contaminated by practice, by everydayness, by hands and legs. We have already hierarchized our faculties, and thereby people around us. We feel we are superior because we think and theorize; and others are just 'workers' engaged in mundane activities of the world! Not solely that. We also give excessive importance to select texts as the ultimate source of knowledge and wisdom. To be a university scholar is to sanctify these texts, legitimate one's being, one's every word, one's gesture through these texts. So *Manusmriti*, *Upanishads* and the *Bhagavad Gita* are now replaced by another set of texts: say, Emile Durkheim's *The Rules of Sociological Method*, Karl Marx's *Capital* or Michel Foucault's *The Archaeology of Knowledge*. But the attitude remains the same. To know the world is to know these texts; and those who can't master these texts are, therefore, not truly knowledgeable; their sense of the world is bound to be inferior!

Moreover, it is to be seen that these texts remain 'sacred'; no dilution should be allowed; no contamination should be permitted to 'pollute' their purity; and hence their popularization, it is thought, is dangerous. Sanskrit is replaced by contemporary academic vocabulary—its heavily loaded and mystified language. Not to speak this language is to miss the rigour of academics!

We continue to engage in this practice. Yet, how paradoxical it is that we call ourselves anti-Brahminical! The fact is that we too are Brahmins—modern/secular/academic Brahmins. I have a sense of discomfort. And out of this discomfort emerges my quest, my search for a new practice of learning. Yes, I am aware that I can be misunderstood. It is possible to allege that I am devaluing these texts; I am bringing the emotive elements of love, poetry and action in a domain that is supposed to be absolutely textual, intellectual and theoretical. And hence I am popularizing or diluting the seriousness of these texts. But as a teacher I need to make my position clear. I am by no means against these texts. I read the *Upanishads*; I read Marx and Durkheim. I read the *Bhagavad Gita*; I read Foucault and Habermas. I read theology, Sufi tales and Puranic narratives; I read about poststructuralism, postcolonialism and postmodernism. But then, no matter how important these texts are, my experience of the world through the movement of my hands and legs, my feeling, my love, my practice are no less important. In fact, it is the richness of my being that helps me to have a conversation with these texts and disseminate in a language that is mine, that is deep and authentic—not borrowed, ornamental and esoteric. And I keep telling my students: read, read these texts, but not even for a second think that your labour, your pain, your love and your historicity are unimportant. Each of us must rediscover, feel, interpret and engage with these texts in unique ways.

Friends, that is why, I do not feel very easy with all these 'orientation programmes' that seek to train, condition and dictate: How to read Marx, how to read Foucault, how to write a thesis, how to write a book review, how to write a research paper. This 'how' business, I am afraid, is Brahminical; it imposes the expertized opinion (or the opinion of the academic priest craft) on you; it devalues you. As a result, it leads to ruthless homogenization. Like a trained dog, everyone seeks to repeat the same jargon, quote the same text, follow the same style. It looks like a manufactured product; it loses its fragrance, its soul. It is ritualistic. In our seminars and conferences we keep reciting the *mantras* of these rituals.

Yes, friends, let me tell you my own story. I read Karl Marx not just through my 'intellect' and 'cognitive power'; I read Marx not just in a sanitized library, in a seminar hall amidst experts. I read Marx as I visit a mall—the magical/surgical space that global capitalism has created, see the spectacular display of goods and commodities and look at their mythologies; I read Marx as I see the power of credit card—its instantaneity that stimulates the urge to consume, possess and define one's essence in terms of the vicarious pleasure of consumption. I find my Marx. I understand 'commodity fetishism'; I understand 'alienation'; I understand the 'power of money'. In fact, I read Marx through love, through pain, through anger, through dream. Yes, my eyes look at the treasure of printed words stored in *The German Ideology*, *Economic and Philosophic Manuscripts of 1844* and *Capital*; my brain cognizes, analyzes and dissects this huge bundle of information; my pen creates essays that need the certification of scholarship. But I do something more. With love and pain, with laughter and humour, with dream and aspiration, with sunrise and sunset I engage with Marx. I de-Brahminize Marx.

And dear students, I want you to find your Marx, your Foucault, your Simone de Beauvoir in your own way—through your unique journey, through your intellect, experience, hope, disillusionment, love and pain. I don't think that because of this these texts get trivialized. Instead, the texts acquire a soul, and become intimate and experiential. And only then is it possible to communicate authentically, to free these texts from the monopoly of modern/secular Brahmins—our university scholars. You need not cause an obstacle by speaking a mystified/ difficult/esoteric language. We know how through simple, yet revealing tales Ramakrishna could communicate what a 'knowledgeable' scholar (a Brahmin pandit who has just read the scriptures, but failed to experience the light of truth) could not. Kabir could narrate what the institutionalized priest craft could not. And Tagore could write extraordinarily illuminating essays without footnotes and references. This is possible only when love, experience and practice become as important as intellectual cognition. Our academic culture needs its Ramakrishna, Kabir and Tagore to de-scriptualize and de-Brahminize it.

It is sad that we remain indifferent to such a possibility. And its consequences are devastating. For example, we theorize: Can the subaltern speak? But for most of us, it is so difficult to initiate a simple/ non-pretentious conversation with a peasant, a rickshaw puller, a coolie, a vendor, a barber; we fail to realize that they too are people like us; they too love, feel, become angry; they too have envy, jealousy and good will. We theorize labour. But we do not wish to make our hands dirty. So if sweepers do not come, our department rooms and toilets are likely to remain dirty; if peons are on leave no file would move from one corner to another. To work with hands and legs is the experience of a 'worker', and hence unimportant in the domain of knowledge. To feel, to love, to relate is the experience of a poet, and hence unimportant in the making of theories. Friends, that is our secular Brahminism. We ought to overcome it. Believe it, knowledge, love and action, or for that matter, theory and poetry are inseparable. When they are merged, a new being is born—not hierarchical, but essentially integral, communicative and wholistic. And then you read Marx, and you love people, feel their pain, and seek to merge with them. You read feminist theories. And you converse with thousands of ordinary women; with your love and practice you begin to heal them. You read Talcott Parsons; but you do not hesitate to have a cup of tea with the security guard in your university, listen to his narratives, and examine whether the Parsonian grand 'social system' can really accommodate the agony of the security guard. You read Gandhi, and you feel encouraged to experiment with your body, and feel the power of fasting. You no longer remain just a 'knowledgeable' scholar burdened with books, with information, with inflated egos getting dirty, cold and cynical; instead, you are reborn. You become a lover, a bhakta, a worker. Your knowledge acquires its soul; science becomes poetry; information becomes awakening; theory becomes experiential; texts become life's blood. You begin to radiate the waves of love, humility and positivity. That is your religiosity. And true religiosity is always anti-Brahminical. Dear students, if there is any gift I wish to give you, it is precisely this religiosity.

12

The act of teaching/writing is inherently creative; it needs its own rhythm, own moments of intense engagement, contemplation and silence; and when you deny it, treat it as an instant product, a measurable commodity, ideas are bound to suffer.

One thing I have always loved to imagine is that a teacher's life is peaceful. He/she is not in a hurry; reading great books, arousing the imagination of young minds, transforming the classroom into a sacred space, and radiating the waves of positive energy—a teacher, I have imagined, lives meaningfully and gracefully. No competitiveness. No restlessness. Only calmness and immense energy in the finest pedagogic act of sharing and disseminating ideas, visions, theories and practices. I know that I fail. Yet, the ideal has not ceased to exist; from the valley I see the peak; I see its beauty; I seek my inspiration from it.

However, as I see the world, interact with my colleagues, meet new/young teachers, I feel that something is changing. There is restlessness; competitiveness is everywhere; there seems to be no peace inside; there is a constant urge to produce, to perform, to demonstrate, to measure and quantify one's achievements. How many books have you published? How many research papers have you written? How many conferences/seminars have you attended? How many projects have you undertaken? Friends, believe me, it is war... constant war, a reckless race. It seems to be an enactment of a play leading to the survival of the fittest. Why is it happening? An immediate reason is that universities are measuring the qualities of an academic in terms of an absurd scale. Beneath it, it seems, there is a belief that everything has to be measured, nothing exists beyond the scope of quantification, and hence what is immeasurable is immaterial or insignificant. Suppose you are a good thinker. You read great books. You reflect. You work hard to invite your students to the world of ideas. And you love its beauty, its silence, its rhythm. You love this experience because it is immeasurable. But then in the age of numbers you are led to believe that you are nothing if a statistician can't measure the number of seminars you have attended, the number of sessions you have chaired, or the numbers of books/papers you have published. Your contemplation is your fault; your willingness to avoid this fast track, this rat race is your stupidity—your inability to write and prove! Your promotion, your position in the academic hierarchy—everything depends on your 'score': the mythical number of success.

It is, therefore, not surprising if my young colleagues ask me: 'Sir, tell me the number of articles we have to write or the conferences we have to attend or the certificates we have to demonstrate as the proof of our participation in international seminars in order to be eligible for Associate Professorship.' Writing desperately, producing papers in all sorts of conferences, trying to attend any conference in Europe/America, paying a huge registration fee for attending such conferences, or paying money to the publication house for bringing out a book which has to be shown before the selection committee—all these practices which acquire yet another meaning in an essentially corrupt society like ours make the mind perplexed, restless and aggressive. See its damaging consequences. No great work is done when you are in a hurry. Moreover, the act of teaching/writing is inherently creative; it needs its own rhythm, own moments of intense engagement, contemplation and silence; and when you deny it, treat it as an instant product, a measurable commodity, ideas are bound to suffer. True, books are written, edited volumes are published, seminars—national and international—are held, and new journals keep coming. Yet, beneath this 'academic activism' there is a great loss. There is no spontaneity; there is no joy in reading and writing; there is no peace; there is no excitement for coming to the class, meeting young minds, discussing a book, an idea, a theory, and celebrating it without any anxiety whether it can be measured, or whether it can lead to a paper, a deliberation in an international conference. Our finest moments of joy are non-utilitarian; there is no profit, no loss. But it is sad that today everything ought to have its utility. It generates immense anxiety. I can, therefore, understand what my student who is now teaching in a newly formed central university means when he says: 'Sir, I love teaching. I love my students. I read a great deal for every lecture I deliver. But I haven't published much. What will happen to me, Sir?'

I meet them. They come. They articulate their anguish. I do not know whether I can advise them. Who am I to do that? However, I feel deep pain. At times, I tell them: 'Live peacefully. Don't be in a race. Keep growing as a teacher. Read. Reflect. Celebrate. Write when there is a call, when there is something you wish to communicate with all intensity and conviction. Don't disturb your own rhythm. Surrender yourself before this rhythm. Everything else will be taken care of.' It is difficult, I know. The 'system' wants them to become restless and competitive; their 'career' depends on their 'measurable' performance. And at a time when because of the general decline in the quality of higher education and corrupt university administration there is no trust, the mechanism of 'quality control' assumes this absurd dimension. But the tragedy is that while it promotes the 'smart' players to prove their worth through all sorts of academic products (when numbers alone matter, who is bothering about quality?), it demoralizes those who are honest and authentic, who love to work—and work creatively—in their own rhythm. That is the ultimate irony.

I begin to look at myself. Am I free from this pressure, this tyranny of numbers? Possibly my location is different. With grey hair and years of experience, I can say 'no' to many of these practices; but, I admit, it is not so easy for young minds who have just joined the vocation. Yet, it should not be forgotten that I too experienced immense pressure. However, my faith, my ideal, my priorities, my inner voice helped me. It was not easy. Even now I keep working on myself in order to retain my sanity. Yes, I have written books; but these books have emerged out of pain, dream, longing; my books serve my existential need; I do not know whether they fit into what the academic bureaucracy regards as 'useful' production. I have attended seminars and conferences; but I keep no record because, more often than not, I laugh at this play of words. I play and then I forget. I do not carry it. My bio-data is empty. They ask me: 'Why don't you go abroad?' I teach in a leading university; almost all my colleagues go abroad quite frequently; I am expected to follow the same practice; that is the pressure. Yes, I wish to see the world as a wanderer; I wish to see its people, its cultures, its rivers, forests, mountains, seas, deserts, islands. But I have now acquired the courage to question the fetish—'There is no other way. You have to go abroad if you are a good academic.' To my mind, this is slavery—a symptom of our colonized consciousness, our failure to believe in our own worth, our inability to differ and create our own reference point. I know that it is not easy to live like this, particularly when everyone around you—your students, your colleagues, your friends, your relatives—begin to see you as somewhat 'abnormal'. Yet, I seek to live on my own terms, and I am happy about it.

'Why don't you have your books published by an international publication house?'—the question confronts me; colleagues ask me, students ask me. I remain silent. Or, I laugh. I feel that even people like us can't avoid the temptation of 'brand' names. It is a 'brand' publication house that defines you, the substance of your book. What you write is not so important; what acquires importance is the name of the publication house. What else is it other than academic consumerism? Your 'prestige' rests on the 'brands' you consume. I differ. I believe that if your book is meaningful, if your writings emanate from the authenticity of your being, even an 'unknown' publishing house—provided it is sincere in its endeavour, and does its work with a reasonable degree of technical/professional perfection—would take your book to the reader; it would be read, sold, reviewed and discussed. You need to believe in yourself. Why is it—I ask myself—that we become excessively 'brand conscious'? Why is it that we lose faith in ourselves? Why is it that we are perpetually restless for acquiring a 'name'—a foreign university, an international publication and so on and so forth? I fight my battle. I choose to live without these ornaments. I have made a choice. It makes me light. It frees me from the trap of never-ending insecurity and restlessness.

I can imagine what the new generation is facing. I can imagine their anxiety, restlessness and ambivalence. I do not know whether I have an answer to their questions. But then, I can pray; I can express my good will; I can share my stories, my failure, my efforts. As I see myself in a world characterized by reckless competition and restlessness, I feel that I am still fortunate. I am in a vocation that continues to give me calmness, peace and creative freedom. I do not wish to lose it. Why should I lose it in the name of 'success'? What I receive is immeasurable. Why should I always think in terms of concrete/tangible numbers? I recall a very memorable semester. I taught a course on sociological theory. For six months I lived with theory; I breathed theory; and I sought to communicate it in a manner so that my young students overcome 'theory phobia', and experience the rhythmic connectedness between theory and lived reality. Every moment, for me, was a celebration; I loved to play with pedagogy and theory. Yes, I could have written a research paper in a trendy journal on the modes of teaching theory. Or, I could have attended a couple of conferences, and delivered lectures on theory and pedagogy. But I did nothing of the sort. No publication, no conference; yet, so much learning and inner development! Those who love numbers would conclude that in that semester I did nothing. But those who have not yet lost their sanity would realize that what I gained was immeasurable. Yes, I evolved as a teacher; and my understanding of sociological theories acquired a new meaning.

Dear students, in your eyes I wish to see that calmness, that peace, that depth which I have always idealized. I trust you. And hence I acquire the courage to tell you a story, a fairy tale. It is midnight. I have studied. I have listened to music. I have thought, reflected and prepared my lecture. And I have just come to my balcony. I look at the sky. I see a star. I see you. I pray. And I feel immensely happy that tomorrow my lecture would be a gift to you: a gift of positive energy and good will. I enter the domain of the immeasurable. I realize the poetry of my vocation. Al that is 'official' and measurable—number of publications, conferences, edited volumes, projects, positions in academic bodies and committees—seems utterly superficial. What remains is just a longing: a teacher walking with his students, and watching the eternity of sunrise and sunset.

13

Life becomes my book; a living engagement with nature becomes my inspiration; and my notion of being an academic undergoes a dramatic transformation. I do not conquer. I relate. I am not just a specialist. I become a lover of life. My pen becomes my brush, my intellect becomes my colour, my awareness becomes my canvas, my teaching/learning/ writing becomes my painting.

I have borrowed a book from one of my students. He loved the book, and wanted me to read it. It is a wonderful book entitled *Being a University* written by Ronald Barnett. Here is a book that reveals the subtle consciousness of an educationist: his sharp reflections on the state of higher education—the way universities all over the world are fast becoming instrumental, losing mysteries, wonder and deep philosophy, and the way in the name of 'useful' research and market demands universities are becoming 'entrepreneurial'. True, there is rapid progress in knowledge-production, there is 'efficiency', and there is reckless competition for 'world ranking'. Yet, there is something fundamental we seem to be missing: our quest for a meaning, for love, for care, for connectedness with the world. And it is in this context that the author constructs his utopia: his plea that it is the right time to strive for an 'ecological' university—a university that seeks to restore all that we have lost, a university that cares, a university that makes us sensitive, humane and deeply ethical/ spiritual.

The book moves me. However, one question confronts me: Why is it that my young student loves the book? And why is it that he intends to write his PhD thesis on an issue having a similar concern: how the ethos of marketization in the neo-liberal era is altering the character of our universities—the way we define ourselves as teachers and researchers, or the way we legitimate certain branches of knowledge and devalue others? Possibly my student has refused to become 'pragmatic'; he retains his dream. Possibly he feels that it is high time we began to restore humanness and moral sensibilities in our universities, and appreciate a domain which exists beyond what the market captures. Possibly he feels that only then can we move towards love, care, mystery, connectedness and what the author of the book regards as an 'ecological university'.

My student's dream fascinates me. And it arouses hope in human possibilities. He comes from a modest background; society must be telling him that he needs money, he needs a job or what these days we regard as a 'placement with a lucrative package', he needs to survive; he too would be asked to marry, to settle down, to buy a car, an apartment, to take his family to Dubai or Singapore for a vacation. He is not naïve. He knows the world. He knows that ideals do not fill one's stomach. He knows that Tagore or Barnett would not provide him with a job. He knows that a course in information technology or management studies is a more 'guaranteed' road to 'success' in life. He knows that for many a technical job assures survival, and it is more important than a philosophic reflection. He knows that it is absurd to imagine everyone pursuing liberal/humanistic education. He knows that it is not easy to overcome the 'constraint' of the Durkheimian 'social fact'. He knows that the emerging private universities—with their 'market-friendly' courses—are becoming the order of the day because the aspiring middle class wants 'success' and quick results, and sees no other alternative to neo-liberalism and its 'pragmatic' discourses on education. He knows; he is intelligent enough to know all these hard facts of existence. Yet, he dreams; he seems to have a mission; he does not wish to write just another 'value- neutral' PhD thesis; he seeks to inject his mission, dreams and utopias into it.

And I am moved. I realize once again that it is wonderful to be a teacher. Your students—not necessarily always your colleagues—illumine your being. It is sad that many of us, despite our secure jobs and academic locations, are not in a position to speak the language that my student wishes to utter. Possibly we are becoming too pragmatic. Knowledge, we tend to think, ought to be produced as a 'product'. Our research, our publications, our projects must sell. At a time when because of this survival anxiety in the domain of market-driven academics we are depriving ourselves of poetry, mystery and wonder, my student comes as a refreshing departure. And possibly an association with students like him makes me move, experiment, and do things which, I am afraid, my 'pragmatic' colleagues may not always appreciate. How often I tell my students that a university is a place for celebration. Learning is celebration; teaching is celebration; studentship is celebration. A university need not be seen as just a 'serious' place without laughter, without music, without colours, without festivals, without dreams. A university need not be seen as just a place that trains one for a lucrative/professional job. A university, I keep telling my students, is a celebration of life. As I see my university, I feel that it is also about its trees that whisper in my ears, its flowers that make me see the beauty of illumination in silence, its curved paths that wait for a mystical embrace with the full moon night, its birds that give a melancholic meaning to the colourful sky at the time of sunset. I learn from my long walk, from those tiny butterflies which soften my intellect, from the old woman who touches my head and blesses me, from an old man and his wife who come every morning from a neighbouring locality to feed the animals. Life becomes my book; a living engagement with nature becomes my inspiration; and my notion of being an academic undergoes a dramatic transformation. I do not conquer. I relate. I am not just a specialist. I become a lover of life. My pen becomes my brush, my intellect becomes my colour, my awareness becomes my canvas, my teaching/learning/writing becomes my painting.

I, therefore, dare. I ask my students to celebrate the entire process of learning. I ask them to travel, to see places, to connect with people (irrespective of 'field work'), to communicate, to see films, to listen to good music, to read great biographies, to draw beautiful sketches, to create colourful wall magazines, to decorate the classroom with flowers, to take a camera, to move around the campus, explore the natural beauty of the campus and make a documentary film. I ask them to arouse their potential, to realize that they are not just 'resources' for the nation's economic growth; they are essentially poets, singers, dancers, writers, lovers of nature. I ask them to believe that they are creating a sane culture: a culture that defies the colonization of what the market-driven culture industry dictates—loud music, noise, meaningless speed, inner void amidst outer glamour. I do not know whether I succeed. Possibly not. Yet, the book that my student loves, and gives me to read makes me believe that I ought to try. To fail is not your tragedy; to give up is your ultimate fall. So I tell them; 'Don't mind even if it does not count in your bio-data. Don't mind even if it is not useful for 'world ranking'. Don't mind even if some of your professors refuse to acknowledge or appreciate your effort. But realize that you are finding yourself. You are giving life, mystery, colour, beauty, connectedness to a university. You are trying to make it ecological'.

Life goes on. It surprises. I find a letter from one of my students:

> *I hardly dream during daytime sleep.... I don't, but this afternoon I did. And surprisingly I also remember it. I saw the 'sea'. Yes, I have never visited one and this afternoon I dreamt of it. It was so blue and slightly greenish.... I could even see colours in my dream, there is a rose occurrence. I would often imagine myself standing on top of a cliff, and I am wearing white loose clothes, the wind brushing against me and the sound of the waves....Oh so beautiful....Of course that is something which has not happened yet, but I imagine and this time in my dream I saw it and I saw myself jumping from the cliff to the water....I didn't seem to be scared of the sea....I was swimming and swimming and then suddenly I was back on top of the cliff...*

Your dream, my dear, is a beautiful gift. What else does a teacher want? You keep me alive. My university touches the sea, the cliff...

14

A teacher carries a lamp: a small, beautiful lamp. Its light softens one's heart, illumines one's being; it is not gorgeous because all that is gorgeous is noisy and pretentious; what is beautiful is simple and unassuming. And hence a classroom where a teacher is engaged in a deep communion with his students is the abode of God.

I think. I read. I contemplate. I come to my class, deliver a lecture, engage with my students, seek to arouse their imagination, and open the windows of their minds. What else can a teacher do? Here is a teacher: simple and unknown. Here is a teacher engaged in an art that is neither big nor spectacular. No 24*7 live coverage; something non-glamorous is happening in silence—a teacher interacts with a group of students. Meanwhile, the world—the 'real' world—is showing its theatrical play, displaying its packages, its mythologies. There are leaders, and they are promising 'development'; television channels are projecting them as ad products; people are voting, getting carried away by the 'wave'; the mantra of success is proclaimed loudly. And the leader, it is declared, has finally arrived; he is strong and assertive; he means business; he delivers! At times, I find myself completely irrelevant and insignificant in a noisy environment of this kind. I find myself as a stranger in this landscape. What then do I do as a teacher? Is my art relevant any more? Does it make any difference? These are difficult questions; I keep thinking, reflecting, contemplating.

Television doesn't fascinate me much. Yet, at times, with a remote in my hand I pass through innumerable channels. I see the glorification of the trivia. Television news readers—they are smart, English-speaking, good looking; yet, beneath these externalities (glamour, instant stardom, narcissism) there is absolute superficiality. Seldom does one see a serious engagement with an issue, a sincere effort to understand what we are passing through—acute poverty amidst vulgar affluence; express highways, flyovers, malls, multiplexes amidst lack of basic facilities for a large section of people; exclusive international schools and private universities amidst poor quality government schools; growth rate and IPL amidst hunger and malnutrition. Yes, development becomes a myth. It is an external decorum seeking to hide the dark interior. Development becomes a playground for corporate capitalism, for real estate mafias, for the aspiring consumptionist middle class. Its hardness manifests itself in the mantra of unlimited desire, competitiveness and recklessness. Television anchors celebrate it;

they invite their chosen 'experts'; they generate noise. And we keep consuming it. See the cultural landscape. Television serials are loud; music is loud; ads are loud. There is only one message—consume everything, consume food, consume cars, consume bullet trains, consume bank loans, consume property, consume happiness, consume nirvana and salvation, consume mountains, deserts, oceans, consume sex, consume pleasure. This principle of consumption is inherently aggressive and intolerant. It abhors softness, simplicity, poetry and depth. Television news, everyday political discourses, soap operas, loud music, express highways, speedy cars and drunk driving, gated communities, multiplexes, malls—all are deeply related and connected.

And, as the heart of a teacher whispers, everything is related to education—the kind of education that is seen as 'useful', 'productive' and 'success-oriented'. Imagine the fate of a schoolchild. As she completes Standard VIII, her 'coaching' begins; innumerable education shops exist to train her, discipline her, prepare her for quick, smart, correct answers that medical/engineering/management institutions would demand in their entrance tests. This drilling, or this ruthless exercise deprives the experience of education of any feeling of joy, contemplation, plurality of ideas, deeper domains of life. The fetish of objective/multiple choice tests kills the spirit of creative learning.

The mind becomes 'efficient', yet dull. It 'solves' problems; but it cannot enter the domain of creativity, imagination and reflexivity. It is violent, ruthless, one-dimensional. This sort of education is devoid of art. There is no music, no prayer, no time to see the sky. Einstein's creativity doesn't exist in such a world; Tagore is a waste of time; Whitman is irrelevant. Creative articulations are not needed; ambiguities are discouraged; contemplative moments for inner growth are prohibited. What matters is the cultivation of 'objective reasoning' that identifies *one and only one* 'correct' answer—quickly, efficiently, smartly. And see the basic driving force beneath this sort of education. It is 'success'—success at any cost; and success is a measurable commodity—it is your salary package, your dowry rate. It begins with schools; it gains its peak in technical institutions; and it culminates into the creation of a 'product': an engineering/management graduate who knows only 'success', who earns, who seeks to earn more, who loathes whatever does not fit into his restricted vision of the world, who is finished from inside.

No wonder, there is no critical thought. You can be violent. You can be instrumental in the mass annihilation of people. You can spread poison for your political victory. You can be restless, totalitarian. But everything is forgotten. Because you promise development! That is the only correct answer; everything else is an ideological fluctuation! Likewise, our 'brightest' young minds can forget everything: poetry, wonder, music, life's mystery so long as a 'placement with an attractive package' is assured. And the aspiring middle class can forget everything—communal violence, naked injustice, poverty, malnutrition, so long as they can drive their cars on smooth express highways, visit malls and multiplexes, find 24-hour water and electricity supply in their fortified housing societies. Authoritarianism comes out of this constant interplay of militant nationalist discourse, aggression of development, bombardment of culture industry, and above all, a system of education that has lost its poetry and metaphysics. And the irony of our times is that democracy legitimates it, people's choices make it sacrosanct, education experts add to its use value, and the media-market alliance causes some sort of *maya* which becomes exceedingly difficult to escape.

Who am I as a teacher in such an environment? It appears that I am nothing; I am irrelevant. I tend to fall down; I begin to crumble. Yet, there is something that keeps me alive. I hear the voice of the ancient sage: *avidya* is darkness; it causes *maya*, arrogance, pride, violence; it is *vidya*—an awakening of the spirit that takes us from the unreal to the real. I acquire the courage to realize—and realize once again—that truth is not propaganda, music is not noise, development is not aggression, meaningful living is not narcissism, and education is not technical efficiency. I realize that the task of a teacher is to continue this search, this urge to speak of light, even if the mob outside is intoxicated and hypnotized. I become aware of the *swadharma* of a teacher. A teacher carries a lamp: a small, beautiful lamp; its light softens one's heart, illumines one's being; it is not gorgeous because all that is gorgeous is noisy and pretentious; what is beautiful is simple and unassuming. And hence a classroom where a teacher is engaged in a deep communion with his students is the abode of God. It generates the waves of love, reciprocity, plurality, empathy, sensitivity and understanding. It is dialogic. It defies authoritarianism. It is musical. It is poetic. It is spiritual. True, the epic battle does not end; the forces of untruth strike with all sorts of spectacular weapons: media-induced hallucinations and narratives of mega professors with huge fund-generating projects in a networking society. Will the truth survive? You cannot remain a teacher unless you keep carrying the lamp of truth, no matter how hostile the circumstances are.

As I pass through this emotional churning, a student arrives. The violence, the propaganda machinery and the loudness all around seem to have disturbed her. 'Sir, what are you thinking? What is going to happen?' I see a great quest in her eyes. I take her to my garden, and give her a lemon, a mango: two wonderful gifts from nature. I touch her head, bless her: 'My dear, truth is this simple act, this act of prayer and offering. So long as we have the sensitivity to celebrate this beauty, there is hope. Take the lamp from me. I wish to follow you.'

15

Education, it ought to be realized, is about the cultivation of a mind that sees the infinite in the finite. Tagore was born in Bengal. You are a Maharashtrian; yet, you can engage with Tagore because deep poetry transcends barriers. I am not a Dalit. Yet, I can study Ambedkar because a libertarian urge is also my urge. Education is about overcoming these constraining identity markers and associated barriers; it is a quest for the universal.

How often I realize that teaching a course is not just about completing the syllabus, and evaluating the assignments of students. With every course you teach you are reborn. You grow—intellectually, ethically and spiritually. It is this perpetual evolution towards a higher centre of being that transforms one's pedagogy into an aesthetic play. Difficulties come, obstacles confront you, and as a teacher you realize that with these difficulties, resistances and challenges you grow. Possibly, as every seeker feels, difficulties become your blessings. I have taught many courses. However, one course that I have found most difficult and challenging to pursue is called *Modern Indian Social Thought*. Emotive outbursts and passions, heated argumentations, conflicting perspectives, ideology and rhetoric, stereotypes and branding: every moment generates turmoil and restlessness. Yet, I need to remain calm, and encourage my students to sharpen the art of listening. I admit that it is not easy; the process is emotionally intense and excessively challenging. But I wish to accept this challenge with absolute humility.

Why is it that this course causes so much passion? One important reason, I believe, is that it is deeply intimate; it is about our own history, our politico-social biographies, our destinies. As I feel, it is possible for a student to reduce Giddens, Habermas and Foucault into an academic puzzle, a fascinating item for cultural capital. True, these thinkers are immensely appealing; but then, their distance from our everydayness reduces the possibility of an extreme form of emotional reaction. However, things acquire a different character when one begins to speak of Vivekananda, Ambedkar and Gandhi. Social identities, political ideologies, religious beliefs, historical memories, everyday gossip, cultural stereotypes: everything emerges as a stumbling block. As a result, one tends to miss the calmness and endurance to go deeper; instead, one hates, one worships, one shouts, one stops others. So for some, Gandhi was simply a Hindu/Gujarati *bania* who was against the interests of the marginalized castes and the working class. For some, Ambedkar was God; there is nothing that can be said to be problematic about him. For some, Indian philosophy is heavily Brahminical, and hence to refer to it in the class is a waste of time and energy. And for some, the course acquires a meaning only when you speak of the Marxian contribution to the making of Indian social thought. See the paradox. When you do a course in Social Theories, you have no problem, you are willing to submit; even if you are a committed Marxist you cannot demand: ' I will study only Karl Marx. I will not study Emile Durkheim or Talcott Parsons.' But the moment something about India is taught, there is impatience, there is always some sort of an identity/stereotype attached to a thinker: 'Oh, Sir speaks of Tagore in the class because he is a Bengali; or, Oh, Sir has delivered three lectures on Jotiba Phule, but only one lecture on Narayana Guru; see his biases, he neglects the South!'

Another difficulty emanates from a largely left-centric ideological milieu prevalent in the campus. As it becomes reductionist and deterministic, one tends to write slogans, and reduce a serious philosophic debate into a mere rhetoric, a stereotype. Hence if you refer to Swami Vivekananda and Vedanta, it is quite likely that you are suspected as a 'rightist'. ' Oh, Sir is quoting the Upanishads in the class. See the hidden curriculum—a Brahminical conspiracy!' We lose patience; we refuse to go deeper; the easy task of labelling comforts us; we miss the subtle beauty of a thinker. Our strong political likes and dislikes disturb the rhythm of a meaningful conversation.

Vivekananda—a Hindu nationalist; Sri Aurobindo—a mere idealist; Tagore—a bhadralok romantic; and a teacher asking his students to study them as seriously as they study Pierre Bourdieu and Jurgen Habermas is certainly deviating from what a progressive university ought to do!

I am growing up with these challenges. There are moments when I too have become excited, lost my temper. I have felt: 'Why am I taking this trouble? It is easy to teach theory, it is safe to speak of Michel Foucault and Levi Strauss. Why am I coming to the class with Gandhi's Experiments, Tagore's religiosity, Sri Aurobindo's path-breaking Uttarpara speech? Why am I allowing myself to be perceived as a philosopher, not an empirical sociologist; a dreamer filled with poetry, not a progressive rationalist with a baggage of political correctness?'Yes, there are moments of doubt. Yet, I rise, close my eyes, and begin to see a series of episodes unfolding before my eyes. I begin to realize that despite all these challenges and resistances, some flowers have bloomed, some new insights have emerged, some stereotypes are broken, and some possibilities have charmed us.

I am introducing Allama Iqbal: a gifted poet-thinker—his evolution, his essays on Islam, politics and culture, his engagement with the Muslim League, his not so easy relationship with Mohammad Ali Jinnah, and his remarkably brilliant poetry. The class gains its momentum. I refer to some of his poems—the way these poems enrich our sociological imagination, and reveal the poet's sensitivity, his pain, his utopia, his anguish. But then, a student asks: 'Sir, why Iqbal? Why not a Tamil poet, a Telugu poet, a Punjabi poet? Why this special preference for Iqbal?' I feel the question; it is emerging out of a terrible anxiety over 'democratic representation'. India's diversity, heterogeneity, plurality, it is thought, must be adequately and democratically represented in everything I teach. So, as the argument goes, Iqbal can be taught only if all great poets from all Indian languages are taught. Otherwise, to teach Iqbal is to do injustice to others! Is it possible in a course that continues only for a semester? Or, for that matter, is it at all desirable? Is education about voting and a clever strategy for making everyone 'happy'—the way our power-hungry/ambitious politicians visit a Dalit household, organize the Iftar party, and speak broken regional languages while campaigning for elections? Education, it ought to be realized, is about the cultivation of a mind that sees the infinite in the finite. Tagore was born in Bengal. You are a Maharashtrian; yet, you can engage with Tagore because deep poetry transcends barriers. I am not a Dalit. Yet, I can study Ambedkar because a libertarian urge is also my urge. Education is about overcoming these constraining identity markers and associated barriers; it is a quest for the universal.

As all these thoughts come to my mind, a student rises up. 'Sir, may I say something?' 'Why not? Go ahead', I reply. The young boy from Karnataka smiles, and with absolute calmness makes a revealing statement: 'To understand one great poet is to understand all great poets. To study Iqbal is to become sensitive to the world of poetry—the essence of the poetic imagination. It is enriching, fulfilling.' I feel immensely happy. A symmetry takes place between the teacher and the taught. My student's remarks come as soothing rains after a heavy storm in the class.

Gandhi was bad; Ambedkar was good. Gandhi was a casteist; Ambedkar sought to annihilate caste. Gandhi remained a Hindu; Ambedkar debunked Hinduism. Gandhi was anti-modern, superstitious; Ambedkar was modern and progressive. Gandhi was a reactionary; Ambedkar was a magician with answers to everything. Yes, these stereotypes and superficialities keep spreading even in a university like ours. The reasons are many: assertive identity politics, quick/instant political correctness, and refusal to probe, to go deeper, to see beyond posters and slogans. To speak of Gandhi and Ambedkar in the class, needless to add, is not easy. How easy it is to communicate Emile Durkheim's *Elementary Forms of Religious Life*; how difficult it is to invite young students growing up with scepticism and doubt to Gandhi's engagement with the *Bhagavad Gita*! It is easy to communicate Karl Marx's *The Communist Manifesto*, and the theory of class conflict; it is, however, extremely difficult to invite these young students to Gandhi's art of resistance: how the cultivation of 'soul force' and the process of 'self-purification' play an important role in *satyagraha*, in the act of resistance against untruth. Furthermore, an environment has been created in which it is expected that if you speak of Ambedkar, you have to demolish Gandhi. It is almost like reproducing the script of a standardized Hindi film: if there is a hero, there ought to be a villain! Yet, I come, retain my stamina, and run the risk of being branded as a 'sympathizer' of Gandhi. I refer to Gandhi's engagement with the *Bhagavad Gita* and the *Sermon on the Mount*, I narrate his experiments, and try to make them feel that his practices are more important than his words. I tell them how he learned from John Ruskin, realized the importance of labour, and thereby interrogated the Brahminical principle of 'purity vs. pollution'. I refer to Ambedkar's brilliant essay on Buddha and Marx, how even the 'rationalist' Ambedkar realized the need for changing man's conscience for overcoming the caste system, how he engaged with Buddha's *Dhammapada*, and how Ambedkar too became a man of prayer. I ask them to enquire whether Gandhi's

Bhagavad Gita and Ambedkar's Buddhism are irreconcilable. I ask them to enquire whether in our quest for a just society one's ideas and contributions have to be vehemently denied for the glorification of the other. It is at this juncture that a student comes forward, surprises the proponents of identity politics, chooses to write an essay (while invoking the late scholar Professor Nagraj's contributions), and argues why we have to see beyond the fetishization of Ambedkar and hatred of Gandhi; and how a nuanced philosophy of justice ought to negotiate with both. At that moment, my class acquires a different character—not a party school, not a place for writing pamphlets and slogans, but a creative/dialogic space that encourages us to go deeper, and break stereotypes.

With difficulties and possibilities I too grow. As a teacher I learn the fundamental lesson of calmness. Even if students become impatient and restless, I ought to remain calm; I ought to listen; and slowly and steadily I have to create a pedagogic environment that creates the ground for the art of listening. This calmness—or, the wisdom to receive all sorts of condemnations with a smile—is, I believe, an essential characteristic of a teacher. It is extremely difficult to practise. I fail. I fail when I become terribly upset or angry. Yet, I rise because I believe in the virtue of this journey. Moreover, I learn another important lesson—

criticality is not cynicism; criticality is not nihilistic negativity; instead, criticality is the ability to filter, to accept what is enduring and beautiful, and to reject what has lost its meanings; criticality is the art of possibilities. For example, in a plural society like ours, or in a society that runs the risk of experiencing the tyranny of majoritarianism, Swami Vivekananda's references to the glory of 'Hindu culture' might sound somewhat odd and disturbing; yet, it should not prevent me from coming to the class with a series of lectures Swamiji delivered on 'practical Vedanta': how the realization of fundamental 'oneness' or what is felt as Eternal and Deathless can regenerate us, enable us to overcome our fear, limitedness and inertia, and create the foundation of a new civilization—egalitarian and spiritually enriched. I admit that Jawaharlal Nehru's 'developmental' policies might have its discontents; but it should not prevent me from coming to the class with a copy of *The Discovery of India*, and encourage my students to see how the 'modernist' Nehru was becoming ambivalent, how he was realizing the limitations of his Reason nurtured by Charles Darwin, Karl Marx and Sigmund Freud to understand the continual flow of an old civilization like ours, and how he was seeking to engage with its culture, its epics, its literature, its historical trajectory. The Indian Left may not have made its presence felt significantly in the making of our collective imagination. But how can I forget to invite my students to an extraordinary and illuminating life-trajectory of M.N. Roy—his Marxism, his critical engagement with the Communist International, and eventually his radical humanism, his plea for a decentralized partyless democracy?

My criticality has not made me cynical. I have not lost a sense of beauty. And it is indeed a wonderful journey. I tell my students: 'Imagine...imagine you are walking through a dense forest. And you see a marvellous tree called Mohandas Karamchand Gandhi. Have patience. Don't be in a hurry. Sit under the tree. Feel the fragrance, the shade. Undertake a journey with him—towards South Africa, towards Champaran and Dandi, towards Noakhali and Kolkata. But then, you have to move further. Here is yet another magnificent tree called B.R. Ambedkar. Feel his determinism, his ability to overcome all sorts of obstacles, his extraordinary scholarship, his resistance and criticality. Stand up, stand up, friends. It is a huge forest. You have to explore and see. Trees after trees—Sri Aurobindo, Jotiba Phule, Rabindranath Tagore, Allama Iqbal, M.N. Roy. Carry on the journey.'

Yes, I keep walking. And I ask my students to walk. What else is learning except this constant walking? Walking is my ultimate pilgrimage.

16

We are more than what we appear to be. We are the children of the divine, and the divine is boundless. What else is teaching? It is an act of prayer that transforms us. Is the politics of doubt devaluing this prayer, and instead of healing the wound, intensifying it further?

16

W
vocation
just
spiritual
sorts of
walk
class
become
being is
religion
Univers
connects
and wond
do not bot
at the
seekers
matter
Tamil,
Brahmin?

What is so remarkable about the vocation I am engaged in? Oh, I tell myself, my vocation enables me to grow, to expand—not just intellectually, but also ethically and spiritually. I cross boundaries. I overcome all sorts of limiting identities. As every morning I walk towards the university and come to my class, I undergo a process of transformation. I become a teacher. What spreads out from my being is a flow of energy that has no caste, no religion, no gender, no ethnicity. I realize the Universal in me; I realize what unites and connects. In the eyes of my students I see love and wonder, curiosity and eagerness to learn. I do not bother to know their caste, their religion; at the moment of the communion we are all seekers and fellow travellers. How does it matter whether my student is a Bengali or a Tamil, a Muslim or a Christian, a Dalit or a Brahmin? I am a teacher, and they are my students. Nothing else matters. We are learning together, exploring together. And what an extraordinarily liberating feeling it is! I become more than my caste, my religion, my ethnicity, my gender. Even though I speak Bengali, a Tamil student enchants me. I am born in a Hindu family; a Muslim student enters my inner world. I am supposed to be a 'forward caste' intellectual; yet, someone not belonging to my caste makes me realize the sweetness of divinity. All stereotypes crumble. I grow. I realize the beauty of an expanded horizon. It elevates; it does not limit. It expands; it does not restrict. It includes; it does not exclude. Thanks to my vocation; it has helped me to experience what transcends boundaries, to become truly cosmopolitan.

Are we losing this beauty, this grace? There are moments when some sort of anxiety confronts me. I smell a danger. See, for instance, the negative power of caste as one's permanent identity. It divides and separates. It excludes, and limits one's horizon. It erects a wall, and causes doubt and scepticism about others. It sees conspiracy. Yes, caste exists in our society, in our polity. Yes, caste causes atrocities and violence. Yes, even in a university like ours it may not be impossible to find a professor who carries his caste identity. And at a time when social scientists write more and more on caste, when caste-based mobilization and movement—particularly, if it has got a subaltern touch—is seen as legitimate, when anything universal is seen with doubt and suspicion, and when in an extremely charged political campus like ours not to mention caste is seen as hypocrisy, it is not easy to retain the grace I am talking about. Doubt and mistrust begin to pollute the relationship. Here is a 'Brahmin' professor—he is not very sensitive to the needs of Dalit students, he victimizes them. Or, here is a 'Dalit' professor—see how forward caste students avoid him, and do not want him to be their supervisor! In fact, these days we often hear these whispers, and feel these waves of negativity, doubt and scepticism.

I am not saying that my university is a solitary island, and hence it is free from caste prejudices. But to allow this scepticism to grow, or to begin our educational journey with this doubt is to destroy the basic trust which is needed for a healthy relationship between the teacher and the taught. Yes, we need to be alert. We must fight all sorts of caste prejudice and victimization. But this alertness does not mean that we lose hope. How can higher education evolve if we fail to see the possibility of redemption? My birth, as I feel, is not my final destiny. I may be born in a 'forward caste' family; but my life-philosophies and concrete practices would decide whether I am casteist, or whether I am simply a carrier of the Universal Energy. And as I join the vocation of teaching, I like my students to see this possibility in me; I like them to see me as just humane—a fellow traveller, a comrade, a being who does not stigmatize the so-called 'backward caste' students; nor does he fix the so-called 'forward caste' students, and make them feel eternally guilty. Instead, I love to see the road ahead; I tell myself and my students: 'We are more than our ascriptive identities. We are more than what we appear to be. We are the children of the divine, and the divine is boundless.' What else is teaching? It is an act of prayer that transforms us. Is the politics of doubt devaluing this prayer, and instead of healing the wound, intensifying it further?

Again, it is unfortunate that we live at a time when a male professor's orientation to a female student is seen with suspicion. True, it is the larger society—its perpetual episodes of male violence, sexual assault, abuse of women—that affects the environment of the university. It is also true that not everyone is capable of living with power; for instance, a supervisor may harass his female PhD student, take advantage of the fact that she is at the receiving end. It is also possible that a professor, despite his scholarship, may not be free from sexual lust, and his sexual gaze might disturb and distort the rhythmic relationship between the teacher and the taught. Again at a time when, thanks to women's initiatives, there is increasing awareness of sexual harassment in workplaces, we see the growing mistrust. The question is how the culture of learning retains its sanity and grace, even when it remains acutely aware of the harsh reality. There is no hope without trust. Imagine how pathetic it would be if we find ourselves in an environment in which a female student feels continually suspicious of her professor's moves, if she feels threatened to come to his chamber, meet him at his residence. Or, how terrible it would be if a male professor becomes extremely apprehensive and laments: 'I am afraid. They can do anything. I am not going to accept any woman as my PhD student.' Or, how crude it is when male students keep spreading rumours: 'See this professor. He favours good looking girls. He gives them good grades.' It is slow poisoning. It does not help. It pollutes the environment further. We have to trust ourselves.

One thing I myself have realized through my teaching engagement is that it is one of the most beautiful/graceful relationships one can think of. My horizon expands. I see immensely bright women. Their scholarship, their struggles, their cultural sensitivity and their spirit of hard work enrich my consciousness. I redefine womanhood. This bond has its beauty, grace and dignity. It takes the relationship to a higher domain filled with boundless affections, blessings and songs of prayer. Sexual exploitation, objectification, lust and greed become impossible. What remains is just poetry. And what else is life-affirming education except the celebration of poetry?

Yes, I am aware of the fact that the life of a teacher I idealize or seek to experience need not be generalized. My aspirations may be ridiculed, and seen as, to use Dostoyevsky's expressions, 'the dream of a ridiculous man.' Teachers, it may be said, are not from a different planet; they are not with any lofty mission; like any other group of professionals they are doing their job and earning money; and they carry the entire baggage of societal vices: caste prejudice and patriarchal violence. It may also be argued that the age of innocence never existed. And we live at a time when nothing can be trusted, and hence the need of the hour is to intensify the machinery of perpetual doubt, surveillance and legal/disciplinary measures. Committees are formed, posters are written, students conduct protest marches, enquiry commissions are constituted, and an environment is created in which students doubt the integrity of their teachers, and teachers begin to fear their students. Trust disappears; spontaneity withers away. Can a university function like this? Yet, even at the risk of being regarded as 'unreal', I continue to hope. I cannot function with fear and mistrust. I seek to live and function in the way my heart dictates. I invite my students to my residence. I share a cup of coffee and poetry with them. I ask them to come with me and discover the magical landscape of the university on a full moon night. Photography, cinema, music, art, philosophy—there seems to be no end to this flow of communication. Is it possible that one day I too may be accused as a notorious 'forward caste/ male professor' with all sorts of pathologies? Who knows? I don't bother. I live. I listen to my inner voice. I keep travelling with my students—as a teacher, as a friend, as a potential colleague, as a seeker, as a father. Meanwhile, they come. Someone knocks on my door, and surprises me with beautiful flowers as a gift of gratitude; someone sends a message: 'Sir, it is raining. It seems you are inspired; you must be thinking of your next lecture.' Someone comes forward, her words emanate from eternity; 'Sir, you have just delivered a lecture. Let me bring you a cup of coffee.' It goes on. With sociology and spirituality, with poetry and music, with flowers and books, with mountains and rivers the teacher and the taught become one. Love conquers fear, my dear.

17

It is important to remember that when the burden of 'knowledge' destroys the child within us, some terrible damage to our inner selves takes place. To live with children, to communicate with them, to enchant them, and to be enchanted by them—I believe—is the ultimate strength of a teacher.

Schools continue to fascinate me. My location in a leading university, or my 'status' as a professor has never prevented me from taking an active interest in school education. I do not hierarchize. I do not subscribe to a dualistic division: 'knowledgeable/research-oriented' university professors engaging with serious epistemological issues vs. school teachers merely imparting the lessons of elementary physics, mathematics and language to young children. Instead, I feel a sense of connectedness with schools, with children. Possibly I have never become an 'adult'; I remain a child. I love children's books; at the high altitude of the mountains as I see schoolchildren walking towards their school, I feel I am witnessing divinity; they look as beautiful as the mountains, the clouds, the peaks. Even now in my dreams I see my school; I see my teachers, my classrooms, the playground, the football match, the cultural evening. I read books on school education. From John Dewey to Jidu Krishnamurti—I love to swim into the ocean of pedagogic experimentations. I feel eager to meet school teachers who inspire, motivate, and arouse hope in the tender mind of the child. And on my part I encourage my students to write their dissertations and theses on the dynamics of school education. At a time when my university looks extremely intellectualized—a place where seminars after seminars, publications after publications produce only discontent, a place that celebrates the narcissism of the intellectual elite, a place that does not touch one's heart, I feel like leaving, walking through a village, entering a school, and playing with children. It is not romantic indulgence. Instead, I feel that it is important to remember that when the burden of 'knowledge' destroys the child within us, some terrible damage to our inner selves takes place. To live with children, to communicate with them, to enchant them, and to be enchanted by them—I believe—is the ultimate strength of a teacher.

Possibly from my own engagement with my daughter's education I have realized what it means to grow up with a child. I worked with her, with her books, pencils and colours. My 'scholarship' didn't matter. It didn't matter how many PhD students I had supervised. What really mattered was my patience—the ability to remain calm, despite her naughtiness, the urge to enter her world, and become a child once again. What a great feeling it was when I saw her writing a simple sentence, and then one day a story, solving a mathematical puzzle, making a scientific experiment, reading a book, and asking questions! And at every moment of this journey I realized the beauty of this vocation: how challenging and creative it is to engage with a child, to make her understand that 1/3 is less than 1/2, that an apple falls down from the tree because of the law of gravitation. I have never felt that I am doing something dull, something intellectually inferior. Instead, I have always felt that while, because of my practice, it is not so difficult to communicate with university scholars, it is not so easy for me to engage with children. They make me humble. Once I was asked to interact with the children of Standard VIII, and initiate a discussion on Mohandas Karamchand Gandhi. I still remember my nervousness, the kind of work I did, the seriousness with which I studied Gandhi's 'experiments'. I was becoming a child, and imagining how as a child I would have found Gandhi—quite often received as an old-fashioned gentleman with strange ideas—interesting and meaningful. I thought; I reflected. I was completely engrossed. I rediscovered Gandhi—not necessarily Ashis Nandy's Gandhi, or the Gandhi of *Economic and Political Weekly*, but the Gandhi who lied, who failed, who repented, yet tried to stand up. That is the truth. To become a child, or, to arouse a child's interest in biography, in history, in literature is the most challenging task. Yes, I am fortunate. My experiences have enabled me to overcome the hierarchy: university vs. school, higher education vs. school education. A teacher is a teacher. No matter who her/his students are, at every stage a teacher ought to be creative and alive—intellectually, ethically, spiritually.

Now I understand why some of our finest minds gave so much attention to school education. The fate of our civilization depends on how our children grow up, how their innate possibilities are allowed to develop, how they make sense of the world, and how, despite life's long journey, they retain what they are gifted with—spontaneity, laughter, wonder, love and boundless energy. It was, therefore, not surprising that a gifted poet like Rabindranath Tagore could dare to experiment with a deeply aesthetic/ emancipatory form of education; never could the poet appreciate a typical 'schooled' consciousness that restrains the child, and dissociates her/him from a sense of the infinite prevalent in the abundance of nature. And Gandhi, despite his intense engagement in the freedom struggle, could manage to elaborate his philosophy of basic and integral education. To know about Leo Tolstoy and his experiment with education is a great feeling. Illich and Freire fascinate us. And who would like to miss Jidu Krishnamurti's revealing conversation with the children and teachers of Rishi Valley School? Great thoughts, great efforts! Yet, it is tragic that we do not take school education seriously. 'Anybody can do it. It does not require much talent or intelligence. Just manage to get a B Ed degree from any of the existing education shops, and become a school teacher!' That is the way the larger society looks at it. See its devastating consequences. Not many creative people wish to become school teachers; societal perception, poor salary, life-negating hierarchy—everything seems to prevent the growth of an appropriate ambience for school teachers. The result is that barring exceptions, they remain demotivated with a negative self-perception. The job is seen to be 'inferior'—not for the best minds! Our universities, as a result, remain dissociated from schools. Our professors, researchers and scholars love to live in their own world of 'academic excellence'; and school teachers continue to complete the syllabus imposed from above, reproduce the prescribed texts, receive the dictates of the Principal and school management, and earn some extra money through the notorious chain of private tuitions. The routine goes on. There is no creativity, no light from the world of ideas and research.

My heart aches. This duality must be broken. I feel that university professors must spend some time in teaching schoolchildren, and working with school teachers. Apart from the dissemination of ideas, it would make them humble, enable them to regain their lost innocence, and experience once again that laughter, that spontaneity, that wonder, that naughtiness. And I believe that school teachers should be encouraged to come to the university, attend workshops, visit libraries and laboratories, and interact with researchers and professors. This would enable them to keep the flame of knowledge alive. In the ultimate analysis this constant interaction would create a brilliant community of teachers. I know that what I am imagining does not exist. Yet, I keep dreaming of this bridge. And dreams are indeed powerful; dreams inspire, shape my pedagogic practices. I teach a course on Sociology of Education. My students study Michael Apple and Pierre Bourdieu, and evolve a rigorous critique of school texts—their politics, their ideological messages, their biases. That alone is not sufficient, I tell them. I give them an assignment: 'Visit a school. Interact with the children. Explore the way they look at these texts. And then, if you are critical of the existing text, write a sample chapter—an alternative chapter—that you would want the children to read.' The assignment leads to immense dynamism. My students see beyond the university library, enter the school, rediscover their childhood; they write, intervene and contribute. 'What is the feeling?' I ask them. 'Sir, it is great. We have learned so much while writing for schoolchildren'. I keep moving. Yet, another batch, another group of students—I send them to a school, ask them to choose a group of children, interact with them and their parents. I persuade them to invite the children and their parents to our Centre. I inspire them to organize a day long workshop with them. They become sufficiently enthusiastic. They invite some university professors—a physicist, a theatre personality, a historian, a literary figure, and request them to interact with the children and their parents, and initiate a participatory discussion on education, vocation and life's multiple pursuits. The wall breaks down; university professors and schoolchildren share some golden moments.

The machine that has emerged in the name of education, I admit, is life-threatening. Sometimes I feel that the machine is destroying the child, and transforming her/him into an adult: dreamless, armoured, cynical. Is it that schools, because of reckless competition, obsession with 'success' and exam performance, and overloaded curriculum combined with the parental pressure, are writing the obituary of childhood—its wonder, its laughter, its boundless energy? I begin to look at myself. I thank God; the machine has not yet succeeded in killing the child within me. I look at my students. I pray: let the child within them remain alive; let them see the world, pass through a spectrum of experiences; yet, let them retain their innocence, wonder and joy. The child within me begins to communicate with the child within them. True, they are serious students; they are researchers; they read thick books, write complex essays. Yet, I seek to arouse their hidden childhood. I persuade them to sing and dance, to laugh and cry, to use pencils and colours, to decorate the walls of the Centre with aesthetically designed magazines, to organize cultural programmes, to enjoy the aesthetics of food and laughter. My university becomes my school; my school becomes my university. Dear students, whisper...whisper in my ears William Blake's 'songs of innocence'. I wish to seek refuge in my mother's womb.

18

Give, my dear, give the way you breathe. Give your compassion, your love, your energy, your positive vibrations, and realize that your resources are infinite. Let education be a song of offering.

How wonderful it is to offer, to give, to flow like a fountain. What an extraordinary feeling it is when one melts, loves, shares, gives oneself. These are the moments when one feels that one's true richness lies in the act of becoming empty—the act of sharing, not possessing; the act of giving, not holding. To possess or to accumulate is to remain in an eternal trap of fear and anxiety leading to the poverty of consciousness. Yet, how sad it is that this simple truth is seldom realized in our educational enterprise! Instead, we have been told—and told repeatedly by our parents, teachers and the larger society—that if you are educated you invariably acquire the right to possess, to accumulate, to gain extra privileges. The more educated you are the more privileged you are. You gain a 'position'; your 'status' is your ability to differentiate yourself from others; you are supposed to be ambitious, rich and powerful. It is, therefore, not surprising that all the time we are talking about our rights, our privileges, our salaries. Professors are measuring their 'intelligence'—you get a project, a lucrative one, and hence your department room must have an AC! Or, for that matter, a student thinks that her success must be measured in terms of her placement—the package she receives. The entire discourse, it seems, is centred on the principle of having and possessing. And it is sanctified through a culture of learning that has already conditioned our minds.

I am not different. I have become an integral component of this culture. How much have I gained? What have I got? Should I get more? These questions confront me, and paradoxically I realize that the more I raise these questions the more mean, anxiety-ridden and insecure I become. I realize that I am in a trap. The more I get, the more I demand; the more I seek to possess, the more poverty-stricken I become in my consciousness. Because poverty is not just an economic index; poverty is also a state of consciousness. I keep desiring and desiring. I become a beggar. I can't share. I can't offer. I can't give. There is fear; there is fear that if I give, if I share, I would lose. I fail to realize that only when I give I become truly rich. Is it that universities are making us neurotically restless? We are becoming discontented—living with fear, psychic poverty and chronic anxiety.

Yet, there are moments when I realize the cost of this pathology. And then comes the saner moments—the moments of deep contemplation. I look at the sun; I realize that it is giving me life, warmth and energy. I look at the moon; I realize that it gives me the aesthetics of beauty, the sublime light of illumination. I approach a tree; it gives me its shade, its perseverance, its companionship. I see a flower; it gives me its fragrance. I see a bird in the blue sky; it gives me the beauty of imagination, the urge to touch the sky. Mountains, rivers, oceans—they all give me. And I realize that in the act of giving nature is truly rich; its abundance is its beauty; it doesn't hold, it flows; it doesn't possess, it offers. And then I pray: let nature be my guru, my ultimate tutor. Something happens. There is calmness. Fear tends to wither away. Every act of ours, I tell myself, should emanate from the principle of giving. It is sad that our schools, colleges and universities have lost this rhythmic connectedness with nature. Our science 'conquers' nature; our closed classrooms dissociate ourselves from the infinite space that nature provides; our burden of knowledge makes us incapable of becoming sufficiently light to fly; our ego-boosting exercise through the rituals of seminars and placement cells makes us forget that life is not just about possessing, it is essentially about giving.

However, I rise. I feel inspired to narrate yet another possibility, another story of education. As a teacher I ask myself: What is teaching? Thank God, I find an answer—an answer that makes me calm. Teaching is nothing but an act of giving, sharing, offering. True, it is a job; I receive a decent salary; the university gives me comfortable accommodation. Possibly I receive more than I deserve. Yet, there is something in the vocation of teaching that takes it beyond the logic of calculation. The art of teaching emanates from the urge to share. A teacher's ultimate fulfilment lies in the act of giving everything that he has—ideas, thoughts, realizations, discoveries, interpretations, facts, theories, and above all the flow of life-energy. And in that act of giving a teacher finds everything: love, clarity, wisdom. Dualities disappear; fear vanishes; giving becomes receiving. And what about studentship? Is it possible to bloom without giving, without offering oneself? But what does one give? No, it is not a question of money. In fact, the act of giving becomes deeply meaningful when one gives one's fragrance, one's positivity, one's concern, one's humanity, one's realization that at a deeper level one is inseparable from others. It is in this sense that to give is not the privilege of only those who are materially rich and wealthy. Quote often, that 'richness' itself might prove to be an obstacle to the art of giving. That is why, dear students, I seek to tell you: you can give only when you realize that to love is to give. How wonderful it would have been had our studentship been filled with this principle of giving! As I see our campus, I see that our students with their hyper- political sensibilities are conscious of their rights. They are demanding, demanding all the time because as modern political citizens they are concerned about their rights. They demand fellowships; they demand new hostels; they demand transparency in the admission process. Granted, these demands have their legitimacy. Yet, seldom does one see a similar concern with the ethos of giving. Imagine how the culture of the university would have changed had they given their love to the natural landscape, reduced their dependence on motor cycles, planted and protected trees, and created an environment conducive to bio-diversity. Imagine what would have happened had our students opened a night school for those young boys working day and night at our *dhabas*. Imagine what a difference it would have made to the vibrations of our university had our students visited a neighbouring MCD school and offered a beautiful gift—their passion for books and ideas—to the children. Or, for that matter, imagine what would have happened had we—university professors—minimized the use of costly cars for coming to the department, reduced our dependence on ACs and other electronic appliances to create a more eco-sensitive campus. How graceful it would have been had we all planted and nurtured trees, instead of demolishing these for creating a parking space for our ever growing cars and bikes. I am aware that these simple acts or gestures may not seem like sufficiently political or radical or even intellectually stimulating to charm the academic community. But then, how do we forget that to create is to love, and it is always simple and unassuming?

The ethos of giving/offering I am talking about is not charity. Because charity means the celebration of the inflated ego of the giver; it is like asserting: 'I am privileged. I am rich. And you need my sympathy. I am protecting you.' In fact, in charity one does not really give; instead, the ego gets inflated; one acquires a 'name'. It humiliates the receiver; the receiver is objectified. It fails to realize that we are all givers and receivers at the same time. As a matter of fact, in my offering I receive my ultimate treasure. That is why, the ethos of giving I am talking about is not a separate act; it is as normal as breathing; it is not conscious of itself. It is one's being, one's rhythm, one's existence. An awakening of the naturalness of giving is what education ought to be. It is sad that education has become unnatural. And hence the enterprise of giving is seen as a separate/specialized act which the academic establishment regards as 'social work'—a professional course that trains and manufactures 'social workers' for NGOs. While 'social work' as a specialized course may have its meanings, I am suggesting something else. I am suggesting that to offer, to give, to serve one need not hold a degree; let it be a natural process. Let the spirit of giving characterize every aspect of one's being.

It is at this juncture that I recall an incident. I have asked my students to visit a series of old age homes, interview the inmates, and write their life-histories. Yes, it is an exercise which, academically speaking, is very important for the students doing a course on Methods of Social Sciences. Yet, despite this technical task, something happens. It becomes difficult for some of my students to just interview the inmates. They get involved; and the relationship no longer remains that of a 'researcher-respondent' relationship. My students begin to offer—naturally, spontaneously. What do they offer? No, not money. But they offer their concern, their smiles, their tales, their touch, their vibrations, their prayer. And as I see, my students become richer. Because in that act of giving they receive something special; they receive the feeling that they are not just technical people; they have a heart that aches, that loves. With tears and pain, with love and prayer, with ambiguities (I am a researcher; I can't stay with them forever; yet, I can't remain aloof) and existential questions relating to old age and life's inexplicable suffering they grow, they rediscover themselves. And I learn a lesson. We must alter the dominant notion of 'field work' in which we are primarily interested in taking and accumulating facts, information and interviews for our research publications. It is instrumental. Is it possible to bring the ethic of care into the domain of our field work? I believe it is. Only then does research becomes an act of offering.

True, we live in an unnatural world. What is simple and profound is forgotten. Instead of the ethos of giving, the urge to receive becomes important. And that leads to all that we see in our times: exploitation, poverty, violence, injustice, war. Dear students, believe it: Marx's 'class conflict' exists because there is no giving, there is only an urge to hoard, accumulate and exploit; Simone de Beauvoir's 'patriarchy' prevails because men have forgotten to love and surrender, they know only possession—possession of women as their private property; Foucault's 'surveillance' machinery functions because power has become the power to hierarchize and normalize, and we have forgotten to realize the beauty of the power to be powerless. And hence don't just theorize. Live, and what else is living except the art of giving, the art that makes one abundant and profound? Give, my dear, give the way you breathe. Give your compassion, your love, your energy, your positive vibrations, and realize that your inner resources are infinite. Let education be a song of offering.

19

I have no 'original' idea; I am incapable of revolutionizing human thought. I know that this temporal existence of mine will be forgotten as soon as I die. There is no reason to believe that as a teacher or a writer, my words have an impact on anybody....I exist for some time. I enjoy. But then, I will be forgotten; I will be reduced into zero. That is the reality. Everything else is an illusion.

The other day a young Associate Professor from a leading university in the capital came to see me. Her academic brilliance was quite visible and evident. Yet, I felt some sort of anger and restlessness in her persona. 'Is everyone in the department equally serious? Are they writing anything substantial? Or, are they just producing papers which virtually have no *impact factor*?' She kept alleging and comparing; and this preoccupation with what academicians are fond of regarding as 'impact factor', I felt, seems to have generated a lot of negativity in her being. It seems that it is no longer possible for her to work with joy and ease—without comparing, without measuring, without thinking how bad others are, and how good she is. 'Maybe I haven't published much. But whatever I have done has got tremendous impact factor,' she reminded me. She, I felt, must have done commendable work, and written something which her discipline regards as substantial. Yet, there was no positivity, no contentment, no joy. In her pride there was anger; in her assertion there was a scale for measurement. It was not graceful. What would have happened to her, had there been no impact factor? Would she stop writing, creating, thinking? I kept asking myself.

I made her a cup of tea. In order to lighten the ambience I started talking about politics, cricket, the weather and television serials. But academicians are pretty serious people. They do not smile easily. She left. But then, I started thinking about the much discussed 'impact factor'. What sort of 'impact' are we talking about? You write a paper. And I quote you in the paper I write. Or, I include your book in the bibliography of the book I write. And more and more scholars do so. It satisfies you. You feel that your writing has been taken seriously, and you have acquired a 'name' in the field. In other words, you are having an impact! The game goes on—the game of quotes, references, citation index, journals with good 'impact factor', and the intoxication with measurement —almost like the number of centuries cricket commentators calculate when they talk about Sachin Tendulkar. And this causes restlessness. The worth of everything that you do has to be seen in terms of this scale. No matter how paradoxical it may sound, the fact is that in the process you lose confidence and faith in yourself because if others do not refer to your work, you feel yourself worthless. And in a not so innocent world there is also the politics of who quotes whom, who neglects whom, who gives awards to whom. And once you fall into this trap you lose the grace that a truly gifted thinker or a reflexive mind needs; you lose calmness, humility, the eternal smile—the ability to laugh at yourself.

And then I begin to locate myself in this culture of high academics. Do I have an impact? I ask myself. 'No, not at all,' I assure myself. My emptiness gives me immense freedom. I write what I feel I should write. I value my inner voice, my own rhythm rather than the 'impact factor' of the journals. I do not know whether I am being quoted or not; but what I know is that I am ordinary and temporal, and I need not take myself so seriously; like the tides in the ocean people like me are coming and disappearing. The only thing I can do is to act with this clarity, and celebrate it without pretention, without arrogance. And hence I write not out of compulsion (see the way the pressure operates—you must write, otherwise what would your colleagues think about you), not because I have to prove something (see the way they whisper in your ears—you are nothing if you are not sought after at seminars, conferences and selection committees); I write when my heart embraces my brain, and there is a dance in my entire being. True, I have no 'original' idea; I am incapable of revolutionizing human thought. I know that this temporal existence of mine will be forgotten as soon as I die. There is no reason to believe that as a teacher or a writer, my words have an impact on anybody. But I have some wonder, some curiosity, some urge to communicate my experiences, my ways of seeing, rediscovering culture, life and politics; and that leads me to write—not so frequently, but occasionally—on modernity, on education, on culture, on religiosity. I am sure there is no 'impact'. However, if there are moments when someone writes an encouraging review, sends a letter, conveys a message that she/he has been touched by my writings or teaching, I feel that it is something extra, it is my bonus. But my work does not depend on whether or not it has its 'impact'—the way in the early hours of the morning I come to the balcony, and wait eagerly for the sunrise without bothering whether my communion with this miracle does have an impact on the economy of the nation. I exist for some time. I enjoy. But then, I will be forgotten; I will be reduced into zero. That is the reality. Everything else is an illusion.

My enquiry doesn't stop. I know that I don't have an impact. But what is it that has had an impact on me? I ask myself. Yes, I am a professor. I teach. My students write their dissertations and theses. I read books, research papers, and mention these in lectures and seminars. But is it really true that these writings—even if as a professional sociologist, as a supervisor I am required to mention these—have a genuine impact on me—the way I think, see the world, make sense of my life? I don't think so. Yes, if I teach a course in Social Stratification, I will mention all sorts of writings on caste produced by some of our celebrity sociologists; but, frankly speaking, as I see myself, most of these have no impact on me. I am not touched. My heart does not ache; tears do not flow; there is no inspiration to create a better world. And given a chance, I would not read these works for the second time; I would not like to touch, smell and keep these books in my bed. But no matter where I am, I would love to read Premchand's short stories to feel the pathology of caste; I would like to know more and more about Gandhi's experiments for overcoming the hierarchy of caste; or a gardener with the so-called 'low caste' origin nurturing flowers that would bring the likes of Blake and Wordsworth closer to him would make me see the absurdity of the casteist division between the mental and the manual. The paradox is that the scholars I refer to in my lectures, and occasionally in my bibliography (because of a purely professional reason) need not necessarily have a powerful impact on me. Possibly I do not fit into the model academic box. Because I do not divorce my head from my heart, my science from my poetry, my academics from my life, my discourses from my tears. For example, if someone tells me: 'You are intelligent. You are a scholar. You have read so much', I do not feel very happy. Instead, if someone says: 'What you have said or written has made me feel. It has touched me. I have shared it with my mother, my friend, my beloved', I feel God is blessing me. Likewise, I am not touched by the mere 'intelligence' of a scholar; nor am I touched by his/her academic profile—how many books, papers, prizes.... What influences me is one's ability to touch my entire being. To take yet another illustration, these days in the arena of higher academics, we see the proliferation of scholars in the field of 'cultural studies'; they, as it is said, are highly valued; with their publications in all sorts of trendy journals, they must have a huge 'impact factor'; but they have no impact on me, because most of the time I do not understand them, I do not understand their complex prose, their references, their vocabulary. However, a film by Ray (what an extraordinary poetry on celluloid!), or say, an autobiography of Kamala Das (written with great lucidity and honesty) does have a tremendous impact on me, on my modes of understanding meaningful cinema, or the location of women in a patriarchal society. It enriches my sensitivity to culture, aesthetics and gender.

One may allege that I am deviating; I am denying the logic of the academic discipline; I am emphasizing spiritual/aesthetic influences rather than the 'academic' impact. I need not defend myself. Yet, I can say that I am dealing with the domain of human sciences; I am not talking about mathematics or physics; and how is it possible to enter the domain of human sciences without referring to aesthetics, poetry and spirituality? I learn about the way human societies function not just through the pages of *The Contributions to Indian Sociology*, or *Economic and Political Weekly*, I learn through literature and philosophy, through films and music, through biographies and reflexive writings. And is it necessary that I have to be necessarily influenced by professional sociologists and their publications? I don't think so. As I have already indicated, disembodied/heavily reference-oriented prose, statistics, theoretical complexity and the density of loaded words alone are not sufficient to have an impact on me. Maybe something very simple and yet immensely profound—say, a poem by Muktibodh, an Upanishadic prayer, a short story by Saadat Hasan Manto—influences me more than these academic writings. This is not to suggest that nobody from the academic world has made an impact on me. I have survived because even today I love to read Karl Marx's *Economic and Philosophic Manuscripts of 1844*; my romance with Erich Fromm and Herbert Marcuse has not stopped; Max Weber's reflections on 'science as a vocation' make me think; I feel like going back to Emile Durkheim's penetrating insights into symbolism in the study of the 'elementary forms of religious life'; Ashis Nandy's notes on the 'intimate enemy' in the context of our colonial history have charmed me; and yes, there are many more examples. But then, most of the publications we are compelled to quote and refer (what else can you do because your professors ask you to write a lengthy review of literature in your theses, or the journals/ publication houses demand that you must quote a particular kind of texts?) do not have much impact on me. I am well aware of the fact that my liking/disliking does not mean anything in the way the academic world looks at itself. But at the same time I am sufficiently free to reclaim my space, and say that I need not be always influenced by their criterion of 'impact factor'.

Meanwhile, I ask myself strange questions. Did Jesus Christ or Gautam Buddha have an 'impact factor'? True, they influenced us, and influenced us deeply. Yet, at one level nothing seems to have changed. We do not love our neighbours; we cause war; the Sermon on the Mount is almost forgotten. We do not strive for *nirvana*; we find ourselves trapped into the cycle of *samsara*; instead of the four 'noble truths', we live in a jungle of lies. Where is then the lasting impact? Intellectual cognition is one thing; and the real impact on the life we lead is quite another. But see the irony. We academicians, because of some publications in trendy journals, begin to think that we have a great impact (what sort of impact it is?) Is it ignorance? Or, is it the culture of narcissism? Or, is it a very shallow notion of impact—merely intellectual impact, but no impact on the *dharma* of everyday life? I find no easy answer. Meanwhile, the mountains call me. The radiant sun sends its divine message to the snowy peaks. I become a witness. I forget the grammar of citation index and impact factor; I realize the superficiality of the game of publications because I see the most beautiful book unfolding itself before my own eyes. No dispute any more; it is the moment of silence.

20

I realize that it is difficult to exist as just a 'supervisor'; a relationship is established—a relationship that transcends the boundaries of statistics, empiricism, ethnography, review of literature and post-PhD publications. I do not wish to eradicate or deny this tension because, I believe, a teacher lives in many domains simultaneously.

I was a research scholar pursuing my doctoral work; and my father used to remind me: 'You should always remain polite, and whenever there is a crisis in life consult your 'guide', and do whatever he suggests.' He was not from the world of academics; he was not used to the idea of a 'supervisor' as a mere subject specialist; for him, unlike many of us who assert the need for a hard core professional relationship between the teacher and the taught, a guide was not just a supervisor; a guide, he felt, should be like Krishna taking his disciple Arjuna to a higher level of realization. His task, my father must have thought, was more than just instructing his student how to collect data, how to theorize, how to arrange chapters, and write a thesis to which the external examiner would find no reason to object; a guide, for him, should be a philosopher, a counsellor, a true friend.

And today I find myself in a new situation.

I am no longer a research scholar; instead, I teach, and research scholars work with me. Who am I? Am I a 'guide' in the way my father visualized it? Or, am I just a 'supervisor'—a subject specialist concerned only with the academic life of the student? These questions haunt me; and I find no easy answer. True, I know my limitations; I don't have the wisdom that my father thought a 'guide' ought to have. But at the same time I realize that it is difficult to exist as just a 'supervisor'; a relationship is established—a relationship that transcends the boundaries of statistics, empiricism, ethnography, review of literature and post-PhD publications. I do not wish to eradicate or deny this tension because, I believe, a teacher lives in many domains simultaneously.

To begin with, let me ask myself a pertinent question: Am I a true researcher capable of supervising my M Phil/PhD students? I am not very sure. I love to see myself primarily as a teacher, not a researcher. Yes, I am aware of the fact that good teaching involves a fair degree of familiarity with the latest research trends, and a good researcher can also be a great teacher. However, I cannot imagine myself engaging only in research and publications; my *swadharma*, I feel, is that of a teacher engaging in an act of communion with students. And, therefore, I have no hesitation to say that I am not a very solid researcher—a researcher who is excessively focused, specialized, and a master of a tiny domain of enquiry. I move; I fly; I transcend boundaries; literature, sociology, metaphysics—everything attracts; and as a result, life itself—modernity, culture, education, social theory—becomes my area of interest. It is this passion—not necessarily a very focused/ specialized knowledge—that makes me communicate with my research students. I do not know whether as a supervisor I am of any help to them. However, there is only one thing I can do. My passion inspires me; ideas strike my imagination; I share those ideas with my students; and as a result, something happens. They too get inspired, and find a theme for further research. I remember my first M Phil student. He was a young man with a political dream. He read Marx; but he was not a conventional Marxist. And then one day I asked him to study Erich Fromm's *The Sane Society*. He read; he was excited; and then, I whispered in his ears: 'You can write an M Phil dissertation on Erich Fromm's notion of freedom.' He got it, and wrote a reasonably good dissertation. It was his work. I am sure there were more equipped professors in the department to tell him about Erich Fromm: his critical engagement with Sigmund Freud and Karl Marx, his plea for humanistic psychoanalysis, his critique of authoritarianism, his dissenting voice against the culture of consumption, and his quest for the art of loving. In that sense I didn't help him much. But I only acted as a catalyst. Nothing more. Nothing less. Time passed. And again, to take yet another example, a young man arrived who was not very sure about his research area. My engagement with him began; and slowly I realized that he was deeply religious; and his interest in the ashram life was truly remarkable. I suggested to him: 'Choose an ashram, do a rigorous ethnography of the ashram, see its notion of time, space, food, prayer and speech, and write a thesis on the ashram as a site for alternative culture.' I saw light in his face. 'Sir, now I have got the topic. For me, it is not just the academic question; it is my life's quest.' And he came forward with a reasonably meaningful thesis. True, I didn't know anything about the ashram he studied; nor did I know much about the particular religious sect he was referring to. He could have got a better supervisor specialized in the field of the sociology of religion. My only satisfaction was that I could become a companion in his search for a research enquiry.

I know my limitations. I am not a researcher. I am a teacher. Never did I try to hide this fact from my students. Yet, I am fortunate; many bright students have come forward and worked with me; and as a result, I have grown, and learned immensely from them. Their interests were diverse and many; my horizon kept expanding. How wonderful it is to recall those days—an Iranian student reading his chapters on the intellectual traditions in post-Ayotollah

Khomeni Iran, and I am listening with great care, learning and at the same time suggesting some possibilities to further improve the thesis; a student sharing his field notes collected from the Hindi film industry, and we are engaged in a discussion on the changing notion of 'masculinity' in our Hindi films, and this act of mutual learning inspiring my student to write an innovative thesis; a student writing about Allama Iqbal, his poetry and politics, and I am continually moving from one world to another—from Tagore to Iqbal, from Iqbal to Tagore. In a way, my research students become my young tutors, and I enjoy this experience. The story goes on. One writes an M Phil dissertation on partition violence and Saadat Hasan Manto's writings; my literary sensibilities develop; Manto enters my inner world. Or for that matter, when an Assamese student chooses to write her dissertation on Bhupen Hazarika and the sociology of music, I grow and learn many details about the great singer which I didn't know earlier. True, my age, my experience might have helped me to give some kind of coherence and direction to their dissertations and theses. But how can I deny that they have enabled me to grow and evolve with them? Possibly I am not a supervisor. I am more like a wanderer, a co-traveller.

And in the process something happened. I ceased to exist as just a 'supervisor'—an expert who directs and only talks about chapters, references, logical coherence and argumentation. No, as I have already said, I do not have the wisdom to become the kind of 'guide' that my father idealized. However, I found myself in a fluid zone. We could not make a clear demarcation between the thesis and the curve of human life; and as a result, many of my research students took me to a world beyond footnotes, methods and theories. A student of mine wrote a good dissertation on culture and gender. There was a promise in her work; and I suggested to her a tentative PhD theme on feminism and women ascetics. She was prepared and enthusiastic. And then she became a mother; her child, needless to add, became her book, her thesis; it was becoming increasingly difficult for her to continue her university life. 'What should I do, Sir? I know that home is not everything for a woman; all my friends are writing their theses. But Sir, I feel guilty if I do not give adequate attention to my child. At this stage God wants me to be with my child. Sir, what do you think?' she asked me. I could not say: 'Why are you bothering me? It is your personal problem. I am here only to look at your chapters.' Instead, I listened, listened with great care, and then one day I suggested to her: 'For the time being you can withdraw and de-register yourself from the university because at this juncture you need to fulfil yourself as a mother, and it is this life-affirming experience that will enrich you immensely. You will miss nothing. Instead, when after a couple years you come back, your entry into the discourse of feminism is likely to acquire a new meaning.' She gave her consent. Who was I at that moment—a 'supervisor', a subject specialist, a 'guide', or a concerned friend who empathizes, who listens? The journey with research students has its ups and downs; and I too realize that I cannot exist as merely an 'expert'; I enter into the domain of life—its moments of glory and its moments of pain and disorder. 'Sir, I have to consult a psychiatrist. For quite some time I am not in a position to concentrate. Sorry Sir, I can't show you my work', a student expressed her utter helplessness. 'Don't worry. Tell me what has happened to you?' I sought to assure her. 'I don't know, Sir. I find no inspiration, no meaning in what I am doing. Moreover, I can't escape the trap of anxiety. What will happen to me? Can I take care of myself, of my old parents?' I forgot her research plan; I began to walk with her. And the dialogue continued. I don't know whether our conversation really helped her to find herself—her innate potential, her ability to find joy and meaning in simple and profound things of life, her eternal spirit that knows that anxiety takes us nowhere because the next moment is unknown, and hence what makes sense is to live this very moment, and live intensely. But I know that

God whispered in my ears: 'It is not easy, my dear, to become a guide. It is a long journey.'

Meanwhile, my students keep writing and submitting their dissertations and theses. And I continue to learn—a young researcher tells me that the changing dynamics of the relationship between the two major religious communities can be seen in the streets of Kolkata; the phenomenal growth of play schools in the city makes a student of mine think, and she relates it to the sociology of urban/middle class living; and to take yet another example, a bright researcher keeps informing me of the new readings on Mohandas Karamchand Gandhi—his presence (even presence in absence) in diverse social movements. And at this juncture an external examiner returns the PhD thesis of one of my students. The examiner wants her to revise her thesis. She falls down; she becomes upset; she is angry; and she tells me: 'I am giving up, Sir. I have an ideological position; the examiner has not understood it. To revise the thesis is to go against my conviction.' I sit with her; I try to make her calm; I want her to see that there is nothing unusual if the examiner asks a researcher to make some revisions; and there is no harm if she does it; and with more maturity and hard work she can always sharpen her arguments and eventually publish her work. She passes through emotional turmoil. I play a role—a minimal role—in making her rise once again. In the process, I do not know when

I have ceased to become a mere supervisor. But who am I? I look at the sky, and ask myself how many times I have to be born in this world in order to come closer to my father's visualization of a true 'guide'.